£20.99

SPORT, RACE, AND ETHNICITY
NARRATIVES OF DIFFERENCE AND DIVERSITY

SPORT, RACE, AND ETHNICITY
NARRATIVES OF DIFFERENCE AND DIVERSITY

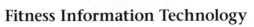

Fitness Information Technology

A Division of the International Center for Performance Excellence
262 Coliseum, WVU-CPASS ▪ P O Box 6116
Morgantown, WV 26506-6116

Library of Congress Card Catalog Number: 2011920470

ISBN: 978-1-935412-09-0

Production Editor: Aaron Geiger
Cover Design: 40 West Studios
Typesetter: 40 West Studios
Copyeditor: Aaron Geiger
Proofing: Maria denBoer
Indexing: David C. denBoer
Printed by: Thomson-Shore

Cover image: Nicky Winmar lifts his jumper and proudly shows off his skin color after being vilified by Magpie fans during a St. Kilda vs. Collingwood AFL game on April 26, 1993, in Melbourne, VIC. Photo courtesy of *The Daily Telegraph*.

10 9 8 7 6 5 4 3 2 1

Fitness Information Technology
A Division of the International Center for Performance Excellence
West Virginia University
262 Coliseum, WVU-CPASS
PO Box 6116
Morgantown, WV 26506-6116
800.477.4348 (toll free)
304.293.6888 (phone)
304.293.6658 (fax)
Email: fitcustomerservice@mail.wvu.edu
Website: www.fitinfotech.com

CONTENTS

FOREWORD

They are terms that, through extensive use and regular circulation, have acquired a certain currency. "Race," "ethnicity," "difference," and "diversity": terms that are familiar, rooted in a certain mode of political discourse. In *Sport, Race, and Ethnicity: Narratives of Difference and Diversity* the authors challenge us to think about these concepts again. This collection of essays does not only explore how these terms function, what they mean in society, but how they might be thought in relation to sport. What is different or particular about race or diversity in relation to sport, a practice that has historically served as one of the key sites where issues around ethnicity or aboriginality are played out? What role does difference perform in the selection of a nation's sports team?

In many ways, this collection turns that question on its head. More through implication than direct address, *Sport, Race, and Ethnicity* asks: how could difference or race not be a critical component of that process? In sport, race, and ethnicity, difference and diversity find not only a very particular articulation, but the stakes that pertain to these issues assumes a very public visage. As some of the contributors argue, it is either often or it becomes a matter for and of intense political debate. How the nation sees itself, how the ethnic community understands its representation, how the excess or lack of difference and diversity fail to articulate the proper difference or diversity within a said community, all constitute key questions and lines of inquiry in this volume. In taking up these issues, *Sport, Race, and Ethnicity's* contributors demonstrate not only the urgency and veracity of these questions, but it provides a lineage of how these issues have informed debates in a variety of historical sites—from apartheid South Africa to the USA to an Australian political that has, it seems, always been haunted by the spectre of the Other, of the Aboriginal as a figure who is alternately, in short order, ridiculed and feared, excluded and admired.

It is for this reason that this volume is able to bring into critical view an icon such as Evonne Goolagong . Is this famous Australian female tennis star an Australian or Aboriginal? First one and then the o/Other? Which Aboriginal does the settler community claim for itself? And, why? As all the contributors argue, in one or another, the Other must be accounted for: the politics that append to it must explained. Of course, in iterating the name "Evonne Goolagong" other such disruptive presences are stirred to political life: Jim Thorpe, Jim Brown, Muhammad Ali are all part of the conversation that takes place in *Sport, Race, and Ethnicity*. One could easily add: Mark Ella, Basil D'Oliveira, Andrew Symonds, John Smith, Tommie Carlos. There are certainly others, omitted here for no reason other than these were the first names to come to mind.

That these names come so easily to mind because of their association with sport, that they in themselves constitute a memorable cultural event, demonstrates how sport brings a particular kind of political life to race or ethnicity, to difference or diversity. We are reminded by the authors in this volume, who all evince a real investment in the subject, that sport matters, and that it matters most publicly because sport is a singular repository of politics. That is, sport is never just (about) sport, especially when those who are opposed to difference and diversity insist most strenuously that all politics should be kept out of sport. The authors here show, often with a deft touch, the fallacy of that argument. If sport did not matter as much, it would not matter so much that this form of cultural activity addressed—or, redressed, might be the proper term—racial diversity or ethnic difference. It is not simply a matter of suggesting that sport constitutes its own kind of politics, or that politics is unthinkable without sport, but that sport is always indistinguishable from politics, sport is always burdened with the history of race or racism, it is often a bulwark against ethnic violence or a refuge for ethnocentrists. Appropriately, then, the title of the volume, *Sport, Race, and Ethnicity,* foregrounds the unbreakable linkage between the cultural practice ("sport") and the core political issues ("race," "ethnicity").

The value of *Sport, Race, and Ethnicity,* then, is that it demonstrates where, when and why sport functions as the site of contestation of a nation or a community's most dearly held political beliefs. These essays provide a sense of how these issues are addressed, or not, and what the efficacy, or not, of the "solutions" are. Of course, race or ethnicity is rarely ever thought without reference to other foundational categories – say, class or gender or sexual orientation. In making sport the pivotal social practice, these essays reveal both the kinds of difficulty inherent in how sport is practiced and, paradoxically (a matter of some relief, one imagines), how much sport still retains a certain sovereignty. The game is both just a game and, all the contributors make clear, so much more than a game. It is this complexity, this knotty place of conjuncture, that the contributors in their diverse and different ways, address themselves to: it is only through sport that particular political stakes can be properly understood; in sport, because of sport, these stakes are, sometimes more regrettably than others, disguised. All the authors in *Sport, Race, and Ethnicity* are committed to undoing the knot without ever suggesting that sport can be, for good or ill, either just one thing or the other. Some things get lost in translation, some get their just critical deserts because cultural history would be so much poorer if the place of sport in the politics of a society were not properly understood.

—**Grant Farred**, Director of Graduate Studies in Africana and Associate Chair in English at Cornell University. Farred has published in a wide spectrum of studies, such as culture, postcolonialism, literary theory, and sport. Farred is the author of *What's My Name? Black Vernacular Intellectuals* (2003); *Phantom Calls: Race and the Globalization of the NBA* (2006); and *Long Distance Love: A Passion for Football* (2008).

ACKNOWLEDGMENTS

This book stems from a selection of outstanding papers delivered to the *Sport, Race and Ethnicity* conference staged in Sydney, December 2008. Thanks go to conference partners the Australian Human Rights Commission and the Department of Immigration and Citizenship, both of which providing funding and logistical support. I would also like to recognise the School of Leisure, Sport and Tourism at University of Technology Sydney for providing an opportunity to stage the event. I appreciate, in particular, the support of Bruce Hayllar, Simon Darcy, Nicole Gruber, Brad McCarroll, Angela Powell, Alana Thomson and Colin Tatz in the conference management process.

The journey from conference papers to fully fledged book chapters was encouraged by Fitness Information Technology's (FiT) Steven Pope, whose patience and collegiality are much appreciated. Aaron Geiger of FiT provided meticulous feedback on manuscripts and proved to be a first class sub-editor. The contributors to the book deserve the most thanks: their energies and intellect have produced a collection of essays that, we hope, will be of interest to both academic and general readers.

Daryl Adair

Introduction: Perceptions of Skin and Kin: Sport as an Arena of Difference and Diversity

BY **DARYL ADAIR**

S port is a deceptively rich area for the investigation of community attitudes, values, and power relations. It is a public display within which behavioral norms and social hierarchies are played out. Sport can variously include or exclude, and engage or marginalize, depending on a complex mix of values, attitudes, and power structures. Like society, the ideas and purposes of sport are subject to competing forces of conservatism and change, the impacts of localism and globalization, and the influence of divergent ideologies. Sport, in that sense, is neither inherently virtuous nor heinous. It is a human creation that continues to evolve. Depending on context, sport can either reinforce prevailing orthodoxies or be part of reformist or radical agendas (Sugden, 2010).

Sport, "Race," and Ethnicity: Narratives of Difference and Diversity, focuses on two key areas of contention, negotiation, and accommodation in sport—the domains of "race" and ethnicity. Sport is a site for the articulation of group identities, processes of collective identification, and means

1

of mass representation. Socially conceived ideas about skin color, ancestry, and kinship have, at varying times and places, made sport an arena of disdain for difference, or, by contrast, a realm in which diversity is welcomed. During the 19th century and for much of the 20th century, sport was an arena in which participants were "racially" segregated or marginalized (Miller and Wiggins, 2003). There were, for instance, "negro" and white leagues in American baseball until Jackie Robinson became a catalyst for change. Moreover, the West Indies cricket team, though dominated numerically by non-whites, did not have a black captain until the 1960s. Slowly, and amidst trenchant opposition, sport has evolved to the point where, in some contexts, it even appears to be an exemplar of cosmopolitanism. High performance, professional sports are now less likely than in the past to exclude participants with minority backgrounds. Affiliation with a particular "racial," indigenous, or ethnic group is not expected to compromise selection; athletic performance, not skin color or ancestry, is the prime determinant of selection today.

That said, ethno-racial perspectives remain fundamental to attitudes and behaviors both in society and around sport. Although there is no scientific basis to "race," it is simplistically applied to skin color and stereotypical assumptions about identity, status, and physiology associated with racialized appearance. "Race," in this sense, is a human invention by which to classify and separate people: it establishes hierarchies of "value" in respect of whiteness, blackness, and so on (Graves, 2001). Ethnicity, meanwhile, has fundamental links with ancestry but not biology: family, language, religion, and nationality are key bases for ethnic identity. Individuals are born into ethnic communities but may reject this connection, recasting themselves with a different sense of self (Cornell and Hartmann, 2007; Adair and Rowe, 2010). Indigeneity can be connected with "race" and/or ethnicity; certainly Aboriginal peoples, when victims of colonial annexation, have been racialized by processes of Eurocentric hegemony and assumptions of white superiority. However, this camouflages diversity and complexity within indigenous communities: there are vast differences of language, culture, and tradition—each of which demarcate ethnic identities.

Sport is an important barometer of assumptions about "race" and ethnicity: it has long attracted ideas—whether folkloric or scientific—that elite athletic performances can be explained by physical traits thought to be associated with particular groups—such as "racial" minorities, indigenous communities, or ethnic groups. In short, there is a belief that ethnoracial background predisposes people to have different athletic capacities (Hoberman, 1997). Just as importantly, sport remains a site wherein intergroup hatred is expressed—and this type of hostility has been the focus of policy interventions. Anti-racism campaigns, such as "Give Racism the Red Card," are testament to the vitality of hostile and prejudicial attitudes about the "other" in sport. Importantly, ethnic minorities may be just as likely to experience prejudice as "racial" and indigenous minorities, and the bigotry they experience is often described as racism (Tatz and Adair, 2009; Tatz, 2009). So, while sport is often lauded as a site wherein diversity is coveted, it is also a domain in which differences can be exploited in the interests of malevolence.

Historians have examined racial segregation and racial integration in sport; they have investigated the political struggles and conflicts around race on the field and track, in the ring, and across the spectrum of ideologies, practices and institutions. Moreover, several sport historians debunked the idea of race as a biological category and traced the construction of race as a social category. For the most part, historians have engaged with "race" primarily through the lens of social history. Social historians of race and sport primarily direct their attention at those discriminatory racial structures of power and domination that affect participation in sport. Yet, according to contributor Douglas Booth, "while social historians of race and sport largely conceptualize racial discrimination in terms of structures of constraint, when accounting for racial changes over the last fifty years they tend, ironically, to foreground individuals who challenged and set out to transform those structures." Of course there can

3

be influential change agents, such as Jack Johnson in boxing and Jackie Robinson in baseball, but their stories—no matter how evocative—are an incomplete canvas of wider, ongoing struggles for structural change on the part of oppressed peoples.

Over the last decade something of a paradigm shift has begun in sport history, with practitioners engaged more explicitly in hermeneutic and postmodern approaches to the identities and cultures that shape sport and society. Sport is now better understood by historians as a practice that has created diverse and conflicting meanings for an array of groups (local communities, genders, nations and so forth). This view became prominent in sport history from the mid-1990s, when cultural approaches entered the field in concerted fashion. Deconstructionist cultural history, in particular, prompted skeptical and critical perspectives about the "straightforwardness" of historical facts and evidence, and has questioned the sometimes unreflective ways in which historians prefigure and configure their narratives (Hunt, 1989: 20). However, that tension reverberated rather slowly in sport history. Most practitioners continue to have an almost evangelical faith in the sanctity of archival repositories and the "authority of evidence" therein when conceiving their histories (Munslow, 2006: 195). A range of methodological and data collection approaches is useful for research into themes of "race" and ethnicity in sport—particularly as so many of the subjects have been marginalized and therefore too often absent from conventional historical records.

The contributors to *Sport, "Race," and Ethnicity* provide important insights into the negotiation of difference and diversity. It is a multi-disciplinary collection involving historical reflection, political perspective, sociological inquiry, and media analysis. It involves a range of investigative techniques, such as archival exploration, narrative argument, discourse analysis, biographical inquiry, and group evaluation. As the book's title suggests, it includes discussion of "race" and ethnicity, and ways in which these descriptors have been woven into experiences like exclusion or inclusion, and discrimination or engagement. It is hardly a final word on the subject matter; research into difference and diversity in the realm of sport and society has an impressive lineage, but there is still so much to explore, interpret, and evaluate.

"RACE"

Randy Roberts connects issues of race and racism with the concomitant theme of gender—in this collection he examines masculinity. He describes the machismo associated with bare-knuckle boxing in the United States and how it was eventually usurped by prizefighting with gloves; boxing had been "civilized" by the take-up of Britain's Queensberry Rules in the late 19th century. The heavyweight championship of the world became the premier title bout, with unprecedented sums of money in the ring. However, Roberts shows that African-American fighters were excluded from top flight contests by white boxers who drew the "color bar." Jim Crow was alive and well in American sport, with the fight game a cornerstone of race discrimination and white dominance. When a black American eventually took on a white Canadian for the heavyweight title, the bout was staged on the other side of the world. Jack Johnson's (in)famous victory in Sydney, Australia, set a black cat among a flock of white pigeons. Johnson dominated the sport of boxing and, in doing so, helped to change perceptions that the "negro" was physically inferior to the white man. However, as Roberts concludes, Johnson was made to suffer for his ascendancy, spending years in jail on trumped-up charges.

Andrew Ritchie provides a second example of African-American athletes traveling abroad to seek a better deal in sport. Marshall "Major" Taylor, the finest professional cyclist in the United States, regularly toured Europe and Australia in an effort to escape racial vilification in his sport. Ritchie's chapter focuses on the Australian legs of Taylor's overseas jaunts: while he was treated as a celebrity, Major was also subject to dirty tactics by other riders and had run-ins with officials. Overall, though, he experienced—as a black man—adulation and freedoms that were denied to him back in America, where the specter of Jim Crow made it difficult for Taylor to secure a room in white-owned hotels or to eat at white-run restaurants. However, Ritchie also points to the irony of this contrast, for in the antipodes Taylor "was a black-skinned hero in a nation that prided itself on 'White Australia.'"

Sean Brawley considers the role of sport and cultural diplomacy in the context of the high-profile tours to Australia of Japanese swimming stars Katsuo Takaishi and Takahiro Saito in 1926-27. The visit took place during a time in which "Pacific goodwill" was a key platform of diplomacy in the region, and it preceded the overt militarization of Japan in the 1930s. The touring swimmers performed very creditably against well-established Australian competitors, with their efforts sparking debate in the press about the physical prowess of the "European race" versus the "Asian race." It had long been presumed that "Orientals" were inherently inferior athletes to Westerners; the Takaishi/Saito performances suggested that view needed revisiting, particularly in the breaststroke event, where Japanese coaching had initiated new styles of movement. The visitors were feted around the country—they were tourists, not migrants, and so able to be granted an exemption to the otherwise restrictive White Australia policy. Brawley concludes that the Japanese swimmers and Australian officials firmly believed that goodwill had been created between the countries. That they were soon at war had nothing to do with the tour; indeed, the visit showed how Japanese-Australian relationships could thrive under propitious circumstances.

John Hoberman is concerned with the salience of perceived or imagined racial differences. He notes that high performance sport has been a key site for the articulation of ideas and assumptions about "race" and athletic acumen. Sport, in this sense, has been a vehicle through which race-based hierarchies of physical prowess have been conceived. Hoberman nonetheless emphasizes that racialized theories of sport ability have been either pseudo-scientific or folkloric. That said, he acknowledges the persistence of biological notions of race, which have reappeared in American society under a new guise—racial pharmacology. A recently formulated heart drug, BiDil, has had particular success with patients of African-American ancestry. While such a diagnosis is welcome in terms of treating at-risk populations, it has raised a wider epistemological debate. Critics caution against inferences that medicines function differently for "blacks" and "whites," as though there is a race-based resonance to pharmacology. Supporters, meanwhile, have tended to point to race discrimination in America's medical history and argue that, pragmatically, if a drug suits a particular "racial" group then it ought to be approved for that purpose. Hoberman argues that such race-based approaches to medicine have allowed "the 'reauthorization' of racial biology." He concludes that the debates about racialized sport and medicine have something in common—they both focus on the body and biology as cornerstones to ideas of race, and that "neither discussion has been racially defamatory in any explicit sense."

Nicole Neverson and Graham Knight critically examine media representations of the "trash talking" rivalry between two African-American sprinters, Maurice Greene and Michael Johnson. Using a reflexive approach, the authors move beyond the conventional notion of skin color as demarcating "race." Instead, they argue that these two athletes are represented, whether by their own commentary or that of the media, in ways that either accentuate blackness or cultivate whiteness. For Neverson and Knight, race is never static and always under negotiation. Greene and Johnson, as antagonists, have different socio-economic backgrounds, educational backgrounds and cultural profiles; the spectacle of their bitter rivalry played into wider discussions about "race" and the authenticity of blackness versus whiteness.

ETHNICITY

Dean Allen evaluates tensions in South African history over sport, ethnicity, and nationalism. He examines intra-group conflict within the ruling white minority in South Africa—the British and the Afrikaner. He describes how the British game of rugby union was appropriated by Afrikan-

7

ers and reinvented as a symbol to accentuate their own sense of identity and power. In the period 1899-1948, Allen explains, South Africa underwent a political revolution in the interests of an Afrikaner ascendancy, and the physically demanding sport of rugby became a potent expression of courage and pride in white, non-British, Afrikaner power. Rugby thus became a public arena within which inter-ethnic tensions between Afrikaner and Briton were played out. For black and colored South Africans, meanwhile, the heightened emphasis on rugby as the "white man's game" curtailed and constrained their involvement in that sport.

Joseph M. Bradley examines arguments about identity, ethnicity, and nationalism in the context of two essentially white social groups—Scots of Scottish descent and Scots of Irish descent. Like Neverson and Knight, Bradley is concerned with media representations; his concern is with how and why the press and radio have articulated a vision of "Scottishness" that fails to recognize ethnic diversity within Scotland and, in the case of Scots of Irish descent, derides a non-British lineage. Bradley explores what he terms "majority Scottishness" and "minority Irishness" in the context of the Scottish national football team. He asks how contested notions of ancestry, patriotism, politics, and religion have played out in respect of whom the Scottish side is claimed to represent. Just as importantly, how do fans from the dominant ethnic groupings—Scottish and Irish—identify (or otherwise) with the Scottish national football team? Bradley concludes that Association football is a key domain in which dominant ideologies of Scottishness are maintained, and also through which the ethnic minority Irish are depicted negatively as the "other."

Colin Tatz is concerned with "the good, the bad and the ugly" of sport for Australian Aborigines, and Torres Strait and South Sea Islanders over the vast period of 1868 to 2010. He points to trenchant discrimination against indigenous Australians in sport; this was compounded by loathing towards those who excelled in spite of participation constraints. Paradoxically, though, a few prominent aboriginal athletes were widely embraced after making world-class achievements in sport, such as the boxer

Lionel Rose and the tennis player Evonne Goolagong. The inference here is that many whites now saw them more as "Australian" than aboriginal. Tatz concludes that for all its foibles, sport plays a fundamentally positive role for indigenous communities, and that it even acts as a deterrent to feelings of self-harm and anti-social behaviors.

Vicky Paraschak and Janice Forsyth evaluate the experiences of aboriginal women in and around sport. Too often this area of research has been overlooked by an inordinate focus on indigenous males. Such gender disparity is, it must be admitted, similar to that of sports studies generally. But the relatively small amount of research into aboriginal sport means that the evaluation of women within that literature has been limited. Paraschak and Forsyth focus on indigenous females in Canadian sport, and do so by locating their research in the context of that country's first national roundtable on aboriginal women in sport. The authors immersed themselves in this symposium and drew upon its findings; concurrently they conducted semi-structured interviews with several delegates who attended the roundtable. The voices of these aboriginal women were therefore central to the research process, with the authors engaged in free-flowing dialogue with the participants. Listening to them carefully was especially important, argued Paraschak and Forsyth, because "aboriginal women ... have few opportunities to publicly engage in discussions about gender and how it shapes their lives as women in sport." This exploratory study provides a framework for further research into gender issues, sport and Aboriginal communities.

CODA

There is a broad consensus amongst the contributors to this book that scholars ought not be politically neutral toward the findings and implications of their research. While not speaking on behalf of all authors in this volume, Booth argues that scholars should take an overt moral stance for, as he puts it, "knowledge about racism in sport for its own sake serves little purpose: knowledge needs utility." Injustices of the past have legacies; the role of the historian is to articulate the problems of the past and take an active role in addressing them today. This position is predicated upon scholars crafting what Booth characterizes as "socially-responsible narratives" to provide that utility. Sport historians and sociologists could profitably adopt a cultural studies approach which is praxis-driven (not a purely academic endeavor but rather one that attempts to address real, contemporary, socio-cultural-political issues) and self-reflexive (an approach that realizes the potential incongruity and transient nature of the knowledge it produces). In the end, as Richard Gruneau writes, "the challenge is to write theoretically-informed histories that are sensitive to multiple and uneven paths of change, histories where the structuring principles of the field of sporting practice at any given time are recognized to involve complex sets of dominant, residual, and emergent tendencies." I trust that *Sport, Race, and Ethnicity* provides examples of this socially and politically engaged scholarship.

ACKNOWLEDGMENTS

The edited volume *Sport, "Race," and Ethnicity* stems from the conference *Sport, Race, and Ethnicity: Building a Global Understanding,* which was hosted by the School of Leisure, Sport and Tourism, University of Technology Sydney (UTS), and staged at UTS Haymarket Campus, Sydney, Australia, from November 30 to December 2, 2008. This event, which attracted some 150 delegates and 75 speakers from various parts of the world, was a follow up to the inaugural symposium *Sport and Race: Building a Global Understanding,* which was organized by the Dept. of Health and Sports Studies, University of Iowa, from October 12-14, 2006. A third such conference, *Beyond Boundaries: Race and Ethnicity in Modern Sport,* was staged at the University of the West Indies, Cave Hill Campus, Barbados, between July 16-18, 2010, and hosted in partnership with the Academy of International Sport, George Mason University, Virginia, and the CLR James Cricket Research Centre at The University of the West Indies, Cave Hill.

REFERENCES

Adair, D. and Rowe, D., Beyond boundaries? "Race," ethnicity and identity in sport. *International Review for the Sociology of Sport* vol. 45, no. 3, pp. 251-257.

Cornell, S. and Hartmann, D., *Ethnicity and Race: Making Identities in a Changing World,* Thousand Oaks CA: Sage, 2nd ed., 2007.

Graves, J.L. Jr., *The Emperor's New Clothes: Biological Theories of Race at the Millennium,* Piscataway NJ: Rutgers University Press, 2001.

Gruneau, R., *Class, Sports, and Social Development,* 2nd ed., Champaign, IL: Human Kinetics, 1999.

Hoberman, J. *Darwin's Athletes: How Sport has Damaged Black America and Preserved the Myth of Race,* New York: Houghton Mifflin Company, 1997.

Miller, P.B. and Wiggins, D.K. (eds.), *Sport and the Color Line: Black Athletes and Race Relations in Twentieth Century America,* New York: Routledge, 2003.

Sugden, J., "Critical left-realism and sport interventions in divided societies," *International Review for the Sociology of Sport,* vol. 45, no. 3, pp. 258-272.

Tatz, C., 'Coming to terms: "Race", ethnicity, identity and Aboriginality in sport', *Australian Aboriginal Studies,* No. 2, 2009, pp. 15-31.

Tatz, C. and Adair, D., "Darkness and a little light: 'Race' and sport in Australia," *Australian Aboriginal Studies,* No. 2, 2009, pp. 1-14.

FOR MORE INFORMATION ONLINE, PLEASE SEE:

http://www.business.uts.edu.au/lst/sre/index.html

http://www.uiowa.edu/~global/ index.htm

http://www.cavehill.uwi.edu/fhe/beyondboundaries/index.htm

History, Race, Sport: from Objective Knowledge to Socially-Responsible Narratives

BY **DOUGLAS BOOTH**

Conceptualizing history and memory

[T]he photograph of two black athletes standing, on the victory podium, raising black-gloved fists in the "black power" salute, ignoring "The Star-Spangled Banner" ... has been fixed in historical memory. For [Avery] Brundage, [the president of the International Olympic Committee] and his colleagues, this was an inexplicable act (and one to be punished by expulsion from the games), but millions of Afro-Americans knew exactly what Tommy Smith and John Carlos wanted to express by their symbolic gesture. The civil rights movement in the United States, which made significant gains in the early sixties, had slowed ... That the "grunts" fighting and dying in Southeast Asia were disproportionately black intensified the anger felt by Afro-American activists. When the murder of Martin Luther King, Jr., seemed to snuff out the possibility of peaceful progress toward racial justice, many despairing blacks turned to violence (Guttmann, 1992: 130-31).

> [T]he enduring intrigue of the image Smith and Carlos produced can be traced to the way in which these athletes were able to inject "blackness"—in the form of their own black bodies—into a ceremonial system that quite literally had no place for nonnational identities such as race, class, religion, or (in a more complicated case) gender (Hartmann, 2003, xv).

These quotes both describe the famous photograph of protests by Tommy Smith and John Carlos at the 1968 olympic games[1] in Mexico City. They also illustrate two paradigmatic approaches to the analysis of race by historians of sport. Allen Guttmann views the photograph as straightforward evidence of a racial protest, the causes of which emerge when it is placed in the context of race relations in the United States in the late 1960s.[2] Guttmann's assumptions about the evidential, or truth-bearing, properties of the photograph and his contextual approach are classic social history, a form that dominated twentieth-century historical study (Munslow, 2006, 78). Douglas Hartmann, by contrast, poses the question why the photograph continues to attract intense attention nearly four decades after its first publication. The contradiction in Guttmann's phrase "fixed in historical memory" highlights the potency of Hartmann's question: the term "history" typically refers to the ways that "a collectiv[e] relates to its past, whereas *memory* is, strictly speaking, the domain of the individual." Thus "'collective memory'" is "a metaphor whose fruitfulness can always meaningfully be questioned" (Ankersmit, 2005, 5).[3] Indeed, nearly 50 percent of the American population has no personal memory of events in the late 1960s (US Census Bureau, 2000). Hartmann looks beyond the politics of a past event and turns his attention to the nature, and power, of the black body at the world's largest sporting pageant. In so doing he advocates interpreting the symbolism and enduring meaning of the act; Hartmann's interpretative approach aligns with contemporary cultural history that first challenged the status of social history late last century.

SOCIAL HISTORY, RACE, AND SPORT

Along with class and gender, race is a foundation stone of sport history (Pope, 1997; Struna, 2000). Since the history of sport came of age as a recognized area of study in the 1970s, historians have examined racial segregation and racial integration in sport; they have investigated the political struggles and conflicts around race on the field and track, in the ring, and across the spectrum of ideologies, practices and institutions (e.g., Baker, 1986; Booth, 1998; Lapchick, 1975; Murray & Merrett, 2004; Tatz, 1995; Tygiel 1983; Wiggins, 1977, 1980a). Sport historians debunked the idea of race as a biological category and traced the construction of race as a social category (e.g., Wiggins, 1989; Hoberman, 1997, 2006).[4] Summarily dismissing race as a biological category, Niall Ferguson (2006, xlii) writes that modern genetics demonstrate "human beings are remarkably alike. In terms of our DNA we are, without a shadow of a doubt, one species … The differences we associate with racial identities are superficial: pigmentation (which is darker in the melanocytes of peoples whose ancestors lived close to the equator), physiognomy (which makes eyes narrower and noses shorter at the Eastern end of the Eurasian landmass), and hair type. Beneath the skin we are all quite similar" (see also, Pope, 2006, 151-52).[5]

Traditionally, historians of sport approached race largely through the lens of social history (Parratt, 1998; Pope, 1997; Struna, 2000). Reacting against the neo-Rankean emphasis on "political history and great men" (Burke, 2005, 13), social historians embraced the ideas, concepts and theories of anthropology, economics, psychology, and sociology in order to understand the gamut of human activity. Social historians sought to replace political history with a "'wider and more human'" form that "would include all human activities and which would be less concerned with the narrative of events than with the analysis of 'structures'" (Burke, 2005, 14). Whether examining the history of the body, food, gender, language, race, sexuality, medicine, or sport, social historians grounded their studies in structural analysis and structural causation; that is, those "long term ecological conditions, demographic regimes, technological and occupational orders, patterns of exchange, and arrangements of power that people find themselves in and that limit and shape activity" (Licht, 1992, 37). Social historians of race and sport primarily direct their attention at those discriminatory racial structures of power and domination that affect participation in sport. For example, for most of the twentieth century racial structures precluded the vast majority of black South Africans and Aboriginal Australians from even reaching the playing fields, while in the United States they precluded African Americans from positions of authority and responsibility in white-run national sporting associations and federations.[6] Yet, while social historians of race and sport largely conceptualize racial discrimination in terms of structures of constraint, when accounting for racial changes over the last fifty years they tend, ironically, to foreground individuals who challenged and set out to transform those structures. Thus, social historians single out actors such as Jean Claude Ganga, Denis Brutus, and Sam Ramsamy in South Africa, Charles Perkins in Australia, and Harry Edwards in the United States, who led political campaigns against discrimination and whose lives and experiences rarely appear in official national histories.[7]

Social historians identify considerable progress in racial equality on the sporting front. In their documentary history of the African-American sporting experience, David Wiggins and Patrick Miller (2003, 443) describe the "virtual erasure" of the color line on the playing fields; today "African Americans participate in a wide array of sports at all levels of competition." Indeed, scenes of racial integration appear on sports fields around the world, from Australia to Scotland. But Wiggins and Miller (2003, 444) warn that the "ordeal of integration" is far from over, with racism and discrimination "still shadow[ing] African-American success." Statistics reveal a paucity of black coaches, black officials and black team owners; the popular press and media continue to propagate racial typologies that highlight supposed white virtues—mental dexterity, integrity, tenacity, willpower, and teamwork—at the expense of supposed black deficiencies—casual attitudes, showmanship, and individualism. In the broader context of race relations none of this should surprise. "Racial differences may be genetically few," says Ferguson (2006, xlvi), "but human beings seem to be designed to attach importance to them." Indeed, John Hoberman (2006, 224; and 2010 herein) sees the concept of biological race undergoing a resurrection after "decades in disrepute." A key source of this "comeback," he says, is the Human Genome Project and its research into the "distributions of certain genetic variations (alleles) among 'racial' populations that experience corresponding (and differing) rates of medical disorders of genetic origin" (Hoberman, 2006, 224). Citing sociologist Troy Duster, Hoberman (2006, 224) believes this research will "'reinscribe taxonomies of race across a broad range of scientific practices and fields.'"

Social historians do not approach culture in the same wholehearted manner as they embrace other concepts such as class, domination, subordination, hegemony, and resistance. Nonetheless, culture holds currency as a descriptive category (e.g., art, literature, music, sport) and as a social category referring to "the whole way of life of a people" (Jenks, 1993, 12). The latter is particularly apparent among historians of sport interested in class (e.g., Hargreaves, 1986; see also, Booth & Loy, 1999). However, whether they regard culture as a descriptive or social category, social historians tend to conceptualize it as "a kind of superstructure," reflecting a relationship with the economic and social base (Burke, 2005, 120).

In *Learning to Win*, Pamela Grundy (2001) examines sport as part of the cultural superstructure. Seeking to understand how sport became "a model for a conservative view of the American social and economic order," Grundy finds the answer in a nineteenth-century ideology that portrayed competition as an inevitable and generally admirable fact of life. According to Grundy, this new ideology penetrated all walks of life. Underpinning this ideology, she says, was the structure of modern capitalism, which determined nineteenth-century American society, its economy and its culture—including sport. In her words, competitive sport "meshed neatly" with the goals of capitalism; sporting, and capitalist endeavour was one and the same. In both capitalism and sport citizens must not only "win" their places, they must "win [them] anew each day" (Grundy, 2001, 5, 217 & 220). Grundy (2001) in fact makes a concerted effort to step beyond structural analyses and to incorporate non-reductionist notions of agency and culture. For example, she recognizes African Americans negotiating their own cultural space within institutionalized sport. Yet, despite her notions of cultural autonomy, Grundy ultimately privileges structure. As she concludes, the very institution of sport—which is built upon a "model of competition and individual effort"—offers participants little space in which to question the "larger meaning of competition" that structures contemporary American society (Grundy, 2001, 301).

Over the last decade something of a paradigmatic shift has begun in sport history with practitioners increasingly engaging in a more herme-neutic-type approach to sporting identities and cultures. Of interest here is the potential epistemological tension in this shift. Deconstructionist cultural history in particular invites more skeptical and critical perspec-tives of historical facts and evidence and the ways that historians prefig-ure and configure their narratives (Hunt, 1989, 20). However, that tension has yet to demonstrably surface in sport history. Most practitioners re-main committed to the "authority of evidence" in the production of their histories (Munslow, 2006, 195) and have embraced very select elements of decontructionism (e.g., discourse and textual analysis) as supplementary analytical tools. At this point then, let me examine the analysis of race and sport in contemporary cultural history.

CULTURAL HISTORY, RACE, AND SPORT

It is impossible to give either a precise date or a single explanation for the turn from the social to the cultural in history. Victoria Bonnell and Lynn Hunt (1999, 6) refer to the cultural turn running across the 1980s and 1990s, and they identify a raft of contributing factors including "ques-tions about the status of 'the social,' concerns raised by the depiction of culture as a symbolic, linguistic, and representational system, seem-ingly inevitable methodological and epistemological dilemmas, a resulting or perhaps precipitating collapse of explanatory paradigms, and a consequent realignment of the disciplines (including the rise of cultural studies)." In sport history the cultural turn was neither abrupt nor even. Examples of cultural approaches within social history abound as Gerald Early's (1988) analysis of black boxing and Brian Stoddart's (1987) study of Barbadian cricket culture testify; however, C. L. R. James' acclaimed *Beyond a Boundary* (1963/1993) predated Stoddart's work on black West Indian cricket culture by a quarter of a century. Nonetheless, the interest in sport as a medium of identity and as a practice that creates meaning for all kinds of groups (local communities, genders, nations, and so forth), and which became prominent in sport history in the mid-1990s (e.g., Allison, 1993; Jarvie 1993; Nauright & Chandler, 1996), marks at least one distinctive phase of cultural approaches in the field.

Accounts and explanations of cultural history are complicated by the fact that it comprises "varying and vying projects" (Licht, 1992, 41). Walter Licht (1992) distinguishes three basic positions: "social constructionism," "pure deconstructionism," and a "less nihilistic deconstructionism." Historians of sport tend to discuss the two strands of deconstructionism under the heading postmodernism (e.g., Hill, 1996; Parratt, 1998, 9; Phillips, 2006, 7). In this section I will examine the approaches taken by social constructionists and deconstructionists to the analysis of race and sport and some of the methodological issues that they raise.

Social Constructionism, Race, and Sport

Social constructionists conceptualize culture as a "deliberate product, a social construction ... produced out of existing social tensions" (Licht, 1992, 41), and this conceptualization underpins most cultural approaches in sport history. Social constructionists argue that cultural formations may arise under any number of conditions: from "above as an instrument of social control," as a result of "dialogue" between dominant and subordinate groups, stemming from "conflict and negotiation" between dominant and subordinate groups, or simply among "different groups" who seek to "distinguish themselves and sanctify their authority or to eke out separate, autonomous places" (Licht, 1992, 41; see also Nussdorfer, 1993, 79). As stated above, social constructionist approaches to culture have grown in sport history over the last decade. Ben Carrington and Ian McDonald (2001, 4) capture the framework of this approach in their definition of cultures as "lived social processes," always "porous, subject to constant change, and forever being remade."

When discussing the concept of a racially-based culture one must avoid transforming race—a social construction—into a natural or essential category. However, the enforced separation of people of color in Australia, South Africa, the United States, and elsewhere, undoubtedly contributed to the formation of distinct cultures. This separation, and the inevitable deprived material conditions faced by people of color, justifies the term racial culture. In the United States, approximately 1.75 million African Americans left the southern states for northern cities between 1910 and 1940 (Wiggins & Miller, 2003, 85). The social relations in the northern cities, such as New York, Chicago, and Detroit, were less rigid than in the southern states—and certainly less rigid than the *bantustans* (tribal reserves) and townships of South Africa (Booth, 1998) and the rural reserves of Australia (Tatz, 1995). Nonetheless, the color line remained essentially in place in these northern cities. In these spaces, African Americans formed their own institutions including churches, media, and sporting clubs. Influenced by prevailing material conditions, black institutions and groups produced distinct cultures (Wiggins & Miller 2003, 85). Thus, while the organizers of black sporting leagues in the United States may have "crafted organizational plans and operational procedures that mirrored the efforts of their white counterparts," African-American baseball and basketball teams, such as the Harlem Renaissance Five, still "fashioned distinctive patterns of play" (Wiggins & Miller, 2003, 87).

Steven Pope (2006, 155) elaborates nicely on this very example.

Early black professional basketball performance emerged in Harlem as a result of black entrepreneurial interests and was closely linked to after-game dances. Guys and gals watched the Harlem Renaissance Five (the "Rens")—as well as teams such as Cumberland Posey's "Big Five" (the first openly professional team formed in Pittsburgh in 1913)—and afterward danced to the music of leading jazz bands (e.g., Count Basie, Duke Ellington, Chick Webb) at the most popular dance halls. [At] the thirty-five hundred seat capacity Renaissance Casino and Ballroom ... [the "Rens"] provide[d] basketball exhibitions for the throngs of people waiting to dance the night away ... Ballplayers were probably among those who danced after games so that the diffusion of taste flowed from musicians to dancers to basketball players or from players to the dancers and musicians.

Pope (2006, 148) locates the distinguishing style of African-American basketball in its "fast breaks, explosive speed, innovative ball handling, and varied shot selection." According to Gerald Early, this style is an example of how black people "transformed an *American* ludic endeavour into an *African American* cultural expression thereby redefining the meaning of being American in their own terms through the game;" that is, "they took a larger cultural trait, not an inherently racial one, and adapted it as a ritualized style, as a performance ... [so as] to distinguish themselves from whites" (cited in Pope, 2006, 148).

Examples from elsewhere further illustrate the point that distinct sporting cultures will emerge under specific material conditions and as groups set out to variously "distinguish themselves and sanctify their authority." In the South African townships of the Cape Flats around Cape Town during apartheid, Colored[8] soccer players established unique sporting cultures. Grant Farred (2003) shows some players appropriating the names, colors, and playing styles of English professional clubs. But their actions were not simple mimicry. On the contrary, they demonstrated a highly complex—and often disguised—form of agency in which they negotiated between idealized notions of Europe and everyday life in the townships. In this negotiation they created unique identities. Farred (2003) concedes that members of some clubs on the Cape Flats made only minimal and superficial adjustments to their identities. However, he cites the Everton Amateur Football Club of Heideveld as an example of one club that successfully unshackled township football from the English model to achieve cultural autonomy.

Like their brethren at Merseyside, the players at Everton of Heideveld share a loose affiliation with the Anglican Church, wear blue and white, and base their game on a combination of ball skills and defence. Yet, the distinctive offensive bravado and defensive discipline of the Cape Flats' amateurs effectively gave a new meaning to Everton, removing all connotations of Merseyside and transforming it into an independent township soccer team. In Farred's (2003, 142-3) words:

> On the playing fields of the Cape Flats, "Everton" evoked only one identity—the local one, because Everton AFC played a brand of football that was not only different from their English namesake, but one that was more highly regarded than the metropolitan model. The Cape Flats amateurs succeeded in wrestling "Everton" from the county of Lancashire, unmooring it culturally, and then re-inventing it. Everton AFC made the Everton Merseyside institution "undesirable"— Heideveld boys wanted to play like "their" Everton, not the English model.

Thus, rather than seeing one brand of football as superior or inferior to another, or as a mimic of another, Farred examines the specific conditions on the Cape Flats that produced an entirely new brand with its own distinct local cultural identity. Most importantly, this identity helped the players and their supporters cast off the yolk of cultural and psychological "racial dependency."

In their respective examples of African-American basketball and Cape Colored soccer, Pope and Farred provide interpretations that exceed the material evidence and thus highlight the methodological issues of social constructionism. Pope (2006) explicitly tackles this subject. Culture, he reminds us, "is always a vexing process ... to document through traditional sources and methods" (Pope, 2006, 159). This is all the more so when the culture under consideration is a "stylized physical ... primarily non-verbal ... performance" (Pope, 2006, 148). Commenting on basketball, Pope cites historian Stephen Fox who describes the game developing "'spontaneous[ly] ... in thousands of isolated pockets around the country. The game bounced forward in the hands of numberless innovators, most of them now unknown and unknowable'" (Pope, 2006, 159-60). Thus, Pope (2006, 160) concludes, "if it is difficult to substantiate the timing of the sport itself, we must also confess that any documentation on the development of a distinctly *black* style of play is even more elusive and thus open to speculation and historical conjecture [emphasis in the original]."

> Written sources are scarce, much of the oral testimony is contradictory and often impossible to corroborate; and the richest sources of all (black ... basketball players) have died and taken their recollections to the grave. With the exceptions of a few African American newspapers, there was virtually nothing about black basketball in the mainstream media prior to the early 1950s. (Pope, 2006, 161)

How should sport historians deal with this problem of elusive sources? Pope (2006, 163) advocates a "postmodern sensibility" that "allows us 'to know something without claiming to know everything.'" He also urges historians to move beyond seeking objective facts and instead ask questions about the origins of facts and "'how do they operate *in* history, especially insofar as they cultivate the subjects *of* history?'" (Pope, 2006, 164, emphasis in the original). But if Pope's (2006) "postmodern sensibility" expresses deconstructionist sentiments, his preferred approach is a knowledge-based, causally-orientated social constructionism. He still advocates, for example, investigating "the structure and function of cultural production" and "why social groups develop distinctive styles of performance" (Pope, 2006, 164). Such then is the position occupied by contemporary social constructionism in sport history. But what of deconstructionism?

Deconstructionism, Race, and Sport

Pure deconstructionism, promoted by Jacques Derrida (e.g., 1978) and Dominick LaCapra (e.g., 1987) is "truly poststructuralist: nothing can be known. Texts or subjects of analysis are filled with contradictions and voids, and there is no need even to consider the author and his or her intentions" (Licht, 1992, 41). While less nihilistic deconstructionists admit "the past can be studied and known," they still deny all "truths or essences." Rather, "all knowledge is constructed, and it remains for the 'reader' to discern the premises of various constructions" and discourses (e.g., Foucault, 1980) (Licht, 1992, 41). Where historians have translated these approaches into concrete histories, they have typically framed them around "laying bare *meaning*," that is, analyzing how authors inscribe meaning in their texts and how different groups construct meaning in terms of "otherness," and analyzing the multidimensional nature of meaning and the relationships between meaning and the wider context of discourse (Booth, 2005, 18-19, emphasis in the original). For example, laying bare the meaning(s) of the image of Tommy Smith and John Carlos at Mexico City, is Douglas Hartmann's objective in *Race, Culture, and the Revolt of the Black Athlete* (2003).

Deconstructionism has also focused new attention on texts that now include non-literary forms such as paintings, television programs, clothing styles, sports spectacles, and political events. And instead of viewing texts as "concrete phenomenological objects with a fixed meaning," many cultural historians now see them as "systems or structures of meaning flowing from semiotic, social and cultural processes" which they subject to "diverse readings and various interpretations" (Berkhofer, 1995, 21). Among the many implications that this reconceptualization has for historians of sport, two warrant mention. First, textualism tends to direct cultural historians towards smaller units of analysis and micro-interpretations, and the relationships between texts (intertextuality), and both text and context (Iggers, 1997). Douglas Hartmann's analysis of the Smith and Carlos photograph captures many of these themes. Commenting on the shifting meaning(s) of the photograph (text), Hartmann (2003, 10) notes that the two "one-time enemies of the state" are now widely accepted as "heroes of the civil rights movement." The text remains the same but the context in which people look at it has changed dramatically. A new commemorative statue at San Jose University is evidence of the different context (Smith, 2006).

Second, textualism raises new issues and questions about narrative and historical representation. Textualism, for example, has alerted historians to the fact that they "express ... historical knowledge ... by texts rather than by individual statements or explanations" (Ankersmit, 2005, xiii). Logically, then, "history is not something given (waiting to be discovered in 'primary' sources) or as something made (the 'facts') but an activity embodied in 'performance,' in the sense of action enfolded in the resources of representation and of representation as itself a form of action" (Pope, 2006, 164; for the fullest examples in sport history see Phillips, 2002; Sydnor, 1998).

I am not aware of any historians of sport embracing (poststructuralist) deconstructionism to the extent that they conceptualize language as the foundation of reality. Those engaging language (and its corollaries) in any substantive manner generally treat it as a supplementary analytical tool. In other words, language helps shape, rather than constitute, lived experiences (Toews, 1987, 882). In early examples, Patricia Vertinsky (1994, 10) saw "networks of discursive practices" being "moulded and influenced by social institutions," while John Hargreaves (1986) linked discourse to the production system. More recent approaches still follow this path as John Bloom (2000) illustrates in his textual analysis of an interview conducted in 1967 between Arthur Harris, a Native American, and two anthropologists, Elizabeth Euler and Patricia McGee.

Bloom (2000, 105) reads Harris's stories of sporting events as a "counternarrative ... that critically reflects upon race, national identity, and assimilation" in the United States.[9] Upon first reading Harris's narrative, Bloom (2000, 111) found a "rather straightforward celebration of ideologies that have been a core aspect of dominant culture in the United States: ideologies such as those elevating individual success and upward mobility, nonwhite subservience, and white privilege and paternal responsibility." Subsequent readings, however, revealed a series of "hidden transcripts" or conversations. These provide important "clues" into the "complex nature of boarding schools, Native American history, and the role of sports within these." "Harris's story," Bloom (2000, 111) continues, "might seem to accommodate those in power, but it is also about using dominant society to survive and about drawing upon hidden stories to fashion critique."

Harris's decision to leave the San Carlos reservation in Arizona and attend the Hampton Normal and Agricultural Institute in Virginia, an institution originally established to educate freed slaves, is one example of a "hidden transcript." Harris, says Bloom (2000, 114-15),

> recalls that he learned of Hampton while a student at the Phoenix Indian School when a teacher had him read Booker T. Washington's memoir *Up from Slavery*. However, he made the decision to attend the school over the Fourth of July weekend in 1910 while participating in a baseball tournament playing for Phoenix Indian School against both Indian and white teams. Even more significantly, he takes special care to remind his interviewers that July 4, 1910 was an eventful day in sports history. On that date, Jack Johnson, the first African American heavyweight boxing champion, successfully defended his title against a white fighter named Jim Jeffries in Reno, Nevada.

Although Harris makes only fleeting reference to the fight, Bloom (2000, 115) insists that "it shapes his narrative in very important ways." (At this point Bloom provides the racial context of the Johnson-Jeffries bout, referring in particular to the negative sentiments expressed by the American press. On the eve of the fight, the *Chicago Daily Tribune* praised Jeffries, referring to him as a minister's son, while vilifying Johnson as a "coward" and a shirker who gravitated to boxing with the sole desire to make easy money. Bloom also notes that white-led race riots erupted in several cities and towns in the United States following Johnson's victory.) Harris, Bloom believes, uses an ironic trope to frame his decision to leave for Hampton. In Bloom's (2000, 117-18) words,

> Harris constructs an ... ironic narrative in which he is able to resist identification with whiteness during a time of intense hatred toward blacks by embracing African American institutions like Hampton and heroes like Washington. Harris's narrative, particularly in the way that he evokes sports, suggests that beneath the surface, Native Americans and African Americans shared common interests at a particular moment of danger in relation to racial politics.

Bloom finds further support for his argument in Harris's decision to stay at Hampton after the federal government, fearful of, in Harris's words, "Indians ... intermarry[ing] ... Negroes" (cited in Bloom, 2000, 118), refused financial support to Native Americans studying at the Virginian institute. Leaving Hampton and attending an Indian school would have financially benefited Harris. And "he could have followed the lead of someone like Charles Carter, attempting to gain social advancement by embracing the potential privileges of whiteness and, in turn, accepting a racial polarity in which its opposite, blackness, is associated with degradation" (Bloom, 2000, 118-19). However, by remaining at Hampton, Harris "chooses to defy" white definitions of success and "sid[es] his own more ambiguous racial identity with 'blackness'" (Bloom, 2000, 119).

Bloom (2000, 121) argues that the "hidden transcripts" in Harris's narrative offer "a powerful critique of race and racism in the United States from the multiple social locations" Harris occupied: "as a Yavapia who was brutally displaced and as a Native American who played sports, identified with blacks, and became educated into white society."

Bloom's (2000) interpretation of Harris's narrative displays signs of "less nihilistic deconstructionism" (Licht, 1992) in that both the author and his subject construct, rather than discover or find, knowledge. However, there is no doubt that Bloom is also the author—the narrator, the system maker and the authority—who organizes the text in order to promote *his* interpretation, meaning and knowledge of Harris (Berkhofer, 1995, 169). There is little encouragement of, or space for, reader skepticism in Bloom's text. Bloom (2000) reinforces his interpretation with evidence and argument external to the interview. As well as deconstructing Harris's interview, Bloom (2000) employs contextualization (e.g., the Johnson-Jeffries fight as a context for Harris's decision to attend Hampton Institute) to frame the transcripts and to expose the deeper meanings therein. Ultimately, Bloom (2000) engages language, as did Vertinsky (1994) and Hargreaves (1986), as one of several analytical tools to produce knowledge of relationships of power.

Like social historians, cultural historians privilege the analysis of social relationships of power, examining either the functions of culture within such relationships or language as a vehicle for revealing and concealing relations of power. While the interpretative methods of cultural history are more ambiguous with respect to evidence and involve greater speculation and conjecture, cultural historians are no less committed to the production of interpretive knowledge than social historians. Not surprising then, Catriona Parratt (1998, 13) finds "most sport and leisure historians ... quite comfortable" with this form of history; she suggests that some even welcome it as a way to "sharpen and enrich historical study." On the other hand, it is precisely the overriding commitment to knowledge of the past that disturbs postmodern philosophers of history such as Hayden White (2005) and Alun Munslow (2006). They maintain that issues such as racism are contemporary social problems and that if history is to be relevant it must address not only the past, but the present and the future. I will outline and assess these criticisms and arguments in the final section of this chapter.

HISTORY, RACE, SPORT, AND THE
BURDEN OF SCIENCE

Historians of sport have studied aspects of racism in the past to produce a formidable body of knowledge on the subject. Social historians have portrayed the discrimination faced by black people in the realm of sport and their political battles to gain access to sports fields; cultural historians have described the inner worlds of black people who live in racist societies and their attempts to build sporting cultures as expressions of agency and to counter discrimination. But how does this historical knowledge inform us about contemporary racism? Do people invoke this historical knowledge as a reality to challenge essentialist and reductionist notions of race and popular notions of racial and racist hierarchies? Does this historical knowledge provide "moral instruction" through "idealized examples of virtue and vice for imitation?" (White, 2005, 334). Practicing historians rarely consider such philosophical questions. Whether they work within a framework of social (causal) or cultural (interpretative) history, most historians view their discipline as a "science" that frowns on "moral and aesthetic, not to mention political and social, judgements on the present" (White, 2005, 334). For critics, including White (2005) and Munslow (2006), this empiricist stance leaves history languishing and historians unable to intervene in contemporary issues. In this section I take up these criticisms in the light of the fallacy of race as a biological category that continues to vex sport.

International sport, with its focus on national identities (e.g., national achievements and victories), generally relegates to the margins expressions of non-national identities such as race, ethnicity, and gender. This makes political sense: removing opportunities for the expression of non-national identities is critical if organizers are to avoid embarrassments, conflicts, and even disruptions to their events (Forsyth & Wamsley, 2005). But, as Ben Carrington (2004) demonstrates, events such as the olympic games do little to challenge binary perspectives on race; rather, they reinforce them. Carrington (2004) illustrates this in his analysis of two incidents at the 2000 games: Eric Moussambani's swim in the men's 100 metres, and Konstantinos Kenteris's gold medal in the men's 200-meter sprint.

After Moussambani completed his solitary swim, the media positioned the swimmer from Equatorial Guinea as a stereotypical black African: innocent, happy, and unencumbered by the demands of professional sport. And the man who had allegedly learned to swim while evading crocodiles became the infantile African, renamed Eric the Eel (see also, Nauright & Magdalinski, 2003). Some of the discourses around Moussambani were undoubtedly part of a nonracist parody on sport; some could be classified under the rubric of Australian irreverence at the Sydney olympics (McGregor, 1966). But irrespective of whether one classifies these discourses as racist or non-racist, Moussambani's words were all but absent; these discourses denied Moussambani the opportunity to cultivate any sense of self. Janice Forsyth and Kevin Wamsley (2005) reach a similar conclusion in their analysis of the cooptation of indigenous peoples into olympic ceremonies. The nature of the relationship is such that "Olympic organisers reinforce common views of Aboriginal peoples as being rooted in the past and having no place in modern social contexts" (Forsyth & Wamsley, 2005, 242).

In the final of the 200m sprint, Kenteris defeated seven black runners. Carrington (2004) says the result confounded many journalists unaccustomed to seeing a white person win an event long dominated by black people. Kenteris, after all, represented a race supposedly incapable of jumping or sprinting. Some journalists initially explained Kenteris's victory with veiled references to performance-enhancing drugs. However, when his drug tests returned negative, the discourse immediately shifted to racial epithets and to the racial pedigree of Greeks: did Kenteris, a member of the swarthy race, the media asked, really justify a white classification (Kelly, 2000, 57)?

Where was the historical consciousness in these events? Where were the historical discourses to dispel these racist views and practices? Where were the historical discourses to challenge and dissect the racist language and expose it as a relationship of power? White (2005, 335) argues that they vanished during the Enlightenment when professional historians removed the art from their discipline, when they set out to "'tell the truth (and nothing but the truth)' about the past," and when they moved to "isolate [themselves] from the temptations of literary writing, the excesses of philosophy of history, and the seductiveness of ideology." "Professional historiography," White (2005, 335-36) insists, "cannot honorably participate in discussions of the main political, ethical, and ideological issues that beset a society which ... has little more than 'history' as a basis for making cognitively justified judgments on current issues." As soon as professional historiography staked its academic credibility to "'objectivity' ... in the study of the past," it "sold out any claim to relevance to present existential concerns" (White, 2005, 336).

Why should concerns for objectivity and truth in the past preclude academic historians from contributing to the resolution of contemporary issues? Some insight into this equation emerges from an analysis of David Wiggins's work on race and sport. Over three decades of research and writing, Wiggins has demonstrated great empathy with the injustices suffered, and struggles endured, by black sports people. He is particularly familiar with the institutional neglect, social isolation, racial insensitivity and prejudice suffered by African-American athletes on white university campuses (e.g., Wiggins, 1991, 164-65, 174 & 175). At the same time, however, he has also subscribed to "the spirit of science" (Wiggins, 1989, 185) and the objectivity of history (e.g., Wiggins, 1980b, 221). More recently, in the introduction to *Glory Bound*, Wiggins (1997, xiv) describes historical research in terms of locating primary source material, organizing historical materials and careful writing. Elsewhere he warns historians against adopting the role of "moral critic" (Wiggins, 1980b, 221). Although Wiggins (1980b, 221) admits that historians should "be willing to confront ethical issues," these competing positions leave little space to judge current issues. First, objectivity means giving equal weight to all sides. But in race relations equal weight ends up favoring the white perspective over

31

the black perspective because the two sides are so unequal in the first place. Second, the a-political stance does not preserve the neutrality that historians apparently seek to convey. As the historian of social policy and gender issues Linda Gordon reminds us, "the pose of objectivity is worse than explicit partisanship, because those who claim neutrality are misleading people about their actual positions, and worse, ... they lack a viewpoint from which to be critical of their own culture" (Berkhofer, 1995, 215). Indeed, it is not at all clear that Wiggins wants to critique sport (e.g., Booth, 2005, 220) or, for that matter, history.

Does this mean that historians should abandon objectivity and the quest for truth in the past? White (2005, 338) thinks so:

> we need much more than a discipline devoted to establishing "the facts of the matter" ... . History-writing is more about meaning than about knowledge. Our knowledge of the Holocaust could hardly be more complete or more compelling in regard to its "facticity;" what we need are imagination and poetic insight to help us divine ... meaning.

This argument applies equally to the study of race and racism in sport. Historians have established the always demeaning, often nasty, and occasionally violent facts of racial discrimination in sport. But establishing these facts has hardly countered the emergence, or stemmed the appeal, of Moussambani- and Kenteris-type narratives of racially-based styles and performances as grounded in biology, much less exposed them as the products of uneven relations of power. The best way to counter a narrative that abuses historical facts "is a better narrative," argues White (2005, 336). Such a narrative is "not one with *more* historical facts, but [one] with greater artistic integrity and poetic force of meaning" (White, 2005, 336, emphasis in the original).

Of course, the critical question remains, which meaning? Alun Munslow (2006, 13) claims that "historical meaning flows from what is ... socially responsible to believe about the evidence of the past." Socially responsible narratives of race and sport should emphasize human commonalities, "recognise human variability without the concept (and classification system) of race" (Munslow, 2006, 214), combat stereotypical images of black (sports) people, expose racial explanations of differences in style, performance and access as the products of racist discourses and social relations of power, privilege the voices of those who suffer most from racism, challenge the social relevance and benefits of scientific investigations into race, and remind readers of their inevitable roles as bystanders to racist practices and deeds. While no one should underestimate the difficulties associated with such a project (e.g., Bloxham & Kushner, 1998), longstanding examples already exist. In *The South African Game,* Robert Archer and Antoine Bouillon (1982) reported rich and vibrant rugby, soccer, and cricket competitions and cultures in different black communities during apartheid. Their specific aim was to correct white South African ignorance of black sporting culture, and to challenge official history as relayed by the organs of the apartheid state. Citing an incident during police interrogation of the South African Black Consciousness leader Steve Biko, who later died of brutality in police detention, they show black people using their knowledge of sport to unsettle white stereotypes. Biko's

> interrogators had been astonished by his interest in what they regarded as exclusively "white" matters. For example, a rugby tour by the New Zealanders was in progress at the time, and the Security Police asked if he was following the tour. He told them he was. What did he think of the Springbok team? Steve replied: "I wouldn't have Bosch at fly-half, I'd pick Gavin Cowley." This he said appeared to flabbergast them. Such black knowledge of white sport ... (Archer & Bouillon, 1982, 60).

It is an immensely powerful and socially responsible narrative.

CONCLUSION

Historians of sport interested in race increasingly incorporate into their narratives elements of cultural history including social constructionism and both discourse and textual analysis. Mostly, they regard these elements as supplementary analytical tools to assist their quest for knowledge about the past and have not employed them, as have practitioners in other subfields of history, to reflect on their discipline. Some time before the cultural turn had emerged in sport history, Lynn Hunt (1989) predicted that rigorous cultural analysis will sharpen the methods and goals of history. In her words, "as historians learn to analyze their subjects' representations of their worlds, they inevitably begin to reflect on the nature of their own efforts to represent history; the practice of history is, after all, a process of text creating and of 'seeing,' that is, giving form to subjects" (Hunt, 1989, 20). Thus far Hunt's (1989) prediction shows few signs of materializing in sport history; could this be to the detriment of the field?

Throughout this chapter I have suggested that knowledge about racism in sport for its own sake serves little purpose: knowledge needs utility. I have also suggested that socially responsible narratives might provide that utility. But in order to produce such works historians of sport need to reconceptualize history into both a present-centred and ethically grounded discipline. Notwithstanding those practitioners motivated by a backward-looking curiosity, most historians actually ground their work in the present; their interests in, and concerns about, the present provide the perspectives that lie at the heart of their questions. Conservatives, of course, condemn presentism as an anathema to the discipline and insist that the experiences, thoughts and actions of the people of the past, not those of the present, must be at the fore (e.g., Elton, 2002, 43; Appleby, 1998, 12). By contrast, a present-minded perspective situates "the study of the past and its 'living existence' in the present" (Burton, 2003, 138). In the words of Canadian novelist Margaret Atwood (1998, 1516), "the past no longer belongs to those who once lived in it; the past belongs to those who claim it, and are willing to explore it, and to infuse it with meaning for those alive today. The past belongs to us, because we are the ones who need it." Indeed, the need for a past undoubtedly explains why new generations of historians continually proffer new interpretations when raking over bygone events, and why different groups often read the past so differently. The fact that so many historians pose their questions against a backdrop of contemporary events, issues and observations, and that so many questions involve, either directly or indirectly, issues that relate to contemporary identity, social position, and social change, are good evidence of presentism in history.

While presentism always makes historical perspectives the subject of prevailing consciousness and tentative, it does not mean upholding the present as "true, given, natural, foundational, and so on" (Dean, 1994, 32). Nor does it mean forsaking the relationship between knowledge of the past and predictions of the future. On the contrary, many practitioners already employ historical knowledge to warn their readers of "the dangers inherent within certain modes of thought and institutional practice" (Dean, 1994, 29). In *Darwin's Athletes,* John Hoberman (1997) uses historical examples to show that sport perpetuates rather than alleviates racial stereotypes. He argues that the rise of the black athlete gave new life to biological racism that continues to block the social progress of African Americans.

If historians believe that historical knowledge can influence the future, then, logically, they should consider their ethical responsibilities and thus the politics of 'doing' history. Berkhofer (1998, 248) puts this well when he says "ethics stresses as it envisages the 'ought' of ... power and social relations" (see also White, 2005, 338; Paraschak, Heine & McAra, 1995). And in addressing issues about how people ought to live and conduct their lives, the historian has to decide whether to promote a status quo or oppositional efforts.

ENDNOTES

[1] Author's note: There is no grammatical law that these words ("olympic" and "games") should be capitalized. The olympic movement uses the capital "o" in olympics and olympism to, in part, decorate and venerate itself.

[2] Elsewhere I argue that contextualization and causation are two distinct explanatory paradigms (Booth, 2005: 180).

[3] As well as describing historical memory as a "contradiction in terms," Hayden White (2005: 335 & 336) refers to collective memory as a "scam" of "practical historiography."

[4] Praise for the early contributions made by sport historians has not been unanimous. Referring to the 1987 special edition on race and sport edited by David Wiggins in the *Journal of Sport History*, Jeffrey Sammons (1994: 258) describes it as "signal[ing] a new albeit tardy appreciation for blacks and sport by the forces of [the North American Society for Sport History]." Moreover, Patricia Vertinsky and Gwendolyn Captain (1998: 539) criticize historians of sport for largely "disregarding" the experiences of black women. Those delving into the topic have focused primarily on "the selective achievements of high-achieving African American sportswomen such as Alice Coachman, Wilma Rudolph and Althea Gibson, often explaining their use of sport as a means of social mobility or as an expression of their 'natural' physicality or lack of femininity" (Vertinsky & Captain, 1998: 540). Two important exceptions are the works by Susan Cahn (1995) and Pamela Grundy (2001). Cahn (1995: 127) believes that "the silence surrounding black [female] athletes reflects the power of [dominant discourses] to restrict African American women to the margins of cultural life, occupying a status as distant 'others.'"

[5] In an historiographical sense, historians "devise and deploy" concepts such as race "to organise the data of the past", and "like all concepts ... race derive[s] only in part from the sources that contain references to it. It is, equally, an invention built to meet the insatiable demands of historians for 'mechanisms of explanation,' but also for larger political purposes. Inevitably historians re-view and re-construct such ideas as the needs of contemporary society and, therefore, history change. For this reason, like all concepts employed in history, race is both found (in the evidence/sources) and also continually re-imagined and re-invented" (Munslow, 2006: 212).

[6] Jeffrey Sammons (1994) questions the depth of 20th century social history in this area. He described the majority of books on blacks and sport as "overwhelmingly narrative, largely devoid of theory, rarely pathbreaking, and often behind the curve" (Sammons, 1994: 254).

[7] As Vertinsky and Captain (1998) comment, see note 3 above, there is a striking absence of women in these studies.

[8] In South African parlance, "Colored" refers to people of mixed race, in particular the descendants of liaisons between Europeans and Africans.

[9] Bloom (2000: xiii) sees sport as a "polysemic cultural form," one that "gives voice to a variety of historical perspectives, social contexts, and cultural interpretations."

REFERENCES

Allison, L. (1993). "The Changing Context of Sporting Life," *The Changing Politics of Sport*, Manchester, Manchester University Press, pp. 1-14.

Ankersmit, F. (2005). *Sublime Historical Experience*, Stanford, Stanford University Press.

Appleby, J. (1998). "The Power of History," *American Historical Review, 103*, 1: 1-14.

Archer, R., and Bouillon, A. (1982). *The South African Game: Sport and Racism*, London, Zed Press.

Atwood, M. (1998). "In Search of Alias Grace: On Writing Canadian Historical Fiction," *American Historical Review, 103*, 5: 1503-16.

Baker, W. (1986). *Jesse Owens: An American Life*, New York, The Free Press.

Berkhofer, R. (1995). *Beyond the Great Story: History as Text and Discourse,* Cambridge, Harvard University Press.

Bloom, J. (2000). *To Show What an Indian Can Do: Sports at Native American Boarding Schools,* Minneapolis, University of Minnesota Press.

Bloxham, D., and Kushner, T. (1998). "Exhibiting Racism: Cultural Imperialism, Genocide and Representation," *Rethinking History, 2,* 3: 349-58.

Booth, D. (1998). *The Race Game: Sport and Politics in South Africa,* London, Frank Cass.

Booth, D. (2005). *The Field: Truth and Fiction in Sport History,* London, Routledge.

Booth, D., & Loy, J., (1999). "Sport, Status, Style," *Sport History Review, 30,* 1: 1-26.

Bonnell, V., & Hunt, L. (1999). "Introduction," in *Beyond the Cultural Turn: New Directions in the Study of Society and Culture,* Berkeley, University of California Press, pp. 1-32.

Burke, P. (2005). *History and Social Theory,* second edition, Cambridge, Polity.

Burton, A. (2003). *Dwelling in the Archive: Women Writing House, Home and History in Late Colonial India,* Oxford, Oxford University Press.

Cahn, S. (1995). *Coming on Strong: Gender and Sexuality in Twentieth-Century Women's Sport,* Cambridge, Harvard University Press.

Carrington, B. (2004). "Cosmopolitan Olympism, Humanism and the Spectacle of 'Race,'" in J. Bale and M. Christensen (eds.), *Post-Olympism? Questioning Sport in the Twenty-first Century,* Oxford, Berg, pp. 81-97.

Carrington, B., & McDonald, I. (2001). "Introduction: 'Race', Sport and British Society," "Race", *Sport and British Society,* London, Routledge, pp. 1-26.

Dean, M. (1994). *Critical and Effective Histories: Foucault's Methods and Historical Sociology,* London, Routledge.

Derrida J. (1978). *Writing and Difference,* translated by A. Bass, Chicago, University of Chicago Press.

Early, G. (1988). "The Black Intellectual and the Sport of Prizefighting," *The Kenyon Review, 10,* 3: 102-17.

Elton, G. (2002). *The Practice of History,* second edition, Oxford, Blackwell.

Farred, G. (2003). "'Theatre of Dreams': Mimicry and Difference in Cape Flats Township Football," in J. Bale and M. Cronin (eds.), *Sport and Postcolonialism,* Oxford, Berg, pp. 123-45.

Ferguson, N. (2006). *The War of the World: History's Age of Hatred,* London, Allen Lane.

Forsyth, J., & Wamsley, K. (2005). "Symbols Without Substance: Aboriginal Peoples and the Illusions of Olympic Ceremonies," in K. Young and K. Wamsley (eds.), *Global Olympics: Historical and Sociological Studies of the Modern Games,* Amsterdam, Elsevier, pp. 227-47.

Foucault, M. (1980). *Power / Knowledge: Selected Interviews and Other Writings,* Brighton, Harvester Press.

Grundy, P. (2001). *Learning to Win: Sports, Education, and Social Change in Twentieth-Century North Carolina,* Chapel Hill, University of North Carolina Press.

Guttmann, A. (1992). *The Olympics: A History of the Modern Games,* Urbana, University of Illinois Press.

Hartmann, D. (2003). *Race, Culture, and the Revolt of the Black Athlete,* Chicago, University of Chicago Press.

Hargreaves, J. (1986). *Sport, Power and Culture: A Social and Historical Analysis of Popular Sports in Britain,* Cambridge, Polity Press.

Hill, J. (1996). "British Sports History: A Post-modern Future?," *Journal of Sport History, 23,* 1: 1-19.

Hoberman, J. (1997). *Darwin's Athletes: How Sport Has Damaged Black America and Preserved the Myth of Race,* Boston, Mariner Books.

Hoberman, J. (2006). "Race and Athletics in the Twenty-first Century," in J. Hargreaves & P. Vertinsky (eds.), *Physical Culture, Power, and the Body,* London, Routledge, pp. 208-31.

Hunt, L. (1989). "Introduction: History, Culture, and Text," *The New Cultural History*, Berkeley, University of California Press, pp. 1-22.

Iggers, G. (1997). *Historiography in the Twentieth Century*, Middletown, Wesleyan University Press.

James, C. L. R. (1963/1993). *Beyond a Boundary*, Durham, Duke University Press.

Jarvie, G. (1993)."Sport, Nationalism and Cultural Identity," in L. Allison (ed.), *The Changing Politics of Sport*, Manchester, Manchester University Press, pp. 58-83.

Jenks, C. (1993). *Culture*, London, Routledge.

Kelly, D. (2000). 'He's All-White', *The Mirror*, London, 29 September, 57.

LaCapra, D. (1987). *History and Criticism*, Ithaca, Cornell University Press.

Lapchick, R. (1975). *The Politics of Race and International Sport*, Westport, Greenwood Press.

Licht, W. (1992). "Cultural History / Social History: A Review Essay," *Historical Methods, 25*, 1: 37-41.

McGregor, C. (1966). *Profile of Australia*, London, Hodder & Stoughton.

Munslow, A. (2006). *The Routledge Companion to Historical Studies*, second edition, London, Routledge.

Murray, B., & Merrett, C. (2003). *Caught Behind: Race and Politics in Springbok Cricket*, Johannesburg, Wits University Press.

Nauright, J., & Chandler, T. (1996). *Making Men: Rugby and Masculine Identity*, London, Frank Cass.

Nauright, J., & Magdalinski, T. (2003). "'A Hapless Attempt at Swimming:' Representing Eric Moussambani," *Critical Arts, 17*, 2: 106-122.

Nussdorfer, L. (1993). "The New Cultural History," *History and Theory, 32*, 1: 74-83.

Paraschak, V., Heine, M., & McAra, J. (1995). "Native and Academic Knowledge Interests: A Dilemma," in K. Wamsley, *Method and Methodology in Sport and Cultural History*, Dubuque, Brown and Benchmark Publishers, pp. 62-8.

Parratt, C. (1998). "Reflecting on Sport History in the 1990s," *Sport History Review, 29*, 1: 4-17.

Phillips, M. (2002). "A Critical Appraisal of Narrative in Sport History: Reading the Surf Lifesaving Debate," *Journal of Sport History, 29*, 1: 25-40.

Phillips, M. (2006). *Deconstructing Sport History: A Postmodern Analysis*, Albany, State University of New York Press.

Pope, S. (1997). "Sport History: Toward a New Paradigm," *The New American History: Recent Approaches and Perspectives*, Urbana, University of Illinois Press, pp. 1-31.

Pope, S. (2006). "Decentering 'Race' and (Re)presenting 'Black' Performance in Sport History: Basketball and Jazz in American Culture, 1920-1950," in M. Phillips, *Deconstructing Sport History: A Postmodern Analysis*, Albany, State University of New York Press, pp. 147-177.

Sammons, J. (1994). "'Race' and Sport: A Critical Examination," *Journal of Sport History, 21*, 3: 203-77.

Smith, M. (2006). "Frozen Fists in Speed City: The Statue as 21st Century Reparations," paper presented at the North American Society for Sport History Conference, Glenwood Springs, Colorado, May 20.

Stoddart, B. (1987). "Cricket, Social Formation and Cultural Continuity in Barbados: A Preliminary Ethnohistory," *Journal of Sport History, 14*, 3: 317-40.

Struna, N. (2000). "Social History and Sport," in J. Coakley & E. Dunning (eds.), *Handbook of Sports Studies*, London, Sage, pp. 187-203.

Sydnor, S. (1998). "A History of Synchronized Swimming," *Journal of Sport History, 25*, 2: 252-67.

Tatz, C. (1995). *Obstacle Race: Aborigines in Sport*, Sydney, University of New South Wales Press.

Toews, J. (1987). "Intellectual History After the Linguistic Turn: The Autonomy of Meaning and the Irreducibility of Experience," *American Historical Review, 92,* 4: 879-907.

Tygiel, J. (1983). *Baseball's Great Experiment: Jackie Robinson and His Legacy,* New York, Oxford University Press.

US Census Bureau (2000). "Demographic Profiles," available from: http://censtats.census.gov/data/US/01000.pdf

Vertinsky, P. (1994). *The Eternally Wounded Woman: Women, Doctors, and Exercise in the Late Nineteenth Century,* Urbana, University Of Illinois Press.

Vertinsky, P. & Captain, G. (1998). "More Myth than History: American Culture and Representations of the Black Female's Athletic Ability," *Journal of Sport History, 25,* 3: 532-61.

White, H. (2005). "The Public Relevance of Historical Studies: A Reply to Dirk Moses," *History and Theory, 44,* 3: 333-8.

Wiggins, D. (1977). "Good Times on the Old Plantation: Popular Recreations of the Black Slave in Antebellum South, 1810-1860," *Journal of Sport History, 4,* 3: 260-84.

Wiggins, D. (1980a). "The Play of Slave Children in the Plantation Communities of the Old South, 1820-1860," *Journal of Sport History, 7,* 2: 21-39.

Wiggins, D. (1980b). "Clio and the Black Athlete in America: Myths, Heroes, and Realities," *Quest, 32,* 2: 217-25.

Wiggins, D. (1988). "The Black Athlete in American Sport," special edition, *Journal of Sport History, 15,* 3: 239-355.

Wiggins, D. (1989). "'Great Speed But Little Stamina:' The Historical Debate Over Black Athlete Superiority," *Journal of Sport History, 16,* 2: 158-185.

Wiggins, D. (1991). "Prized Performers, but Frequently Overlooked Students: The Involvement of Black Athletes in Intercollegiate Sports on Predominantly White University Campuses, 1890-1972," *Research Quarterly for Exercise and Sport, 62,* 2: 164-77.

Wiggins, D. (1997). *Glory Bound: Black Athletes in a White America,* Syracuse, Syracuse University Press.

Wiggins, D., & Miller, P. (2003). *The Unlevel Playing Field: A Documentary History of the African American Experience in Sport,* Urbana, University of Illinois Press.

Emperors of Masculinity: John L. Sullivan, Jack Johnson, and Changing Ideas of Manhood and Race in America

BY **RANDY ROBERTS**

*"Boxing is for men, and is about men, and is **men**. A celebration of the lost religion of masculinity all the more trenchant for being lost."* (Oates, 1987, 72)

Willam Lyon Phelps (BA Yale, MA Harvard, and PhD Yale) was the very model of rectitude. In his forty-one years as a literature professor at Yale, he was known for wide-ranging scholarship, astute critical pronouncements, and unimpeachable humanity. He was the quintessence of the gentleman scholar. In fact, it was Phelps who provided a lasting American definition of a gentleman when he pronounced, "This is the first test of a gentleman: his respect for those who can be of no possible value to him" (Ruggiero 2008, 80). Phelps, like many of Yale's students and professors, came from a religious family. His father was an orthodox Baptist minister—New England Baptist, not southern Baptist. Daily, as an act of filial love, he read the news of the day to his elderly father. One day in 1892, as he was working through the newspaper, he read the headline about the outcome of a prize fight—CORBETT DEFEATS SULLIVAN—and then turned the page. Never in his life had he heard his father mention Corbett or Sullivan, nor prize fighting for that matter. Such men and activities were beneath the scope of the Phelps family. The younger Phelps assumed his father did not know "anything on that subject, or cared anything about it." But the son was mistaken. As he turned the page his father "leaned forward and said earnestly, 'Read it by rounds!'" (quoted in Somers, 1972, 185). The statement must have given William Lyon Phelps pause. The world in which he had grown to manhood—the tight, clannish, White Anglo-Saxon Protestant America that he inherited from his father—was changing. The days when the only emotion that a prize fight would elicit from a New England Baptist minister was disgust were drawing to a close. And John L. Sullivan stood as a symbol of a new world.

A fundamental question for this chapter is why professional boxing, and especially the heavyweight championship, mattered to Americans in the first four decades of the twentieth century. For most of modern history, the sport of prize fighting was publically deplored, politically outlawed, and morally condemned. It was considered barbarous and archaic—a throw-back to a time when man walked with his knuckles scraping the ground. But for various reasons a new construction of the meaning of boxing emerged in England in the beginning of the nineteenth century and America at the end of that century. In England bare-knuckle boxing had enjoyed the popularity and patronage of sporting aristocrats. In the mid-eighteenth century, the early decades of the nineteenth century, and again briefly in the mid-nineteenth century, the prize ring captured the popular imagination. Ideal for betting, easily corruptible for gamblers, and diffused with an argot, traditions, and culture all its own, prize fighting attracted wealthy supports with a healthy *nostalgie de la boue* (Brailsford, 1988).

It also communicated the basic social and cultural instincts of English life. As practiced under the London Prize Ring Rules, it was an uncompromising, violent activity. Fighters battled with their bare fists. A round lasted until one of the contestants threw or knocked his opponent to the ground. The felled fighter then received a thirty second rest, after which period he had to "come up to scratch," a line drawn in the center of the ring. All important matches were battled to the finish, lasting until a fighter was too beaten to "toe the line." Fights could, and often did, last for hours, with the combatants sustaining terrible beatings. In the first two decades of the nineteenth century, when Britons were battling Frenchmen on the waves of the Atlantic and the dirt of the continent, prize fighting symbolized the bulldog tenacity—the refusal to give an inch—of John Bull. Regency boxers showed the nation how to confront danger, absorb frightful punishment, win with grace, and lose with dignity. The very language of the ring—including such phrases as "the manly art of self-defense," "toe the line," "up (or not up) to scratch," and "throwing one's hat into the ring"—connected boxing to the most revered masculine traits of the age. Wellington may have won the Battle of Waterloo on the playing fields of Eton, but his officers and soldiers learned something about being a man from the examples of the English prize ring (Brailsford, 1988).

By comparison, bare-knuckle boxing generally languished in the United States. Not until the 1840s did it begin to dig roots in American soil, and then only with a certain "unsavory" class of men. American prize fighting was a product of ethnic, working-class culture, and most of the earliest American boxers were Irish and, by that time, largely Catholic immigrants. It was generally an illegal fringe activity, populated and patronized by Irish politicians, saloon keepers, emigrant runners, shoulder hitters, pickpockets, second-floor men, pimps, prostitutes, and other sorts of "unworthies," along with a small group of sons of privilege out for a good time. But the bloody, violent sport spoke to working-class men whose lives were similarly violent. As the historian Elliott J. Gorn eloquently observed, "The death sounds of livestock slaughtered in public markets, the smell of open sewers, the feverish cries of children during cholera season, the sight of countless men maimed on the job, all were part of day-to-day street life" (Gorn, 1986, 144). Bare knuckle was brutal, brutish, and occasionally even deadly. But so was the working class life of the immigrant.

In the two decades before the Civil War, interest in the prize ring outgrew its ethnic minority base. Part of the reason was that the sport found a voice. The "penny press" redefined what news was fit to print. Beginning with Benjamin Day's *New York Sun* and James Gordon Bennett's *New York Herald* in the 1830s, newspaper editors discovered that there was an inexhaustible market for stories about murder, violence, mayhem, crime, prostitution, and sordid tales of alcoholics and drug addicts. News, they concluded, was a malleable commodity, and as the stewards of the news, they determined what it was and what it was not—altogether an enviable seat to occupy. Sex, violence, and drugs—especially if they were accompanied by eye-popping illustrations—sold newspapers. And prize fighting, surfeit with blood and violence, nicely fit into their updated definition of the news (Gorn, 1986).

During the 1840s, and especially the 1850s, the penny press gave prize fighters a national audience. "Yankee" Sullivan, Tom Hyer, John Morrissey, and John C. Heenan—three of the four Irish or first generation Irish American boxers—received significant newspaper coverage during the years when hundreds of thousands of hungry, potato-famine Irish were arriving on American shores. Their greatest fights were often against native-born Americans, a dramatic factor that would not be lost on later generations of promoters. A match that pitted a native-born American butcher against an Irish day laborer underscored undeniable American inter-ethnic and working-class rivalries. This mid-century popularity of bare-knuckle boxing reached its pinnacle on the eve of the Civil War when American champion John C. "Benicia Boy" Heenan traveled to England to battle the British champion Tom Sayers (Gorn, 1986).

The Heenan-Sayers fight occupied the attention of English speaking people on both sides of the Atlantic. Currier and Ives made a lithograph of the fighters, sporting magazines offered sage opinions about the combatants, and newspapers documented virtually every drop of sweat the two fighters shed during training. "If you go to the market," a reporter commented,

> the odds are your butcher asks you which man you fancy, and if you want to bet on it. Your newsman smiles as he hands you your daily paper, and informs you that 'there is something new about the great fight in it this morning.' If you drop into Bryant's or Christy's in an evening, you are certain to hear some allusion to the Benicia Boy or Sir Thomas de Sayers that never fails to bring down the house" (Gorn, 1986, 152).

The fight ended in a forty-two round draw. Not long after the bout the Civil War began; Americans no longer needed prize fighting to satisfy their demand for violent action.

Prize fighting fell on hard times after the Heenan-Sayers match. Where once it was a working-class sport, now it became a criminal-class activity. Fixed fights, gang violence, and unruly spectacles were so much the order of the day that even the penny press lost interest. With the likes of fugitives Jesse James and Billy the Kid to report on, journalists saw no reason to follow an arcane, dying sport in which the new golden rule was that the person with a Colt revolver makes the rules. When journalists did write about boxing, they generally waxed eloquently about the golden age of the ring—a time different and infinitely better than their own ragged, corrupt era. For many Americans, prize fighting was a "relic of barbarism," an activity that smacked of bearbaiting and bullbaiting, and which had no place in a civilized society (Gorn, 1986, 222, 224).

Then in the 1880s John L. Sullivan, "The Boston Strong Boy," swaggered onto the pugilistic stage, changing suddenly and dramatically the fortunes of the sport. A son of Irish potato-famine immigrants, Sullivan was born in 1856 in the Boston suburb of Roxbury. His father was a day laborer, and John L. appeared set to follow in his father's muddy shoes, scraping a living by performing back-breaking manual labor during the day, then getting into fights at night. It soon became apparent that he was a better fighter than worker, though in the late 1870s, when Sullivan began fighting for stakes, there was not much money to be made in either endeavor. Still, as a prizefighter he was showered with the cheers and respect of his peers, rewarded in ways that satisfied his enormous ego and diffused his restless, violent energy (Gorn, 1986).

By 1880, the year of Sullivan's first important fight, prize fighting was in a state of transition. The bare-knuckle, fight-to-the-finish London Prize Ring Rules were being replaced by the Queensberry Rules, written by the Welshman John Graham Chambers and named after their Scottish endorser John Sholto Douglas, the ninth Marquis of Queensberry. Written in 1865 and published in 1867, the Queensberry Rules mandated three-minute rounds with a minute rest period between rounds, and a knock out if a felled fighter could not regain his feet in ten seconds. The rules required fighters to wear padded gloves and they barred all wrestling, grappling, and throwing maneuvers, and permitted matches to be contested as fights to the finish or for a pre-determined number of rounds. Essentially the same rules that are in effect today, the Queensberry Rules appeared, at least on the surface, to be less violent, and certainly less bloody, than traditional bare-knuckle prize fighting (Brailsford, 1988, 152-3; Sheard 2004, 17).

Sullivan preferred the new code, but on rare, important occasions he fought under the old London Prize Ring Rules. That was exactly what he did on February 7, 1882, when he battled Paddy Ryan for the heavyweight championship. In a short, brutal, nine-round battle, Sullivan pounded Ryan into submission. After the fight, Ryan confessed, "I never faced a man who could hit as hard. I don't believe there is another man like him in the country ... [A]ny man that Sullivan can hit, he can whip" (quoted in Pollack, 2006, 40). Trying to give reporters a sense of Sullivan's hitting power, he claimed, "When Sullivan struck me, I thought that a telegraph pole had been shoved against me endways" (quoted in Gorn, 1986, 215). The fight was sponsored by Richard Kyle Fox's *National Police Gazette*, the leading prize fighting periodical, and it was billed as "the championship of the world," the first use of that designation in boxing. That title suited Sullivan just fine, and he immediately proceeded to transform it into a cash cow (Gorn, 1986).

John L took the title on the road. During his Grand Tour of 1883-84, he visited twenty-six (of thirty-eight) states, five territories, the District of Columbia, and British Columbia. Travelling to major cities and smaller hamlets, his band of boxers staged demonstrations of the "manly art of self-defense." To prove his own superiority, Sullivan offered a handsome reward to any man who lasted four rounds with him. Few tried, none succeeded. For millions of Americans, Sullivan was Homeric—a cross between Hercules and Paul Bunyan. He was personable and friendly when he was not drunk, and often times frightful and awe-inspiring when he was. But drunk or sober, he was always "the Great John L." (Pollack, 2006).

Sullivan made a small fortune on his Grand Tour, certainly near or more than $90,000 (perhaps as much as several million dollars by the standards of 2010). As a point of comparison, the president of the United States made $25,000 a year, a successful New York City lawyer $50,000, and a university professor $2,500. No American professional athlete of the era made anywhere near Sullivan's income. His biographer accurately claimed that "His name, his face, and his deeds were now known throughout the land" (Isenberg, 1988, 206). Saloon keepers placed his picture above their bars, journalists wrote hundreds of lurid stories about his exploits, and his image regularly appeared on the cover or in the pages of the *National Police Gazette*. He was America's public bad boy—a frequently drunken, brawling spectacle who, nonetheless, captured the hearts of millions of his fellow citizens. Even his standard bar room boast—"My name's John L. Sullivan and I can lick any son-of-a-bitch alive"—seemed more a touching affectation than anything sinister. Such popular songs as "Let Me Shake the Hand that Shook the Hand of Sullivan" attested to his grip on the public's imagination (Isenberg, 1988).

In late 1887 Sullivan took his traveling boxing tour to Great Britain, where he was greeted with the same enthusiasm as in the United States.

He conformed to British stereotypes of the American—big, boisterous, and as open as the American continent—and was an astonishing success. On one cold, foggy December day, he even breakfasted with the elite Scots Guards, followed by an audience with Edward, Prince of Wales. Edward quizzed Sullivan about several of his fights, and the son of Irish-Catholic immigrants asked the future king of England when was the last time he had a fistic go. The two exchanged views on one thing or another, and then the American fighter put on an exhibition of his craft. According to some accounts, when the two exchanged their goodbyes, Sullivan added, "If you ever come to Boston, be sure to look me up. I'll see that you're treated right" (n.a., 1918, 60; Isenberg, 1988, 244). The story might be apocryphal, but given the fighter's casual, egalitarian nature, it might just be true. King or commoner, Sullivan treated every man as an equal, none as a superior.

By the end of his British tour the Sullivan legend seemed complete. And so it would have been for the run-of-the-mill icon, but there was never anything ordinary about John L. Overweight, out-of-shape, road-weary, and drunk much of the time, he was ready to take on another challenge. Fox's *National Police Gazette* considered Sullivan ancient history and had begun touting Jake Kilrain as the new "champion of the world." Sullivan took umbrage. A large panel in the center of his championship belt, given to him by his Boston backers and supporters, bore the legend "Presented to the Champion of Champions, John L. Sullivan, by the Citizens of the United States," and that was how he regarded himself. He was America's champion, the citizen's champion, something akin to the president of pugilism, the first among equals. Even more exaltedly, he was the Emperor of Masculinity. He had a word for Fox's champion, and it was not suitable for the era of the genteel literary tradition. Even in his condition, he was ready once again to toe the line (Isenberg, 1988). An epic battle followed, one that poet Vachel Lindsay appropriated to frame his poem about fin de siècle America:

When I was nine years old, in 1889,
I sent my love a lacy Valentine.
Suffering boys were dressed like Fauntleroys,
While Judge and Puck in giant humor vied.
The Gibson Girl came shining like a bride
To spoil the cult of Tennyson's Elaine.
Louisa Alcott was my gentle guide ...
Then ...
I heard a battle trumpet sound.
Nigh New Orleans
Upon an emerald plain
John L. Sullivan
The strong boy
Of Boston
Fought seventy-five rounds with Jake Kilrain
(Lindsay, 1919, 357-58)

And what a seventy-five rounds it was! Because bare-knuckle prize fighting was illegal in every state in the Union, promoters arranged to hold the contest on a rural patch of turf in Mississippi owned by Charles Rich, a local timber baron. Participants and spectators made the hundred-mile trip from New Orleans to Richburg in trains, and at 10:13, on the morning of July 8, with the sun already hot in the sky, Sullivan and Kilrain toed the line for what would turn out to be the last bare-knuckle world heavyweight championship fight in history (Pollack, 2006, 170-98; Isenberg, 1988, 257-80).

Kilrain ended the first round in fifteen seconds when he threw Sullivan to the turf, landing hard on his opponent. He also scored first blood—always a major betting point—in the sixth with a right to the champion's ear. With blood streaming down his neck, Sullivan "grinned savagely," then quickly responded, dazing and flooring Kilrain with a hard shot (Pollack, 2006, 176). The fight was now barely twenty minutes old, but

Kilrain was hurt and in danger of losing. He responded by going on the defensive, circling away from Sullivan's powerful right, often going down without being hit or thrown, and trying to prolong the fight. Sullivan had trained hard for the match, and he looked in peak condition, but as the temperature rose to over one hundred degrees and humidity rolled in like waves from the Gulf Coast, no one knew how long he could last under the scorching Mississippi sun. And so the fight dragged on, round after round. In the stands, freshly built of pinewood from Rich's sawmill, spectators' pants stuck to the bubbling pitch. The backs and chests of both Irish-American fighters burned and blistered. Everyone sucked in hot mouthfuls of air that seemed filtered through a blast furnace. Against all odds the combatants continued, two determined athletes locked in a fight to the finish, one hurt but patient, the other pressing the attack but impatient (Pollack, 2006, 170-98; Isenberg, 1988, 257-80).

Sullivan tried to goad Kilrain into a slugfest. "You're a champion, eh? A champion of what?" he yelled, his dark eyes seeming to some "almost wild." (Pollack, 2006, 178). Kilrain said nothing. Spectators grumbled and jeered at the challenger's delaying tactics. Kilrain said nothing. Sullivan's punches cut and bruised Kilrain's face and caused red blotches on his stomach, chest, sides, and arms. And still Kilrain said nothing. He fought to survive, hoping something would alter the course of the match. Ten rounds, fifteen, twenty, twenty-five, thirty. Sullivan began to tire. His trainer asked how long *he* could keep going: "I can stay here until daybreak tomorrow," he promised (Isenberg, 1988, 273).

By the fortieth round, Kilrain's seconds had to lift him out of his corner stool and help him to the scratch. He was fighting on guts and hope. Then, in the forty-fourth round, Sullivan began to vomit uncontrollably. Some people in the crowd believed that he had been drinking an elixir of alcohol and tea to bolster his strength, and a wag commented, "Don't worry, John L. is just getting rid of the tea." Seeing an opening, Mike Donovan in Kilrain's corner implored his man to attack, but the fighter refused, saying, "No, I won't, Mike; no I won't ... John, I won't hit you while you are vomiting." Instead he asked the champion, "Will you draw the fight?" "No, you loafer," Sullivan yelled back, and rushed his opponent (Pollack, 2006, 185).

Sullivan recovered. Kilrain lingered. Fifty rounds, fifty-five, sixty, sixty-five, seventy. Blood, mud, sweat, and blisters from the sun covered both men. Kilrain could not outfight Sullivan, and it was now clear that he could not outlast him either. In the seventy-fifth round Sullivan punched Kilrain at will, knocking him down, and sending him wandering dazed along the ropes. One of the challenger's corner men asked Sullivan if he would give Jake a thousand dollars to give up. Although the fight was strictly winner-take-all, Sullivan agreed. But his backers overruled his generosity. "That settles it then," the champion said, "we'll fight." But Mike Donovan, Kilrain's manager, threw in the sponge: "I will not be a party to manslaughter," he said (Pollack, 2006, 191-92). The fight was over—a fight that set a standard for tenacity and fortitude.

Spectators at the match knew with a certainty absolute that they had witnessed an epic moment. Greedily grabbing anything that might by even the most lenient definition be considered a souvenir, they bought what they could and scavenged everything else. The soft hat that Sullivan ritualistically threw into the ring at the start of the proceedings went for fifty dollars, the buckets that held ice water twenty-five dollars. Slivers of the pine ring post that had once flown Sullivan's colors sold for five dollars each. They were the fistic equivalent to pieces of the True Cross (Pollack, 2006).

Across the country, the press treated the fight like an American version of the set-to between Achilles and Hector outside the walls of Troy. The "rage of Achilles," his mixture of bluster, pride, and boyishness, was not a far stretch from the Great John L.'s. Reporters covering the White House received requests from the inside for news of the fight. Thousands of curious people in cities across the country crowded outside telegraph offices waiting for bulletins of the outcome. Even the *New York Times*, the voice of bourgeois sensibility, gave the fight front page coverage under the headline "THE BIGGER BRUTE WON." (New York Times, July 9, 1889).

Sullivan was now the unrivaled emperor of American popular culture. In the ring, on tours, and on the stage, he was cheered, admired, and adored. It did not matter that he put on weight or made drunken spectacles of himself. With no worlds left to conquer, he accepted a champion's final act. On September 7, 1892, a decade after defeating Paddy Ryan for the title, he lost the belt in New Orleans to James J. Corbett, a younger, faster, better-conditioned, and immensely talented fighter. It was a legally staged fight, contested under the Marquis of Queensberry rules. Years of steady drinking and overeating had left John L. in no condition to fight at a championship caliber. It was clear from the start that he would lose. The end came in the twenty-first round of the contest. Sullivan, fighting as he always did by pressing forward, was powerless to catch Corbett and defenseless against his opponent's punishing punches. Finally, Corbett trapped Sullivan in a corner, feinted, and landed a perfectly timed right to the jaw. Sullivan dropped to his knees, but slowly pulled himself up to his feet and stood proud, defenseless, and doomed. Corbett moved in, took aim, and ended Sullivan's reign as champion. Then the unexpected happened. The fight was over, the referee had counted John L. out, and his corner men had revived him as best they could. But instead of staying put in his corner, he stumbled to the ropes and gripped a ring post, holding up his right hand and signaling the spectators to quiet down. "Gentlemen—gentlemen," he began, speaking in exhausted, halting breaths. "I have something to say. All I have to say is that I came into the ring once too often—and if I had to get licked I'm glad I was licked by an American. I remain your warm and personal friend, John L. Sullivan" (quoted in Isenberg, 2006, 318).

To be sure, Sullivan was a reflection of the swaggering, clanging, combative late-nineteenth century. He was all of its strengths and contradictions. "He was a hero and a brute," wrote Elliott Gorn, "a bon vivant and a drunk, a lover of life and a reckless barbarian ... He cut through all restraints, acted rather than contemplated, and paid little regard to the morality or immorality of his behavior. He was totally self-indulgent, even in acts of generosity, totally a hedonist consuming the good things around him and beckoning others to do the same" (Gorn, 1986, 227).

For the sport of boxing, Sullivan was the critical transitional fighter. But his cultural orbit reached well beyond his own sport. For men of his times and later, he was an irresistible icon of strength and masculinity. When Theodore Dreiser was a young journalist he met Sullivan, and the image stuck with him the remainder of his life.

> And then John L. Sullivan, raw, red-faced, big-fisted, broad-shouldered, drunken, with gaudy waistcoat and tie, and rings and pins set with enormous diamonds and rubies—what an impression he made! Surrounded by local sports and politicians of the most rubicund and degraded character ... Cigar boxes, champagne buckets, decanters, beer bottles, overcoats, collars and shirts littered the floor, and lolling back in the midst of it all in ease and splendor his very great self, a sort of prize-fighting J.P. Morgan. (Dreiser, 1922, 150-51).

Dreiser's attempt to interview Sullivan about such subjects as his plans and the value of exercise drew only rich, friendly laughs from the former champion. "Write any damned thing yuh please, young fella, and say that John L. Sullivan said so. That's good enough for me. If they don't believe it, bring it back here and I'll sign it for yuh. But I know it'll be all right, and I won't stop to read it neither." That was enough for Dreiser, who said he "would have written anything [Sullivan] asked me to write." "I adored him," he concluded (Dreiser, 1922, 150-51). Millions of Americans felt the same way as Theodore Dreiser. For American popular culture, Sullivan pioneered the landscape of twentieth-century celebrity culture. For men of his time, he was a flag-waver, a champion of the common man, and the very expression of what an American was. He was all that—and more.

Sullivan was always Sullivan, of course, but his overgrown personality still does not explain why *he* became the central male icon of the late-nineteenth century. What was it about America that was so receptive to John L.'s charms, such as they were, and was not at all receptive to Paddy

Ryan or Joe Goss, the man Ryan knocked out for the title? Americans' notice of Sullivan did not take place in a cultural vacuum. Throughout the country a more spirited and violent popular culture was taking shape. Americans could hear it in the marches of John Philip Sousa, see it in the violent clash of bodies on college gridirons, and read it the sudden explosion of books about Napoleon. Sullivan fought during a national moment that Theodore Roosevelt labeled the "strenuous age," a period of history that witnessed the swelling of Anglo-Saxon chauvinism, deadly confrontations between labor and management, and, at the end of the 1890s, war between the United States and Spain. The entire *mise-en-scene* of the age helps to explain the importance of Sullivan.

But most of the outward manifestations of cultural change—and this included John L. Sullivan—originated in a seismic shift in what it meant to be a white man. Put simply, notions of masculinity were being reformulated. Although sex was biologically determined, gender was a complex social construction. Ideas of "manliness" and "masculinity" are never fixed absolutes, rather fluid and changing. During the eighteenth century, for example, a man's identity was inseparable from his place in society. He was the head of a household and a part of a community, expected to act with decorum and restraint, interacting with his peers in a mild-mannered, soft-spoken, courteous, and pleasant manner. That behavior, so well enshrined in the character and actions of George Washington or Thomas Jefferson, was the outward expression of white manliness (Rotundo, 1993).

In the nineteenth century, as a new construction separated the public and private spheres of men and women, manliness took a slightly different shape. A man was more defined by his position in the workplace. To a large extent, a "man" was defined as being the opposite of a "boy." Boys were wild and careless, and "primitive spirits" full of "animal spirits." They were immature, impulsive, and undependable. Men were different; they controlled their baser urges and met their responsibilities. The ideal mid-Victorian man had a certain softness, a willingness to sentimentally express his deepest feelings, and a firm commitment to his religious faith. He was not a bragger and a bruiser, a swaggerer and boozer who stood ready to out-drink and out-fight the man standing next to him at the bar of a saloon. He was the man who could write to another man confessing his brotherly love, play an active role in a religiously-based reform society, and read to his children each night as they sat in the parlor. (Putney, 2001).

Toward the end of the nineteenth century there was a growing sense—dimly felt at first but gaining strength with each year—that something was dreadfully wrong with American men. They had grown weak and dispirited. Reports of male "neurasthenia," the weakening or loss of the essential "nerve force," and nervous collapse filled countless newspaper and magazine articles. The weekly attendance at local reform societies' meetings, various charitable groups, and church service; the constant reading of social-improvement pamphlets and religious tracts; the talk, talk, talk of a better world and a better mankind and "What would Jesus do?"—it all seemed to be culminating with the feminization of men. The generation of bold, adventurous, brave, virile, white pioneers who had cleared the pass West had been replaced by new generation of men, flat-chested, thin-armed, and pencil-necked (Putney, 2001).

What American men needed was a massive blood transfusion of strength and force. In his influential essay "The Strenuous Life," Theodore Roosevelt decried "the soft spirit of the cloistered life" and challenged American men to "boldly face the life of strife ... for it is only through strife, through hard and dangerous endeavor, that we shall ultimately win the goal of true national greatness" (Roosevelt, 2009 [1900], 8, 20-1. See also Roberts, 1970; Higham, 1972, 78, 84). Roosevelt's sentiment was echoed by bodybuilder Bernarr Macfadden, who in the first issue of his magazine *Physical Culture* (1899) proclaimed the slogan: "Weakness Is a Crime" (Wood, 2003, 93).

The new manliness not only rejected the soft, comfortable life, it also jettisoned anything that smacked of femininity. Temperance reform movements, domesticity, Christianity, women, and language itself had a much circumscribed place in the new realm of masculinity. A new ideal type, epitomized by the emerging protagonist of western novels, was a man unencumbered—no home, no wife, no church, just a gun and a horse (Carnes and Griffen, 1990). Unlike a lawyer or a politician, his power came not from the manipulation of language, but from the absence of language. He spoke, what Norman Mailer dubbed "the language of men" (Lennon, 1988, 18), the sparse vocabulary of Jack London and Ernest Hemingway. He was silent, strong, independent, and deadly, familiar with saloons, prostitutes, animals, and firearms, but a world away from sentimental expressions of love or abstract debates. What mattered was what he did. Like Sullivan, he was defined by his physical feats.

It was to this new sensibility that John L. Sullivan and prize fighting appealed. Charles Dana of the *New York Sun* had only to look at Sullivan to realize that the future of American manhood was safe. "A wonderful specimen is this Sullivan," he bubbled. "He dines like Gargantua. He drinks like Gambrinus. He has the strength of Samson, and the fighting talent of Achilles. When he moves it is with a child's ease, and he hits with a giant's force ... If any one thinks that the physique of the human race is degenerating, let him consider the great John L. He should be reassured" (quoted in Isenberg, 1988, 276).

Unintentionally, Dana captured part of Sullivan's attraction. The fighter was childlike. Modern masculinity worshipped the boy's "animal spirit" and impulsive behavior. As Roosevelt wrote in an article for *Outlook*, "Powerful, vigorous men of strong animal development must have some way in which their animal spirits can find vent" (Roosevelt, 1913, 42). A man was no longer the opposite of a boy; he needed to release the elemental boy inside of him. Here, again, Sullivan was the cultural yardstick. He was "the Boston Strong Boy," "the Boston Boy," or just "the Boy." To be a boy in a man's body, to be in the prize ring with John L. Sullivan, or perhaps alone on an Arizona mesa, riding on the frontier of bare-chested American masculinity—that's what it meant to be a man in the age of TR and John L. Explaining why a man of fifty-five years, a former president of the United States, and a father of six children, would want to shuck it all and risk his life on a dangerous jungle trip to trace the River of Doubt's route to the Amazon. Roosevelt wrote, "I had to go. It was my last chance to be a boy" (Ornig, 1994, 3). Roosevelt admired the qualities that made a great boxer, football player, cowboy, and soldier. He had tried his hand at each. But always, he just wanted to be "one of the boys." His friend John L. Sullivan would have understood—and so would millions of other American men— whatever their race or ethnicity.

Under the reign of Sullivan, then, the heavyweight championship became *the* symbol of the toughest man/boy in the world, a symbol that rested comfortably on the brow of a white American. At a moment when Social Darwinism was the final word of the pecking order of ethnic and racial groups, when such phrases as "survival of the fittest" and "the struggle for survival" were attached to just about every aspect of life, this was a significant achievement. Early in Sullivan's career an editor for the jingoistic *New York Sun* labeled him "the most phenomenal production of the prize ring that has been evoluted during the nineteenth century" (quoted in Somers, 1972, 160. See also Roberts, 1981, 31). And during his years as champion a rough syllogism took shape: Sullivan is the greatest fighter in the world; Sullivan is an American; ergo, American is the greatest country in the world. Nor did this notion die with the end of Sullivan's reign. In the late 1960s, Black Panther leader Eldridge Cleaver wrote, "The boxing ring is the ultimate focus of masculinity in America, the two-fisted testing ground of manhood, and the heavyweight champion, as a symbol, is the real Mr. America" (quoted in Cleaver, 1968, 85).

Freighting the title with such cultural weight, however, created problems. As long as the heavyweight champion was an American—a white American—the syllogism provided endless opportunities for international and racial bragging rights. But what if a non-Anglo Celtic foreigner captured the crown? Or even worse for millions of race-conscious white Americans, what if a black American won the title? During Sullivan's years as champion there were several outstanding black heavyweight boxers, including the great West-Indian born, Australian champion Peter Jackson, who had once fought a sixty-one round draw with Jim Corbett. Sullivan, in his usual fashion, attacked the issue head-on. In 1892 he issued a general challenge to fight for a purse of $25,000 and a side bet of $10,000. He preferred to fight a foreign opponent, he said, "as I would rather whip them than any of my own countrymen." But he made one exception: "[I]n this challenge I include all fighters—first come, first served—who are white. I will not fight a negro. I never have and never shall" (quoted in Isenberg, 1988, 301).

In one stroke, Sullivan banned black boxers from the empire of American masculinity. He set a precedent—Jim Crowing the most important athletic title at a time when "separate but equal" was becoming the law of the land. The heavyweight crown was too valuable a cultural artifact to risk losing in an interracial bout. The champions who followed Sullivan reinforced the same barrier—James J. Corbett, Robert Fitzsimmons, James J. Jeffries, Marvin Hart. Each, even if they had fought blacks before they won the title, drew the color line once they were champion. The very best black boxers of the late-nineteenth and early-twentieth centuries—such as Peter Jackson, Joe Jeannette, Sam McVey, and especially Sam Langford—were simply erased from the title picture. They were the invisible fighters, there but not seen when it mattered, more often than not forced to fight each other because they could not get a decent payday against a white heavyweight (Wiggins, 1985). The legendary black Canadian boxer Sam Langford, for instance, spent much of his brilliant career battling other black fighters for small purses. He fought Jeff Clark eleven times, Jim Barry twelve times, Joe Jeannette fourteen times, Sam McVey fifteen times, and Harry Wills twenty-three times. He fought more than three hundred matches, but never saw a title shot. By the 1940s he was penniless and blind (Mulvaney, 2007).

The color line lasted until 1908, when title holder Tommy Burns concluded that it was worth less than $30,000. By then the crown had lost its luster. Even after the change from the London Prize Ring Rules to the

Queensberry Rules, Americans had not universally embraced professional boxing. The heavyweight champion, to be sure, was a national icon whose exploits in and out of the ring made news. Millions of Americans admired and respected the champion, and the finest journalist of the day often covered important fights. But this said, professional boxing was still illegal in almost every state in the Union, and progressive reformers clamored to outlaw it everywhere. Oddly, many reformers decried the money in prize fighting more than the brutality of the sport. That an uneducated, semi-skilled man could make thousands of dollars by pummeling another man struck reformers as socially unhealthy. Even Teddy Roosevelt agreed. Although he advocated boxing for boys and young men, boxed regularly while in the White House, and counted a few prize fighters "among his friends," he felt that the "enormous" amounts of money professionals fought for "are a potent source of demoralization in themselves, while they are often so arranged as either to be a premium on crookedness or else to reward nearly as amply the man who fails as the man who succeeds" (Roosevelt, 1910, 550-51). His professional friends were not losers, and the idea of rewarding losing offended his sense of competition.

The money, the encouragement of gambling, and the association with drinking and prostitution—everything about prizefighting angered reformers. Where once the most important matches were staged in New Orleans and Coney Island, progressive legislation closed legal loopholes that permitted prizefighting. In the early years of the new century, however, prize fighting swept west to cities like Los Angeles, San Francisco, and Colma in California; Reno and Goldfield in Nevada; and Las Vegas, New Mexico. It became a thoroughly western American sport, a dusty gold-town competition between mostly westerners for the amusement of cowboys, ranchers, miners, and assorted western sports, pimps, prostitutes, and gamblers. Eastern journalists began to lose interest, and after the popular James J. Jeffries retired as the undefeated heavyweight champion in 1904, westerners started to ignore the sport as well. The title passed in an elimination contest to Marvin Hart, a fighter who possessed only one good eye and had difficulty even drawing yawns from the sporting public. When he lost the crown to Tommy Burns, it seemed that no one cared. To make any money at all—and that was not very much—Burns packed his bags and sailed the high seas, defending his title against mediocre boxers in London, Dublin, Paris, Sydney, and Melbourne. Americans back in the United States could not have cared less. The heavyweight crown had become a mere bagatelle (Roberts, 1983).

That is, to everyone except Jack Johnson, a magnificently talented black boxer who had followed Burns almost the entire circumference of the globe in effort to get a title match. Repeatedly Burns had drawn the color line, but finally in the heat of Australia he named his price: $30,000. For that sum, and not a penny less, he would give a black man a crack at becoming the emperor of masculinity. An enterprising Australian promoter, Hugh D. "Huge Deal" McIntosh, arranged the money, convinced Johnson to accept only $5,000, and set the match for Boxing Day, December 26, 1908 (Headon, 2009). The Great John L., old and fat but still opinionated, admonished Burns, sniffing, "Shame on the money-mad champion! Shame on the man who upsets good American precedents because there are Dollars, Dollars, Dollars in it" (quoted in Gilmore, 1975, 27). A journalist for the *Australian Star* was even more concerned, writing, "This battle may in the future be looked back upon as the first great battle of an inevitable race war" (quoted in Broome, 1979, 352-53).

The fight took place in Sydney's Rushcutter's Bay in a purpose-built arena freshly washed by a cool rain. In terms of a contest it wasn't much of a fight. Johnson knocked Burns down in the first round and dominated completely until the referee—McIntosh himself—stopped the fight in the fourteenth. By then, Burns was a battered mess. His eyes were bleeding and swollen, his jaw grossly misshaped, and his mouth bloody inside and out. Johnson later wrote that he had "forgotten more about boxing than Burns ever knew," and no one had reason to doubt his words (Ward, 2004, 123). Novelist Jack London, covering the fight for the *New York Herald*, reported: "The fight, there was no fight. No Armenian massacre could

compare with the hopeless slaughter that took place in the Sydney stadium today." For London, it was a contest between a "colossus and a toy
automaton," between a "playful Ethiopian and a small and futile white
man," between a "grown man and a naughty child" (*San Francisco Call*,
December 27, 1908).

Something more than mere victory drove Johnson. He was a black
man, lashing out at the thousands of racial insults and humiliations that
he had absorbed, affirming his manhood and his superiority and, for
want of a better word, his existence. He could have ended the fight earlier,
but wanted to punish and humiliate Burns. Sometimes he hit his white
opponent and physically prevented him from falling, holding him up so
that he could continue the punishment. Constantly he taunted Burns.
Speaking audibly but with a soft, high-pitched southern accent, he asked,
"Poor little Tommy, who told you you were a fighter?" Or, "Poor, poor
Tommy. Who taught you to hit? Your mother? You a woman?" Or, referring to Burns' wife, "Poor little boy, Jewel won't know you when she gets
you back from the fight" (quoted in Roberts, 1983, 63). Always Burns was
"little Tommy," "little boy," or "Tommy Boy." Johnson repeatedly compared Burns to a woman, emasculating insults that carried as much sting
as his blows. For a time Burns attempted to respond in kind, spitting out
racial invectives with mouthfuls of his own blood. But as the fight wore
on, Burns grew quiet, conserving his energy for survival.

When it ended, thousands of spectators—including many white sailors from the visting American fleet—silently exited the stadium. A fight
that had been consciously and purposefully promoted as a clash for racial supremacy had ended with the raising of a black man's gloved fist.
The crown worn by Sullivan, Corbett, and Jeffries was now on the head
of Jack Johnson. Resorting to doggerel, a reporter for the *Daily Telegraph*
concluded:

And yet for all we know and feel,

For Christ and Shakespeare, knowledge, love,

We watch a white man bleeding reel,

We cheer a black with bloodied glove
(quoted in Broome, 1979, 356)

But the cheers for Johnson were few. In a period when the White Australia Policy was federal government policy, and the masthead slogan of the national magazine *The Bulletin* was "Australia for the white man" any local reporters unsurprisingly portrayed Johnson as a black beast, a shaveheaded serpent, or an apocalyptic anti-Christ extinguishing the light of civilization (Broome, 1979; Headon, 2009). Much of the racial heat was not felt—not yet, anyway—in the United States. But the American black press celebrated the news. "No event in forty years has given more satisfaction to the colored people of this country than has the signal victory of Jack Johnson," wrote a reporter for the *Richmond Planet* (quoted in Gilmore, 1975, 32). The mainstream white press adopted a cautious, wait-and-see position. The general line was that Johnson had not defeated the "real" champion. Jim Jeffries, who in peaceful retirement had ballooned to 300 pounds, was still the "legitimate" title holder, and until Johnson defeated him he was not the true champion (Roberts, 1983).

Jack London undoubtedly spoke for millions of whites. After the match he asserted, "Personally, I was for Burns all the way. He was a white man and so am I. Naturally, I wanted to see the white man win" (Ward, 2004, 132). Watching the fight he witnessed Johnson's superior performance, accepting fully that the best man won. But he was haunted by Johnson's behavior in the ring, and especially the fighter's gold tooth smile as he physically beat and verbally assaulted Burns. "But one thing remains," London wrote from Sydney. "Jeffries must emerge from his alfalfa farm and remove that smile from Johnson's face. Jeff, it's up to you" (*San Francisco Call*, December 27, 1908).

Suddenly for a sport that Americans had forgotten, a down-on-its-luck, punch-drunk, left-for-dead, relic-of-barbarism sport, there was a swift revival of curiosity. Americans perked up their ears and manifested a keen interest in the new heavyweight champion. Jack Johnson had more than captured their attention; the black fighter had gotten under America's skin. Why? What was it about this thirty-year-old, Texas-born, son of former slaves that caused such a ruckus? During the next seven years Johnson served as the national racial lightning rod, channeling white America's fears, anxieties, and hatreds into his soul.

"Well, you see, Jack Johnson didn't know his place," a white southerner explained. A black northerner speculated, "See, Johnson was a pure individual. He did everything exactly the way he wanted to. I don't think it ever crossed his mind that he should be anybody else's version of Jack Johnson." (quoted in Burns, 2005). What was the proper place of African Americans? That was at the nub of the public debate over Johnson. Americans were obsessed by the debate. It echoed in the editorials in northern and southern newspapers about the "race issue," lingered in the halls of the Capitol where Congressmen railed about the "Negro problem," and hung like strange fruit on the trees of the nation beside the hundreds of blacks who were lynched. Booker T. Washington and W.E.B. DuBois addressed it, as did Theodore Roosevelt and Woodrow Wilson. It was the eight hundred pound gorilla at the Fourth of July celebrations.

As heavyweight champion and thus the new emperor of masculinity, Johnson insisted on his rightful share of privileges. Like John L. Sullivan, he enjoyed the high life. He had his front teeth capped in gold, wore diamond rings and stickpins, drank champagne and brandy, traveled with fast company, and consorted with scores of women—most of whom were white. He was a recognized and accepted "sport"—part of a fraternity that included certain athletes, gamblers, confidence men, pimps, and other assorted men open for some action and a romp. The sporting ideal involved living fast and walking slow, winning bets and staying out of jail. It was a tightrope life for most; for a black man it was more like a life on a razor's edge. Especially where white women were concerned. Nothing—not the gold teeth, diamond rings, champagne, or even victories in the ring—enraged white Americans more than Johnson's choice of female company. To be sure, most of his companions were prostitutes. Boxers had a long, rich history of involvement with "working women." It was considered natural. Fighters were a peripatetic breed, traveling about on the rails, living in shabby hotel rooms and dingy training camps, and existing outside the margins of acceptable society. A boxer and a prostitute were the two sides of the same coin. Emerging out of poverty, scraping a livelihood from their bodies, and ultimately arriving at sad ends, the arc of their lives was similar. Johnson, however, took more risks than most other African-American boxers and sportsmen. Just as he did in the ring, he crossed the color line (Roberts, 1983).

His choice was a bold assertion not simply of pride in his race, but also of his masculinity. As was the case with John L. Sullivan, evolving notions of manliness gave meaning to Johnson's actions. It is not to say that they expressed masculinity in the same ways. Although both drank heavily, boasted frequently, and disdained marriage vows, they differed on other points. Sullivan's and Roosevelt's readiness to give expression to their "animal spirits" and embrace of the idea of being "one of the boys" were not part of the African-American sense of masculinity. For a people a generation removed from chattel slavery, and still regarded by many whites as some sort of "insipient species," any talk of "animal spirits" was objectionable foolishness. And the mere word "boy"—a rebuke every black male heard thousands of times during his life—stung like the tip of a whip (Roberts, 1983).

Nor did the new guttural vocabulary of the inarticulate man hold the same attraction for Johnson as it did for many white fighters of the time. Although his formal education was meager, he took pride in his self-education. He read Milton and Shakespeare, frequently quoting a line or two during conversations with reporters; he enjoyed listening to opera, and if asked would accompany the music on the bass viol; he even applied for and was granted several patents, one for a specialized automobile wrench and the other a "theft preventing device for vehicles" (Ward, 2004, 409). When in the mood, Johnson was a delightful and voluble conversationalist who dotted his monologues with references to history, literature, music, art, and his own philosophy on life. Although differing dramatically on many points with Booker T. Washington and W.E.B. Du Bois, he agreed with the two prominent black spokesmen that education, intellectual growth, and verbal dexterity were essential to advancement (Roberts, 1983).

Even the folklore that mushroomed around Johnson's life emphasized his Brer Rabbit ingenuity. One tale told of Johnson speeding in an expensive roadster through some backwater, dusty, red-clay section of the Jim Crow South. A local sheriff pulled him over and explained, "You know you were speeding, boy? Goin' way too fast." Johnson acknowledged the fact. "Well," the sheriff said after glancing at the make of the car and the fighter's fine, costly clothes, "That's gonna cost you fifty dollars, boy." Without looking up, Johnson pulled out from his pocket a thick, heavyweight champion's roll of cash, peeled off a hundred dollar bill, and handed it to the sheriff. "I can't change that big a bill," he said. "Keep the change," Johnson replies, "I'm coming back same way I went through." In another tale Johnson attempted to check into a Jim Crow hotel located in some small, cracker town. Johnson asked for a room and the desk clerk, hardly raising his eyes, said, "We don't serve your kind, boy." Johnson asked again, and received the same answer. He asked a third time and the desk clerk angrily retorted, "You heard me, boy, we don't serve your kind." Johnson rolled back his head laughing and replied, "Oh, there's a misunderstanding. The room isn't for me. It's for my wife. She's one of your kind" (see Wiggins, 1971, 4-19).

These tales are not of heavyweight power, but of lightweight adaptability, featuring Johnson's intelligence and verbal skills rather than his physical attributes. The stories underscore why white Americans considered the champion a threat. They express, implicitly, that this black man can dominate anyone physically *and* mentally. They showcase a man who was his own man, one who drove too fast, spoke his mind, and selected companions to suit his desires. "I am not a slave," Johnson remarked, "and I have the right to choose who my mate shall be without the dictation of any man. I have eyes and I have a heart, and when they fail to tell me who I shall have as mine, I want to be put in a lunatic asylum" (quoted in Burns, 2005).

The more that white Americans learned about Johnson the more they itched with discomfort. No sooner was he back in the United States than boxing managers and promoters began a search for a "White Hope" who could deliver the championship from his black hands. They scoured the country high and low. The journalist John Lardner wrote that "well-muscled white boys more than six feet two inches were not safe out of their mother's sight" (Lardner, 1951, 27). Some carried their search across the Atlantic. Others ventured across the Pacific. Walter "Good-Time Charlie" Friedman, a resourceful talent scout, even hunted for a White Hope among Chinese peasants. And White Hopes they discovered. Some were giants—Jim Coffrey, the Roscommon Giant; Carl Morris, the Sapulpa Giant; Fred Fulton, the Giant of the North; and, eventually, Jess Willard, the Pottawatomie Giant. Others were smaller, but billed as terribly ferocious. However, in the early years of the search, while Johnson was still in his prime, none of the Hopes panned out. In 1909 the champion dispatched a series of them in short order (Roberts, 1983).

Johnson's early victories occurred during white America's "ace-in-the-hole" period. Out West, baling alfalfa—or whatever one did with alfalfa; most journalists were uncertain—was Jim Jeffries, the retired but still undefeated former champion, a big grizzly of a man, said to pack a punch harder than even the Great John L.'s, and the ability to withstand a whack from a poleax. Jack London had called on Jeffries to redeem his race, and so had thousands of other journalists and citizens who wrote about or penned letters to the retired fighter. At first Jeffries refused to budge from his retired status, but he turned out to be a poor businessman. He had opened a saloon and launched a fight club. Both went bust, leaving him with unpaid bills. Fighting, it turned out, was the only business he really knew (Roberts, 1983).

Promoter George Lewis "Tex" Rickard put together a package that

Jeffries could not resist. He guaranteed the fighters $101,000 and two-thirds of the movie rights to meet in the ring on Independence Day, July 4, 1910. The winner would receive two-thirds, the loser one-third. It was a staggeringly large amount of money, higher than had ever been offered to two athletes for a single contest. Although journalists choked over the money, Jeffries and Johnson quickly signed their contracts. The fight was set for San Francisco, but it aroused a firestorm of political protest in California, forcing Governor J.N. Gillett to push the match out of his state. Without missing a beat, Rickard moved the fight to Reno, Nevada, a town so soaked in sin anyway that the staging of a prize fight hardly seemed to make a difference. In fact, fighting appeared a fitting companion for the town's divorce, gambling, and prostitution businesses (Roberts, 1983).

Rickard promoted the fight as a racial reckoning. And reporters covered it that way. It was a fight where people, white and black, felt invested. Whites worried about the implications of the fight. "If the black man wins," a *New York Times* editorialist warned, "thousands and thousands of his ignorant brothers will misinterpret his victory as justifying claims to much more than mere physical equality with their white neighbors" (quoted in Roberts, 1983, 97). Even in Great Britain, where race and empire had long mingled uncomfortably, the idea of the fight sounded alarms. "It is not so much a matter of racial pride as one of racial existence which urges us so ardently to desire [Jeffries'] triumph," commented an editor of a British boxing magazine. The writer knew that the "coloured races outnumber the whites," and that Japan's victory over Russia in 1905 and Johnson's defeat of Burns in 1908 had sent out signals that the position of whites around the world was not secure. "Does anyone imagine for a moment that Johnson's success is without political influence," he continued, "an influence which has only been checked from having full vent by the personality of Jim Jeffries? He may smash Johnson when they meet … and by so doing restore us to something like our old position. We shall never quite regain it, because the recollection of our temporary deposition will always remain to inspire the coloured peoples with hope. While if, after all, Johnson should smash Jeffries—But the thought is too awful to contemplate" (quotes from Ward, 2004, 164-65).

An edgy anticipation marked the Fourth of July celebrations. America's attention leaned toward the sun-baked ring in Reno where thousands of spectators had crowded into a hastily-built arena. The sky was crystalline in the desert air, Reno a perfect jewel edged by mountains. Inside the arena a band played "Just Before the Battle, Mother," "All Coons Look Alike to Me," "America," and "Dixie." Like the music, the mood of the spectators was a cross between a traditional Independence Day festival and a Ku Klux Klan gathering. As flags fluttered and racial epithets flew, the fighters climbed between the ropes and prepared to settle the question foremost on everyone's mind (Roberts, 1983).

The fight started at 2:46pm and by 3:00pm or so it had already settled into a pattern. Perhaps, as Jeffries said later, "I couldn't come back" (Ward, 2004, 211). Perhaps he was too old, shed too much weight too quickly, and no longer had the reflexes to exploit openings and avoid danger. Perhaps he was just facing a better fighter, one whom he could not have beaten on his best day. Whatever the case, Jeffries could not sustain an offense or mount much of a defense. Patiently, Johnson wore him down, cutting and nearly closing his eyes, breaking his nose, and draining his energy. By round ten the thick pelt of hair that covered Jeffries' body was matted with his own blood. His corner man did not even attempt to wash it off. The ring was stained with blood, and the white shirts of spectators at ringside had red spots. In the fifteenth round, Johnson cut loose. Jeffries, who had never been knocked off his feet in his career, went down one, two, three times. Finally, to save the former champion from the humiliation of a knockout, his manager threw in the towel. The Battle of the Century, as it had been billed, was over. But the fighting over its significance wasn't (Ward, 2004).

Telegraph operators in Reno tapped out the fight's outcome immediately, communicating to every corner of the country the news of Johnson's victory. Black Americans rejoiced. In the black section of Chicago, they banged pots, gave thanks, and chanted, "Jack, Jack, J-A-J! Jack, Jack, J-A-J" (Ward, 2004, 213). In African-American saloons in New York and Boston patrons drank champagne on the house. They danced in the streets in Cincinnati and St. Louis. Bubbling celebrations of victory led some black journalists to discuss the meaning of the fight (Roberts, 1983, 110). The fight demonstrated, wrote an editor for the *Baltimore Times,* that "any negro anywhere may reach eminence in peaceful ways by using the Johnson method in his particular trade or calling" (quoted in *Literary Digest*, July 16, 1910, 85). Soon black voices sang a new ballad:

Amaze an' Grace, how sweet it sounds,

Jack Johnson knocked Jim Jeffries down.

Jim Jeffries jumped up an' hit Jack on the chin,

An' then Jack knocked him down again.

The Yankees hold the play,

The White man pull the trigger;

But it makes no difference what the white man say:

The world champion's still a nigger."

(quoted in Gilmore, 1975, 48).

Yes, for the most part the white man did hold the trigger, and even before evening became night they began to squeeze it. There was a long tradition of working-class drinking, gun play, and disorder on Independence Day, and the news of Johnson's victory added another combustible element to the mix. The results were predictable. In Uvalda, Georgia, a gang of whites attacked a camp of black construction workers, killing three and wounding five. In Houston, Texas, a black man openly celebrated Johnson's victory, enraging a white man who "slashed his throat from ear to ear." In New York City a black shouted, "We blacks put one over on you whites, and we're going to do more." A white mob stopped just short of lynching him for his bold exhibition of free speech. And so it continued until dawn. Whites killed two blacks in Little Rock, Arkansas; white assailants killed three blacks in Shreveport, Louisiana; roving white sailors attacked scores of innocent blacks in Norfolk, Virginia; and thirty people were injured in a race riot in Pueblo, Colorado. In almost every section of the country, in big cities and rural hamlets, pitched battles occurred. Although a number of whites were injured, in far more cases blacks were shot, stabbed, and lynched. Interracial violence resulted in the deaths of at least twenty black Americans. In the reform magazine *Independent*, an editor wrote onJuly 7, 1910 that "Like the *Hexenlehrling* these apostles of savagery have unchained the demons of disorder whom they are power-less to lay" (Roberts, 1983, 110).

Never before had a sporting contest—or any other event—unleashed such powerful waves of hate and violence, and not until the assassina-tion of Martin Luther King, Jr., would another such spontaneous outbreak reoccur. Nor was there any question, among either white or black Ameri-cans, over the cause of the civil disturbances. A black man had defeated a white man for what had become the greatest prize in American sports—the heavyweight boxing championship. It was an outcome that raised bile into the throats of thousands of whites, turning a handful into murder-ers. The burst of destructive energy frightened many middle-class blacks, threatening gains they had achieved. But several black commentators re-fused to diminish Johnson's victory by saying that it was *just* a prize fight and did not *mean* anything. William Pickens, president of Talladega Col-lege, commented: "It was a good deal better for Johnson to win and a few Negroes be killed in body for it, than for Johnson to have lost and Negroes to have been killed in spirit by the preachments of inferiority from the combined white press" (quoted in Gilmore, 1975, 71).

In victory Johnson had probed the live nerve of American racism. And the Jeffries fight was only the beginning. White America's violent reaction to the fight, and what white authorities interpreted as Johnson's continued provocative behavior, prompted a virtual coup d'état against the emperor of masculinity. The first phase of the campaign attacked the most visible expressions of Johnson's athletic superiority—the moving pictures of his victories. Throughout the early twentieth century, progressive reformers oozed anxiety about the evil influences of both prizefighting and films. Under certain circumstances, they argued, each encouraged vice, contributed to public disorder, and multiplied moral and social corruption. And combined, they had the power to foster incalculable harm.

In 1912, as Johnson prepared to defend his title against "Fireman" Jim Flynn in another Independence Day contest, Congress stirred into action. Four southerners on Capitol Hill—Thetus Sims (Tennessee) and Seaborn A. Roddenbery (Georgia) in the House, and Furnifold M. Simmons (North Carolina) and Augustus Bacon (Georgia) in the Senate—spearheaded a bill "to prohibit the exhibition of moving pictures of prizefights." Roddenbery made no bones about his position on Johnson's mixed-race fights: "No man descended from the old Saxon race can look upon that kind of a contest without abhorrence and disgust" (62nd Congress, 2nd sess., *Congressional Record* July 19, 1912, 9305; see also Streible, 2008, 245). On July 31, only weeks after Johnson's victory over Flynn, President William Howard Taft signed the Sims bill into law. Although the law did not prohibit the filming of a fight or the exhibition of the motion pictures in the same state as the contest was staged, it did outlaw the interstate transport of the film. At a time when championship fights were contested in such sparsely populated locales as Nevada and New Mexico, the law effectively ended the profitability of prizefight films.

The Sims Law attacked Johnson indirectly by making it more difficult for him to make money (a standard championship contract gave the fighters a share in the film rights). It hit him in the pocketbook, and so might be considered as simply business. But the second phase of the government's campaign against Johnson was personal, amounting to an all-out frontal assault against how he lived his life. As the boxer's fame increased, his relationships with white women became an open, festering wound for many Americans. When he married Etta Terry Duryea in January, 1911, one of his relationships was sanctioned by the courts. Their stormy marriage ended in September, 1912, when Etta committed suicide by shooting herself. Three months later in Chicago, Johnson married again, this time to Lucille Cameron, a white prostitute with whom he had been having an affair for four or five months (Roberts, 1983).

Criticism, ominous and threatening, rained down on Johnson. A group of whites in Louisiana inquired whether the good citizens of Illinois knew what "seagrass ropes are made for." The governor of New York called the marriage "a blot on our civilization." Taking the logic one step further, the governor of South Carolina asked, "If we cannot protect our white women from black fiends, where is our boasted civilization?" Not to be out-bigoted by any governor, Representative Seaborn A. Roddenbery cried out in indignation with indignation on the floor of the House, speculating on the history of race relations and lamenting his own times, "No brutality, no infamy, no degradation in all the years of Southern slavery, possessed such a villainous character and such atrocious qualities as the provisions of the laws of Illinois, New York, Massachusetts, and other states which allow the marriage between negro, Jack Johnson, to a woman of Caucasian strain." With the applause of the gallery ringing in his ears, Roddenbery continued, "Intermarriage between whites and blacks is repulsive and averse to every sentiment of pure American spirit. It is abhorrent and repugnant to the very principles of a pure Saxon government. It is subversive to social peace. It is destructive to moral supremacy, and ultimately this slavery of white women to black beasts will bring this nation to a conflict as fatal and as bloody as ever reddened the soil of Virginia or crimsoned the mountain paths of Pennsylvania." Concluding, he ranted, "Let us uproot and exterminate now this debasing, ultrademoralizing, un-American, and inhuman leprosy" (quotes from Roberts, 1983, 158-160; n.a. 1913, 123-24; and 62nd Congress, 3rd session, *Congressional Record,* January 30, 1913, 502-04).

Behind the scenes, agents of the Justice Department were feverishly compiling a case against Johnson for violating the White Slave Traffic Act (1910). That piece of Progressive legislation, popularly known as the Mann Act after its sponsor, prohibited the interstate transportation of women "for the purpose of prostitution or debauchery, or for any other immoral purposes." It was clearly aimed at commercialized vice, not sexual relations between consenting adults. But its language was as broad as it was vague, leaving ample room for a creative interpretation of the law. To be sure, it could be used to harpoon a madam who was attempting to move some new recruits across country. But justice officials argued it could also be employed to gig any man who traveled across state lines with a female who was not his wife and incidentally engaged in sex. "Debauchery" and "immoral purposes" were like the legendary grandmother's nightshirt that covered just about everything (Roberts, 1983).

Jack Johnson became the test case for the alternate interpretation of the Mann Act. In his line of work he traveled often, and he normally took along women. And almost as often he made love—or something close enough for government work—with them. The government's hope to charge Johnson with a Mann Act violation with Lucille Cameron went up in smoke when she married the champion. But it was not difficult to find another companion of Johnson's who was willing to support the government's case. Belle Schreiber, a well-seasoned prostitute who had plied her trade in Chicago, Pittsburgh, Baltimore, and several other cities, stepped forward and asserted that she had gallivanted about the country with the champion and had sex with him many, many times. And in fact, she had (Ward, 2004).

Johnson was duly arrested, charged, tried, convicted, and sentenced. Judge George Carpenter noted that the boxer was "one of the best known men of his race" (quoted in Roberts, 1983, 179-80) and, therefore, in a manner of speaking, he decided to throw the book at him Instead of just a fine, Carpenter ordered Johnson confined to prison for a year and a day and fined $1,000. Before the sentencing a *Cleveland Daily News* headline blared: "BLACK PUGILIST WILL BE MADE AN EXAMPLE" (quoted in Gilmore, 1975, 121). And he was. But what exactly was he an example of? Not of harming anyone, for he had harmed no one. Not of breaking the law, for he had broken no laws. What then? He had won the title, become the emperor of masculinity, lived like the heavyweight champion of the world, and bedded and married white women. He had lived like a free man—and because he was black, he was now going to pay. The federal government, in its own way, had cut off his balls. It had symbolically lynched Jack Johnson.

W.E.B. Du Bois saw eye-to-eye with Johnson on very few matters, but he did understand the reason for the champion's downfall. It was not just that Johnson "out sparred an Irishman," or that he was unfaithful to his wife. "[W]e have yet to hear, in the case of white America, that marital troubles have disqualified prize fighters or ball players or even statesman." No it was something deeper, an impulse almost primordial. It was the color of his skin, thought Du Bois. "It comes down, then, after all to this unforgivable blackness" (quoted in Ward, 2004, vii).

REFERENCES

Brailsford, D. (1988) *Bareknuckles: a social history of prize-fighting,* Cambridge: Lutterworth.

Broome, R. (1979) "The Australian Reaction to Jack Johnson, Black Pugilist, 1907-9," in Cashman, R. and McKerman, M. (eds), *Sport in history: The making of modern sporting history,* St. Lucia Q: University of Queensland Press: 343-63.

Burns, K. (Director) (2005). *Unforgivable blackness: The rise and all of Jack Johnson,* Florentine Films and WETA, Washington DC in association with PBS.

Carnes, C. and Griffen, C. (eds) (1990) *Meanings for manhood: constructions of masculinity in Victorian America,* Chicago: University of Chicago Press.

Cleaver, E. (1968) *Soul on ice,* New York: McGraw-Hill.

Dreiser, T. (1922) *A book about myself,* New York : Boni and Liveright.

Gilmore, A. (1975) *Bad nigger! The national impact of Jack Johnson,* Port Washington NY, Kennikat Press.

Gorn, E.J. (1986) *The manly art: Bare-knuckle prize fighting in America,* Ithaca NY: Cornell University Press.

Headon, D. (2009) "'World's Fistanic History', Sydney 1908: 'Flash Jack Johnson' vs 'Sinking Tommy Burns,'" *Sporting Traditions 26* (2): 1-14.

Higham, J. (1970) *Writing American history: Essays on modern scholarship,* Bloomington: Indiana University Press.

Isenberg, M.T. (1988) *John L. Sullivan and his America,* Urbana: University of Illinois Press.

Lardner, J. (1951) *White hopes and other tigers,* Philadelphia PA: Lippincott.

Lennon, M. (ed.) (1988) *Conversations with Norman Mailer,* Jackson: University Press of Mississippi.

Lindsay, V. (1919) "John L. Sullivan, The Strong Boy of Boston," *New Republic* 16 July: 357-58.

Mulvaney, K (2007) "The greatest fighter almost nobody knows" *ESPN Black History Month,* 7 February (online) http://sports.espn.go.com/espn/blackhistory2007/news/story?id=2755803 accessed 30 May 2010.

n.a. (1913) "Messrs. Blease and Johnson" *Crisis* January: 123-24.

n.a., "'John L.' (1918) Last of the Bare-fisted Fighters of the Ring" *Literary Digest* 23 February: 60.

Oates, J.C. (1987) *On boxing,* Hopewell NJ: The Ecco Press.

Ornig, J.R. (1994) *My last chance to be a boy: Theodore Roosevelt's South American expedition of 1913-1914,* Mechanicsburg PA : Stackpole Books.

Pollack, A.J. (2006) *John L. Sullivan: The career of the first gloved heavyweight champion,* Jefferson NC: McFarland & Co.

Putney, C. (2001) *Muscular Christianity: Manhood and Sports in Protestant America, 1880-1920,* Boston MA: Harvard University Press.

Roberts, G.F. (1970) "The Strenuous Life: The Cult of Manliness in the Era of Theodore Roosevelt", PhD thesis, Michigan State University.

Roberts, R. (1981) "Boxing and Reform," in Baker, W.J. and Carroll, J.M. (eds), *Sports in modern America,* Montgomery AL: River City Publishers: 27-39.

Roberts, R. (1983) *Papa Jack: Jack Johnson and the era of white hopes,* New York: Free Press.

Roosevelt, T. (1910) "The Recent Prize Fight" *Outlook,* 16 July: 550-51.

Roosevelt, T. (1913) *Theodore Roosevelt: An autobiography,* New York: The Macmillan Company.

Roosevelt, T. (2009 [1900]) "The Strenuous Life," Speech Before the Hamilton Club, Chicago, 10 April 1899, in Roosevelt, T. (ed.) *The strenuous life: Essays and addresses,* Mineola, NY: Dover Publications.

Rotundo, E.A. (1993) *American manhood: Transformations in masculinity from the Revolution to the modern era,* New York: Basic Books.

Ruggiero, V. (2008) *Becoming a critical thinker,* Boston, MA : Houghton Mifflin, 6th ed.

Sheard, K. (2004) "Boxing in the Western Civilizing Process," in Dunning, E. Malcolm, D. and Waddington, I. (eds) *Sport histories: Figurational studies in the development of modern sports,* London: Routledge: 15-30.

Somers, D.A. (1972) *The rise of sports in New Orleans, 1850-1900,* Baton Rouge: Louisiana State University Press.

Streible, D. (2008) *Fight pictures: A history of boxing and early cinema,* Berkeley: University of California Press.

Ward, G.C. (2004) *Unforgivable blackness: The rise and fall of Jack Johnson,* New York: A.A. Knopf.

Wiggins, D.K. (1985), "Peter Jackson and the Elusive Heavyweight Championship: A Black Athlete's Struggle Against the Late Nineteenth Century Color-Line", *Journal of Sport History 12* (2): 143-68.

Wiggins, W.H. (1971, Jan.). "Jack Johnson as Bad Nigger: The Folklore of His Life," *Black Scholar 2* (5): 4-19.

Wood, C. (ed.) (2003 [1929]) *Bernarr Macfadden: A study in success,* Whitefish MT: Kessinger Publishing.

Major Taylor: Understanding the Complex Story of a Champion African-American Cyclist in White Australia, 1903-1904

BY **ANDREW RITCHIE**

INTRODUCTION

Major Taylor, an African American, was born in 1878 and brought up in humble, semi-rural poverty in Indianapolis. He went on to have an extraordinary life as a professional athlete, and in a sport that black Americans were not renowned for. Through a combination of luck, perseverance, intelligence, ability, and the arrival of the bicycle boom in America in the 1890s, Taylor had a meteoric career in professional cycling. From a very young age bicycling lured him in, providing new opportunities and the chance to excel, first as a cycling shop-boy and machinist, then as an amateur racer, and finally as the first outstanding—and ultimately world-famous—black professional in the highly competitive, financially lucrative, and international sport of bicycle racing (Ritchie, 2009).

But this opportunity to become famous was not realized without an epic struggle against racist opposition in America, which sought to exclude Taylor from challenging white riders for championship honors. Indeed, the

League of American Wheelmen, the governing body for amateur cycling in the United States, officially refused to accept blacks as members. Taylor's every move in American cycling was therefore dogged by racist opposition and, frequent, blatant fouling and physical danger from cycling opponents. It is not an exaggeration to say that his struggle for acceptance in American cycling from 1893 until about 1904 was a milestone in the gradual history of integration in American sport. Only outside of the United States, and particularly in Europe, was he able to win a reprieve from constant racist harassment and discrimination. In addition to racing abroad, Major Taylor's other strategy to become more involved in racing was to turn professional; there the color of money was of paramount significance, though the color of one's skin was hardly glossed over. That said, from 1896, when Major Taylor first turned professional, he built an impressive competitive cycling record. He was world champion at Montreal in 1899 at the age of 20 and American champion in 1900 at age 21. In 1901, he had a meteoric season in Europe when he beat all the leading European champions, and invitations to return to Europe followed in 1902 and 1903 (Ritchie, 2009).

Paris was Taylor's adopted European home, and he was one of the brightest stars of the flood-lit races regularly promoted by Breyer and Coquelle on weekday evenings at the famous Buffalo velodrome in Paris. Taylor spent brief periods at home in Worcester, Massachusetts to rest and recuperate, but for much of the time he lived in luxury hotels and fine boarding houses in Paris and the other cities he visited. He slept frequently in first-class accommodations on trains and boats, raced wherever his promoters scheduled him, and performed in a grueling succession of top-class races against all the world's best sprinters. Taylor's skin color, which stood in his way in America, was a foundation for his novel appeal and attraction in other countries he visited, yet it was his speed and style on the bicycle that thrilled spectators in every place he competed. In the early 20th century, Taylor was perhaps the world's most sought-after athlete and probably the most traveled sportsman. He was, without a doubt, the world's most illustrious black athlete. As he was leaving New York on

March 25, 1902, he was visited by a delegation of black students headed by the iconic Booker T. Washington, who came to wish him well on behalf of all black Americans. On board the *Kaiser Wilhelm der Grosse* on that trip, he kept company with Henri Fournier, the famous French racing driver, and Albert Clément, the automobile pioneer. His fame as a racing cyclist preceded him, and there were always crowds to welcome him and cheer him on. Everywhere he toured in Europe white civic dignitaries gave Taylor, a black American, the red-carpet treatment (Ritchie, 2009). Would this be the same when he decided to tour Australia?

FIRST TOUR OF AUSTRALIA: 1902-03

Taylor was aware of the "White Australia" immigration policy and the explicit assumption, therefore, that this was a country for white settlers. But he had received a personal invitation from cycling authorities to race, and thus visit, the country. He was, however, astonished by the scale and warmth of the local welcome. Upon his first arrival in Sydney, on December 22, 1902, a flotilla of small boats greeted his vessel the *Ventura* as it entered the harbor, including one boat carrying a reception committee from the Summer Nights Amusement Committee, which was an arm of the New South Wales League of Wheelmen (NSWLW). The committee was headed by Hugh D. Macintosh, a flamboyant 28-year-old entrepreneur who was also the general secretary of the NSWLW, and who had negotiated the contract to lure Taylor south. Also aboard was Tom D. Scott, one of the best-known figures in Australian cycling (Ritchie, 2009).

"I could not restrain my tears," Taylor remembered later, "as I looked over the side of the liner and saw hundreds of boats ... decked out with American flags with their whistles tooting and men and women aboard them with megaphones greeting me with this salutation, 'Taylor, Taylor! Welcome Major Taylor!'". When the Taylors stepped ashore, they were welcomed by thousands of cheering people. The mayor of Sydney praised him at a press reception as "the Champion Cyclist of the World, who has met and defeated the foremost men in Europe and America and who now comes to Australia to gain fresh victories" (Taylor, 1928, 235).

Taylor and his wife were surprised and elated to be greeted like visiting royalty and deluged with social invitations, many of which they could not accept because of time pressures associated with Taylor's training and racing. While prospective non-white migrants were discouraged by the "White Australia Policy," and local Aboriginal people regarded as undesirable by many Australians with a European ancestry (Cashman, 2002), the African-American Taylor was welcomed—as a touring professional sportsman—with open arms. As Daryl Adair (2009, 418) explains, "short term visitors [to Australia] could, with the support of a local sponsor and the consent of immigration authorities, be provided with an "exemption certificate" that temporarily overlooked their "alien" or "coloured status." In Australia in 1902 a non-Aboriginal "black" person was a rarity. Hence, many people among the thousands who paid to see Taylor's cycling feats were also catching their first glimpse of what to them was an exotic human form, an African American.

Bicycle racing was very popular in Australia at the turn of the century, though Taylor's visit was widely credited with providing the sport with an immense boost as a public spectacle (Grivel, 1954). He brought American class and European finesse to the Australian tracks. His arrival, said local newspapers, was the most exciting thing that had happened in Australian cycling since the American champion, Arthur Zimmerman, had visited in 1895 (Ritchie, 2009a). Indeed, Major Taylor may well have been the greatest athletic sensation Australian crowds had yet witnessed. He was one of the best paid athletes in the world. The syndicate that sponsored his visit had lured him to Australia with an offer of £1,500 appearance money for three months of racing, plus whatever he could win in prizes—at a time when an average Australian worker earned about £100 a year. Taylor's superstar status was spectacularly reinforced by such astonishing earning power (Ritchie 2009).

A flood of press coverage greeted his arrival in Sydney. A profile of him in the *Sydney Morning Herald* headlined "A Great Wheelman" read:

In appearance, Taylor is a cleanly built, neatly packed parcel of humanity. He is short in stature, with good body and hip development and slender legs, with ankles which a fashionable ballet dancer might envy. No comparison for his build would be fitter perhaps than that of the racehorse. His skin shines like satin, and his face smiles pleasantly under his centre-parted, close-cropped curly hair as he walks to the starting point, but the smile does not last long. When he mounts, it gives way to an expression of thoughtfulness. Taylor tests his seat till he finds his position right, and sees to it that his feet are properly strapped to the pedals. When satisfied, he surveys the field ahead of him, and getting a grip on the handlebars, he waits for the pistol." (*Sydney Morning Herald,* Jan. 26, 1903).

Taylor was frequently interviewed by Australian newspapermen. Journalists sought his opinions on local rivals and on the sporting scene in Europe and the United States. They were fascinated by his character and personality, especially his intense religious convictions, which were widely publicized. One long interview he gave to *The Baptist,* a denominational Sydney newspaper, provides a more complete statement of his religious beliefs than can be found in articles written about him in American newspapers. "Thirty Thousand Dollars for Conscience Sake," the article was headlined, referring to the amount of money Taylor estimated that he had lost by refusing to race on Sundays: "For years this man of deep and strong convictions has been preaching to the sporting world a silent but eloquent sermon of example ... He is a most unassuming man, and so modest that almost every word has to be coaxed from him." (*The Baptist,* Jan. 1, 1903). As well as giving earnest interviews about his religious convictions, Taylor was also invited to speak from the pulpits of various churches, where he welcomed the opportunity to carry his message of clean living, good sportsmanship, and Sabbath observance to Australian congregations. There was, at the time, no Sunday bicycle racing in Australia.

The cycle racing during this first Australian tour was a spectacular athletic and commercial success. As in Europe, even Taylor's training sessions were attended by fans eager for a chance to see the champion at work. Crowds of twenty thousand people crammed into tracks in Sydney, Melbourne, and Adelaide to greet "the Worcester Whirlwind" with rapturous applause. Taylor was the idol, the hero of the moment, as he took on the leading Australian champions, Walker, Lewis, Corbett, Gudgeon and Mutton. Spectators paid a shilling each for the privilege of seeing him race. To most observers it was obvious that, in a straight sprint, unhampered by unfair opposition and teaming, Taylor simply outclassed his rivals. Everywhere in Australia, people who met him were impressed by his gentlemanly behavior. The three month visit earned him a total of almost £4,000, equivalent to what an average Australian worker would have made during his entire working lifetime (Ritchie, 2009).

As Taylor became an international cycling star, his career in the United States became extremely difficult. The more famous he became abroad, the more determined his rivals were to crush him at home. Indeed, Taylor had not signed up for the 1902 American championship season before he left for France in March because of his bitter experiences on the track the year before. But his sponsor, Fred Johnson, wanted him to return to America to compete for the championship. So, on Taylor's return from France, he went late into the national circuit races against Kramer, Lawson, and MacFarland. There he encountered a new outbreak of hostility and tactical combinations. The National Cycling Association (the governing body of professional cycling) had changed its rules to allow as many as four riders in championship races, a reform that Taylor alleged was directed specifically against him; for now there was a greater possibility than before to "pocket" him. In a four-man race, two of the riders could obstruct Taylor, leaving the fourth free to win unopposed. His three rivals might then divide the prize money between themselves (Ritchie, 2009). One New York newspaper commented:

> Throughout this season, Major Taylor has been harassed to a
> point of desperation by these cheap fellows who seem deter-

mined that he shall not win the Championship of America again ... In every race a combination seems always in order to defeat Taylor by unfair tricks, even if they themselves fail to score. ... With anything like a fair show, or an equal chance and the honest observation of the rules of bicycle racing, Major Taylor would be Champion of America again.[2]

The hostility between Taylor and his cycling opponents Kramer, Lawson, and MacFarland reached a peak that year. Once, after he had beaten the three of them through skillful tactical maneuvering, Taylor was forced to retreat to his dressing room because MacFarland verbally and physically threatened him. However, Taylor made up his mind to defend himself if necessary: "This is the first time in my racing career that I ever lost my head to the extent of planning to fight for my rights at all costs," he wrote later. And:

> As they came into my room, I was waiting for them with a length of two-by-four which I had picked up from a lumber pile near the grandstand. Before they had a chance to lay a hand on me I made one vicious, healthy swing at MacFarland, but he dodged the blow. Then the entire outfit tried to close in on me, but I was too fast for them even on foot. I dropped my club and made for the dressing room where my trainer and I were obliged to take refuge until the police interfered. Fortunately, there was no bloodshed (Quoted in Ritchie, 1996, 198).

This intensified hostility explains why Taylor was more than ever anxious to make the most of his possibilities to race abroad—particularly during his winter season, when he would have been confined to indoor tracks—and why his participation in American racing became more and more spasmodic. To a journalist who asked him when he visited London in August, 1903, what his future plans were, he responded that they were not yet decided, "But I won't race in America again! No, never!" In addition to his problems with U.S. cycling, the specter of Jim Crow customs and laws added to these problems. It was difficult for a black man, even of his social standing, to secure a hotel room and restaurant service. Even in places as familiar to him as New Haven and Newark, he still had to endure personal rejection and racist insults (Ritchie, 2009).

A revealing article in the *Worcester Telegram* on August 1, 1902, penetrated to the core of his dilemma. "No [Color] Line in Australia!" it was headlined, "Major Taylor Talks of Heading that Way. May Shake the N.C.A. for Keeps. Shabby Treatment Drives Him To It." Taylor told the *Telegram* that he was thinking of giving up his pursuit of the championship after the problems he had had finding a hotel for himself, his wife, and his trainer, Bert Hazard, in New Haven. "The Worcester rider visited several hotels, but at each he was refused admission," the article explained. And:

> Finally quarters were secured for the night, but in the morning when Major went downstairs for breakfast, he was refused service. He visited several restaurants with no success, and then it was that he packed his trunks ... All this shabby treatment, the Major declares, has taken the heart out of him. He is without doubt the best drawing card following the grand circuit game and should the Major follow out his present intention, the track meet promoters would be the biggest sufferers.

Taylor informed the *Telegram* reporter that his chances were very poor that year because of the hostility directed against him. "Man to man," he said, "I have Kramer and all the other cyclists beat to a certainty. I know it and so do they. But I realize that I have little chance the way things are running. Not only do I suffer in the races, but I am unable to get proper food in many of the cities in which I train. With an even break, and I say it without boasting, there is no rider in the world who can defeat me in a match race" (*Worcester Telegram*, Aug. 1, 1902).

Taylor earned a lot of money in those two years. Determined to keep racing, to push himself to his physical and psychological limits, he was driven by the realization that his athletic prime would not last forever, and by the urge to make as much from his career as possible while he was still at the height of his powers. He was still relatively young, at 24 years of age, at the end of the 1902 American season. But the first invitation to Australia arrived just in time to spark renewed interest. He again spoke of retirement on returning from his third trip to Europe in September, 1903. He arrived in New York with his wife and seventeen pieces of baggage, including a motorcycle and a fancy new car he had bought in Paris. This tour had also been an outstanding success. He had been joyfully welcomed in Paris and again won triumphant victories in all the European capitals, traveling frequently that year with Woody Hedspath, another black professional cyclist from Indianapolis. But in spite of the acclaim, he was deeply fatigued (Ritchie, 2009). On that occasion Taylor told the *Worcester Telegram* (Sept. 24, 1903) that his body was letting him know that it was time to retire:

> I can see that years of continued riding are telling on me, and I am satisfied that I have done enough. I shall look around now for the right sort of a position in the business world, and let the other fellows do the racing. I would probably never have gone to Australia this year, had I not wanted to see the country of which I had heard so much, and to give my wife a trip around the world before we settled down to a more quiet life.

Many athletes go through cycles of intense ambivalence about their future. In spite of his determination to retire at the end of 1903, Taylor was not in a position to resist the lucrative offers that came to him again from Australia. Promoters offered him a large sum of cash and all his expenses to race there, plus whatever prizes he could win and a percentage of the gate. In fact, rival promoters competed against each other to secure Taylor's services, such was his attraction. "Major Taylor was flitting about Worcester in his imported automobile, with his poodle dog," the *Telegram* (Sept. 24, 1903) noted, "letting the Australians do the guessing until the offer came that he felt he could not refuse." Once again, Taylor signed a contract with Hugh D. Macintosh, otherwise known as "Huge Deal" Macintosh, the ambitious businessman who later, in 1908, succeeded in persuading the white Canadian boxer Tommy Burns to meet the black champion Jack Johnson in Australia for the world heavyweight boxing title, and who made a fortune selling newsreels of Johnson's victory in Europe and America (Headon, 2009).

SECOND AUSTRALIAN TOUR, 1903-04

Major Taylor's second tour, through the Australian summer of 1903-04, proved to be extremely tiring. It led to a period of mental and physical exhaustion, and temporary retirement from racing for a two-year period, including the remainder of 1904, 1905, and 1906. Taylor was, on this second tour, now a well known personality in Australia. His speed and his athletic qualities were famous, and so was his Christian resolve, which had been widely advertised on his previous visit by articles in various newspapers.

The *Sydney Telegraph* (Jan. 7, 1903), for example, reprinted a recent story from *The Baptist* in which Taylor remarked: "I attribute most of my success entirely to the fact that I have tried to do what was right—live fairly and squarely by every man—and any man who follows these principles is bound to succeed ... I have always said, 'I'm not living for one day or two. I am going to live on and on—I am living for the eternal ... God has always taken care of me and I believe he always will." *The Baptist* (Feb. 1, 1903) reckoned that Taylor's story had "been advertised beyond any article published in Australia for years." And:

> Nearly every daily, weekly, and monthly paper ... has either reprinted the article in whole or in part, or written about it, and thus drawn attention to it ... Scurrilous papers criticized it, and heaped sneers and reproach upon Major Taylor in particular and Baptists in general ... Major Taylor's testimony was a noble one. We were thankful to have been the means of sending it broadcast right through this great continent.

Thousands have read it who never enter a church door, or listen to the preaching of the Gospel in the ordinary way.

The Baptist admitted, however, that Taylor had been "subject to unpleasantness at times when riding. Vile epithets were occasionally flung at him as he flew around the track on his machine. But it is only just to say that this sort of thing came from a comparatively small minority of persons ... By the great majority, he was treated generously." *The Baptist* concluded that Taylor lived up to the testimony he gave. His doings in Sydney were put under a microscope, and "on the racing track, on the training track, in his private association with all classes of people, he proved himself to be one of God's gentlemen." One cycling official told the paper— "He rides to win, and he rides absolutely on his own. He relies entirely on his powers of speed and his judgement. He has nothing to learn, that is evident from the way he uses his head." (*The Baptist,* Feb. 1, 1903).

The well-known national magazine, *The Bulletin*, which printed the motto "Australia for the White Man" on its mast-head, published unpleasant comments and cartoons of Taylor, though it usually stopped short of overt racism. In one of its satirical pieces, which it called "A design for a mural decoration dedicated to the Baptist Denomination," it showed Major Taylor with a bicycle wheel for a halo, and in another entitled "Another interview with Major Taylor," the cyclist is saying "Yes, I always take a friend with me when riding—He keeps me from harm, and in the light of recent events also tells me when a thing's worth going for" (*The Bulletin*, Jan. 17, and March 14, 1903). Certainly, the public airing of Taylor's beliefs on his first visit had given ammunition to those who were inclined towards racism, and saw his public profession of faith as sanctimoniousness. And when he returned in December, 1903, the opposition was again ready for him. *The Bulletin* (Dec. 31, 1903) criticized Taylor openly, saying that it didn't matter whether he won or not since he was being paid so much just to appear at races. The paper suggested that he was in Australia in defiance of the "White Australia" policy. "By the way," it said, "Taylor, being a 'colored' person, should be doubly challenged by the Australian government laws—as colored alien and immigrant under contract."

The atmosphere of the second visit appears to have become somewhat acrimonious, and the racing more bitter and cut-throat. There were two reasons for this. First, sections of the Australian media were uncomfortable with the fact that Taylor was here for a repeat visit. In an article that criticized Taylor's riding in one of the big events, *The Bulletin* said: "If cyclist Taylor isn't careful, there'll be a big slump in his repute [sic] for holiness before he gets away from Australia, and rabbit-fronted parsons will cease to arise and preach sermons on him as a black and brilliant reproach to the White Australia policy" (*The Bulletin*, March 17, 1904). Second, and more importantly, Taylor's hated American rivals, Iver Lawson and Floyd MacFarland, had been engaged in the 1903 tour. They had been lured with the specific purpose of creating a climate of tense athletic excitement, since the hostility between them and Taylor was well known. Indeed, their attitude towards Taylor did not improve in the slightest outside the United States (Warden 2007).

The style of racing in Australia, which put great emphasis on handicap events with big prizes, made illicit teamwork (riders who ought to be opponents working together against other strong riders or favorites, and the big prizes divided up after the event) almost inevitable. This gave Lawson and MacFarland the chances they needed to win. On every occasion they worked together against him, while Taylor, honest and sporting to the core, refused to cooperate or team with any other riders to defend his position on the tracks. Lawson, in fact, was suspended for a year for a foul he committed in a match race in Melbourne which caused Taylor to crash heavily and left him stunned, badly bruised, and lacerated, one of the most serious crashes he had ever had. Lawson was forced to cancel his Australian trip and return to Europe (Ritchie, 2009).

Even the Australian riders saw little enough reason to help Taylor increase his already huge earnings, and so the black American star was isolated, left to fend for himself, against a determined opposition. Unless he paid them, or shared the prize money with them, they argued, they had no reason to work with him in a race. The nature of cycling as a professional sport meant that rival riders might temporarily cooperate and share in the pacing if it was to their mutual advantage in defeating a common rival. The climate was much less friendly than on Taylor's previous tour, with Floyd MacFarland responsible for stirring up much of the negative feeling against Taylor among the previously friendly Australian riders. Commenting on his relationship with Taylor, Iver Lawson told an Australian journalist, "We never speak, and we pass in the street without noticing one another" (Ritchie, 2009).

The increased animosity shown towards Taylor by riders and officials, however, only made him more popular with the crowds, who still crammed into the tracks to enjoy the cut-throat racing between bitter rivals. The *Sydney Morning Herald* reported 10,000 spectators at one of the days of the Sydney Thousand [Cycling] Carnival at the Sydney Cricket Ground, and on the next day, 32,000 were present (*Sydney Morning Herald*, March 24, 1903). The race promoters knew how to create the atmosphere for an impressive spectacle, and the latest technology was at their disposal: "The whole of the stands and pavilions, which almost circle the track, were outlined with thousands of frosted-white electric globes, which shed a soft light over the variegated hues of the ladies' summer costumes." The track itself was lit by "the brilliant and dazzling acetylene light of the many powerful shaded lamps" which were suspended over it (*Table Talk*, March 26, 1903). *The Bulletin* (March 26, 1903) remarked:

> Bicycle racing by acetylene gaslight is a vivid sport. At Sydney Cricket Ground they accentuate the picturesqueness of it by suddenly extinguishing all the lights save those immediately over the course, and then the track becomes a great green ribbon on a quilt of dusky shadows, over which flee a motley crowd of men crouched over spidery bicycles.

On this second tour of Australia, when he was again welcomed warmly again by loyal spectators, Taylor also had to endure corrupt, perhaps racist, decisions from some referees. The match races between Taylor, Mac-Farland, and Lawson were exciting but inconclusive, spoiled as they were by bad judges' decisions, refusals to appear and the muddle of frequent official inquiries and the withholding of prize money. When Taylor left Adelaide in April, 1904, he swore to the press that he would never return: "Don't make any mistake about it. I shall never ride in South Australia again as long as the management of the sport is in the hands of the present officials." Taylor was indignant and "there was a suggestion of vigorous contempt in his demeanor. He thumped the reporter's knee with almost painful emphasis and simultaneously stamped the floor with his feet ... The only condition which would secure my reappearance on your track," he continued, "would be a change in the personnel of the executive. Some of your officials have all along entertained a disgusting prejudice against me," he told the *Adelaide Observer*. "There is no tactful sympathy about them. They have regarded me merely as a revenue-earning machine, nothing more. I could fill up your paper with incidents of how this bias has been displayed" (*Adelaide Observer*, April 23, 1904).

> Off the track, however, there was much for Major and his wife to be excited about. The couple's first and only child, a daughter, was born in Sydney on May 11, 1904. She was christened Rita Sydney after the city in which she was born, and was known thereafter as Sydney. Less than a month after her birth, the Taylors set sail for San Francisco on the liner *Sierra*, accompanied by the Australian cycling champion Don Walker, a staunch Christian who had become a close friend; he was on his way to compete in the world championships in England. They left Australia with what the newspapers referred to as "a small menagerie"—a kangaroo, several brightly colored parrots, and a cockatoo, which had been taught to cry "Major! Major! Hallo, Boy!" (Ritchie, 2009).

A rousing farewell in Australia was followed by a hostile reception in San Francisco. There, wrote Taylor, "we encountered a new epidemic of Colorphobia. ... We found it impossible to dine in the restaurants because the management drew the color line, and the same conditions confronted us at the hotels. We made the rounds of the city, only to be refused shelter and in many cases to be actually insulted" (Taylor, 1928, 408-09). Major Taylor, a household name in France and Australia, was a nobody in California. In the end, at Taylor's suggestion, they resorted to a ruse to be able to eat lunch. Walker went into a restaurant where they had already been refused service and ordered lunch for three, saying that his companions would be coming shortly. When the food was served, he paid the bill and then brought the Taylors in. They were not thrown out. They had planned to rest for a few days in San Francisco, but they were so disgusted with their treatment, they instead left for the East on the midnight sleeper. Such was the respect paid to a great African-American champion in California.

Their Australian companion Don Walker was flabbergasted. "So this is America about which you have been boasting in Australia," Taylor remembered him saying. "From what I have seen of it in the past few days, I cannot understand why you were in such a hurry to get back home here. Do you prefer to live in a country where you are treated like this than to live in my country where you are so well thought of, and where you are treated like a white man, and where many inducements were made you to return to live? I cannot understand this kind of thing." Taylor tried to explain conditions to Walker, he wrote, "but the more I tried to smooth matters over, the more incensed he became" (Taylor, 1928, 408-09). Taylor's daughter, Sydney, later wrote that her parents' experiences in San Francisco were more severe than merely being refused service at hotels and restaurants. She says that a man on the street, mistaking her mother for a white woman, made insulting comments about her being with a black man. She says that Taylor told his wife and Don Walker to go down the street a little further and then turned and confronted the man. A fight broke out, and Taylor, an expert boxer, deftly flattened him (Ritchie, 2009).

In June 1904, Taylor arrived in Worcester with his family and an entourage of animals. He was exhausted, not just from the second Australian tour, where he had ridden close to 100 races, but from the cumulative effect of years of racing, training, and traveling. "I don't know whether I'll ever race again," he told a reporter from the *Worcester Telegram* on July 6, 1904. "During the last six months I raced three or four times a week. The racing was the toughest I ever experienced. In fact, I am sure that the racing I have done in the last six months was harder than all the rest of the racing I ever did." To the reporter he appeared to be in perfect health, but the stress and strain had taken its toll. Taylor himself said that he "suffered a collapse and narrowly averted a nervous breakdown." He canceled his plans to travel on to London and Paris for the rest of the summer season. "You see," he told the *Telegram*, "I can't ask my wife to go around the country and abroad with me like I could before the little girl came, and I won't go away alone. If I could find something congenial to do, I think I'd stay home for awhile."

The complete rest that Taylor took in Worcester for the remainder of 1904 was the first summer break he had had since the beginning of his professional racing career in 1896. He was only twenty-five years old when the curtain fell on the first and most extraordinary phase of his life. Marriage and a child brought a new sense of responsibility. By 1904, he had accomplished the greatest feats of his life and had essentially completed his athletic contribution.

CONCLUSION

As a visiting sports champion of established international caliber and fame, Major Taylor was given official exemption from the racialized immigration control of the "White Australia" policy. In spite of initial misgivings about his first visit, there were no formal objections to his arrival—he was considered a temporary visitor, and an exception. His exceptional status was confirmed by extravagant receptions given by state and civic officials and dignitaries. This, however, did not prevent some newspapers—typified by *The Bulletin*—publishing scathing, racist articles and images about him, revealing other contradictory aspects of the social climate within which Taylor had to compete.

The cycling competition itself was fierce, but that was to be expected. The crowd reaction to Major Taylor at a moment of expansive success for the sport of bicycle racing was overwhelmingly positive. They responded to exciting racing, disliked unsporting behavior, and were interested in the mystique of Taylor. Crowds of 10-20,000 people were reported at these huge promotions. The hostility directed at Taylor on the track during the second tour was fomented by Americans MacFarland and Lawson, and was a continuation of the hostility which had been directed at him in America, and from which he could not escape. The decision of the cycling authorities to include these foreign riders, who had a well-known history of bigotry and physical and verbal hostility towards Taylor, was probably taken with the specific intention of staging exciting sport, but it may have back-fired on the promoters.

The style of the races with the biggest prizes was invariably on a handicap basis, in which the better riders started in groups behind their opponents (on a tiered basis), and needed to work together to overtake those who started ahead of them. This style of racing only served to give Taylor's opposition a better chance to gang up on him. The result was fouling, appeals, official inquiries and hearings, disqualifications—all of which threw the sport into bureaucratic chaos, and disgraced it in the eyes of honest spectators. Taylor had a much greater chance of displaying his abilities—and his athletic superiority—in small-group one-to-one match racing, in which he was practically unbeatable.

From the perspective of cycling as a sport of international popularity and significance at the time, Major Taylor's presence in Australia during those two summer seasons was a logical result of his desire to stay at the very top of the sport, and to profit from his fame and experience. But the stress and strain of the 1904 racing led to a physical and mental break-down which kept Taylor out of competition for the rest of 1904 and the seasons of 1905 and 1906. Upon leaving Australia in June 1904, Taylor spoke openly and critically to the press that he would not return to race if the same officials were in authority within the sport in Australia. Privately and socially, Taylor was treated well in Australia, and was welcomed into the Baptist churches and social circles in all the cities he visited. And he was a huge hit with cycling fans all over the country. He was a black-skinned hero in a nation that prided itself on "White Australia."

ENDNOTES

[1] This article is substantially based on Chapter 10 "World Traveller and International Celebrity" of the new edition (2009) of the author's book: *Major Taylor—The Fastest Bicycle Rider in the World*. It was given in an abbreviated form as a presentation at the Conference, "Sport, Race, and Ethnicity: Building a Global Understanding," held at the University of Technology Sydney, School of Leisure, Sport and Tourism, in December 2008.

[2] Unidentified newspaper clipping in Taylor scrapbook, Indianapolis Historical Museum archive.

Sport, Racism, and Aboriginality: The Australian Experience

BY COLIN TATZ

South Africa's laws never prohibited inter-racial sport. But from 1652, social custom and a fundamentalist religion ensured that sport was rigidly segregated (Lapchick, 1975, Tatz, 1983, Booth, 1998). Until the 1990s, being Black, Asian, or Colored meant that you could roll pitches, mark courts, clean pools, cut grass, erect goalposts, caddie, sell ice-creams, wait tables and clean shoes—but you couldn't play. Racial divides were endemic, pervasive, oppressive, wantonly cruel and often ludicrous. Some inanities linger. In 2009 the rugby union authorities rejected as racist a proposed tour by a New Zealand all-Maori team (totally out of the question in the apartheid era) because there wasn't a White man on the team!

So much for an avowedly race-based society. But what of Australia, "the land of the fair go?" Could the people who see themselves as good colonists commit genocide? Can decent democrats be overtly racist in sport, a domain so essential in and to the national psyche? Can a mateship society disavow its Aboriginal "brethren" in the ring, on the pitch, oval, or stadium?

The answers, of course, are yes. But there are always asterisks, of a kind. A dialectical contradiction is involved, namely, that two apparently contradictory things can both be true at the same time and place. In this brief analysis, we see vilification almost beyond belief *and* adulation of almost equal proportion; denigration *and* veneration; gross contempt and inordinate celebration; total exclusion from teams and competitions *and* active recruitment of players.

LEVELS OF RACISM

There are always degrees of racism. I think Gordon Allport, a noted Harvard psychologist, made a cardinal error in his celebrated classic, *The Nature of Prejudice* (1954). My objection is not to his defining of prejudice but to the causal link he made between his five scales of that phenomenon. Prejudice, he wrote, begets the first step, antilocution, a speaking against or "bad-mouthing" of people, as in "bloody Jew" or "nigger." That begets step two, social exclusion, followed by step three, institutionalized segregation, as in separate neighborhoods or schools. What ensues is step four, physical attacks—swastikas on synagogues, desecration of cemeteries, or lynchings. Then, the endpoint—the physical extermination of people. Unfounded is his insistence on a syndrome, a set of systematic causal connections that flow naturally from one step or scale to the next. History offers endless examples of steps one and two and few, if any, signs of three or four, let alone five.

Wittingly or not, he bequeathed the inference that somehow these overt expressions of prejudice are on a par. In the Western world, accordingly, enormous energy has been devoted by specialized institutions to "treat" verbal vilification (as an illness)—on the premise that if you can cure or somehow even stop the antilocution you can stop the extermination or nip it in the bud.

In the Australian case, access to competition can be illustrated in three forms. One is structural: Because of their place in the political, legal, economic and social system, Aborigines, Torres Strait and South Sea Islanders rarely get onto squash courts or championship golf courses or into ski lodges. They don't hang-glide, play polo, sail yachts, ride bikes for Yamaha (apart from the amazing Chad Reed, now in motorcross in the United

States) or drive cars for Ferrari. The second form is institutional: On remote or rural reserves, where most Aborigines have lived, there was and
is no grass, no facilities, coaches, nutritionists, physiotherapists, personal
trainers, motivators, let alone floodlights or change-rooms. Not much has
changed in the first decade of the twenty-first century. The third form is
political: The blatant and continuing racism which excludes individuals
or teams from competition because they are Aboriginal. That so many are
now eagerly recruited for football codes or nurtured for Olympics, or that
some sports believe there is gold in targeting 'non-White' recruits, doesn't
negate the past or present experiences.

The obviousness of the Aboriginal condition is the most telling indica-
tor of racism in Australia. One example, in passing, will suffice. In 2007,
the federal Liberal Coalition government initiated an "emergency intervention" in the Northern Territory following a report on allegations of sexual
abuse of young children in remote Aboriginal communities (Toohey, 2008).
Reaffirmed by the new Labor government since then, this action across 73
communities has involved suspending the protections of the federal *Racial
Discrimination Act*, quarantining most welfare payments, suspending Aboriginal councils' rights to determine who is allowed into their domains,
and sending in civilian task forces and military troops to act as some new
(untrained) corps of social welfare and health specialists, as "protectors"
and "interveners" in the realm of child safety. Less than a handful of arrests
have been made and no convictions recorded. The reality is that domestic
and personal violence have increased, as has substance abuse. But the police have taken to searching homes, without warrant—for yeast, lest the
natives attempt a home brew. This is 2010, not 1910, and the shibboleth on
which all state and federal policies and practices have rested, that any action is always "in their best interests," hasn't altered in well over a century.

THE BAD AND THE UGLY

Mulvaney and Harcourt (1988) described the famous Aboriginal cricket
tour to England in 1868, a decade before a White team ventured abroad,

as "a dignified episode of race relations." It was a short one, occurring in the gap between the major massacres in Victoria and the creation of the Board for the Protection of Aborigines in 1869. But later researchers have established that there was indignity, even cruelty, as the players went unpaid, were housed inadequately, and regarded as quaint circus-freak performers of various native sports rather than of cricket (Sampson, 2009).

The story is that an Edenhope grazier sent pictures of "his" Aborigines to the owners of the Melbourne Cricket Ground (MCG) refreshment tent. In the Lake Wallace district of Western Victoria, pastoralists had taught their servants the game because they and their sons had no one to play against. The names their "owners" assigned to them illustrated their attitudes: Jim Crow, Sundown, Redcap, Tarpot, King Cole, Mosquito, Tiger, Bullocky. Amid talk of commercial exploitation and associated skulduggery, and despite much illness among the players, hotelier Charles Lawrence agreed to coach the team for an English tour. Two players were ill enough to be sent home and King Cole died of tuberculosis on tour. The team landed in England in May 1868. They played 47 matches for 19 draws, 14 wins and 14 losses.

Romantic, heroic, historic, the subject of three books and innumerable photographic reproductions, the tour was also the beginning of sporting exploitation, bad faith, and ill treatment. The star of the tour, Johnny Mullagh (named after Mullagh Station, where he worked) was the only player to establish a cricket career on his return. A memorial to this man was erected at rural Harrow and the local cricket oval bears his name.

Cricket and pedestrianism, the name for professional track athletics, were two sports open to Aborigines in their period of "freedom," the era before draconian laws for their segregation and protection came into force. Queensland settlers killed some 10,000 Aborigines between 1824 and 1908. The British High Commissioner in Queensland complained to the British Prime Minister about the "wholesale butchery" of Aborigines. Men of refinement, Arthur Gordon wrote to William Gladstone, "talk of the *individual* murder of natives, exactly as they talk of a day's sport, or having to kill some troublesome animal." "Shooting a snipe," wrote one settler, "sounds better than murdering a man." In Central Australia, between the 1860s and 1890s, some 650 Aborigines were shot, mainly by police, in the name of "dispersing kangaroos" (Tatz, 2010).

Yet amid the general carnage there was freedom to play cricket (Tatz 1995). In the 1890s, a number of Aborigines were playing at Deebing Creek, near Ipswich, Queensland. Townspeople felt that "every encouragement should be given to our ebony brethren." People came to watch. They "behaved like white gentlemen," said the *Queensland Times*. The Deebing Creek team won a major trophy in 1895 and then played the National Cricket Union in Brisbane. The Colonial Secretary, shortly before he received a report from Special Commissioner Archibald Meston (1896) on the urgent need to stop the "shameful deeds"—the killings, child abductions, procuring of women through opium—sent the Aborigines two cricket bats "in appreciation of their excellent behaviour and smart turn-out."

Aboriginal fast bowlers have not fared well in cricket, the sport said to define the very ethos of fair play. Jack Marsh played six matches for New South Wales in 1901–03. Branded a "chucker" (that is, that he bent his arm unduly on delivery and was therefore an illegal bowler), he was in reality precluded from an English tour because of his color. Following an unexplained banning from the Sydney Cricket Ground, he drifted into circus life and in 1916 was kicked to death in rural Orange, NSW. His two assailants were charged not with murder but manslaughter; the jury didn't bother to leave their box and in less than an hour acquitted the accused. Judge Walter Bevan's opinion was that Marsh may well have deserved the kicking (Bonnell, 2003). A circle of some kind is now complete: early in 2010, the Sydney Cricket and Sports Ground Trust announced a $A5000 Jack Marsh History Prize for hitherto unpublished work that relates to the history of that venue.

Marsh's colleague, Alec Henry, played seven inter-state matches for Queensland between 1901 and 1904. Like Marsh, he was a champion sprinter; like Marsh, he was branded a "chucker" and hounded out of cricket. Under the new protective legislation of 1897—the *Aboriginals Protection and Restriction of the Sale of Opium Act,* one of the world's first enactments to protect a human species from genocidal killings—Henry was removed to a controlled settlement "for loafing, malingering and defying authority." After a second removal some 1000 miles further north, he died of tuberculosis, aged 29 (Tatz, 1995).

Don Bradman, Australia's most revered sportsman, once said that Eddie Gilbert, whose bowling run-up was no more than three or four yards long, was the fastest bowler he had ever faced. Eddie played 23 representative matches for Queensland between 1930 and 1935. Only one of twenty umpires "called" him for chucking, but that one-off label tended to tarnish him. A "controlled" Aborigine, he needed permission to play interstate matches; he was always chaperoned lest he got too close to White women, and while his teammates often travelled by road to matches, he had to travel by train. When dropped from the state side in 1936, the Queensland Cricket Association informed the Department of Native Affairs, not Eddie, about his non-selection. They also insisted that his cricket clothing issue be laundered and returned to the Association. He died in an overcrowded asylum, having suffered all manner of racial indignities (Coleman and Edwards, 2002). In 2008, a statue of Eddie was unveiled at Queensland cricket headquarters in Brisbane.

In the pretty corrupt sport of pedestrianism from the 1880s to at least the 1930s, Aboriginal "peds" [runners] were prominent and controversial. Races were run on a handicap system over distances varying from 75 yards to a mile, with the fastest man on the back line, or "scratch," and the others allocated anything from a yard to twenty as a start to even up things. The "daddy" of the Gifts, as these races were often called, was the 120-yard handicap Stawell Easter Gift. It remains the world's richest and most prestigious event of its kind. Aborigines, never disbarred, won in 1883, 1910, 1928, 2005, and 2006.

Early in the twentieth century, the Queensland Amateur Athletics Association (QAAA) tried to ban all Aborigines from racing on the spurious grounds that they either "lacked moral character," "had insufficient intelligence," or "couldn't resist white vice." These appalling excuses were rejected by the national athletics body, leading to the QAAA deeming them all professionals in 1903. In 1896, the Northern Territory settlers, very small in number, ordained that "no aborigines or other coloured races be allowed to compete in European events"—a response to the £10 Pine Creek Handicap victory in 1895 of an Aborigine called, unsurprisingly, Bismarck (Stephen, 2009).

Athletes wrote to the governor of Queensland asking him to ban all Aborigines at Fraser Island, Queensland, because they always won. When Aborigines became prominent, separate initials began appearing after each runner's name in the official race programs, indicating that "a" was an Aborigine, "h.c." a "half-caste," and "c.p." a "colored person." It was suggested that "without these distinguishing marks ... the public are misled." This practice lasted from the 1880s until about 1912 (Tatz, 1995).

Queensland was the most draconian of the six Australian colonies that became states in 1901. Archibald Meston, intent on saving Aborigines from the genocidal impulses of settlers, became the first official Protector of Aborigines. He was a keen sportsman, but didn't like cricket. His successor, Dr. W. E. Roth, didn't like any Aborigines playing sport, especially athletics: "They themselves, making plenty of money for a few years on behalf of the betting fraternity ... come back to us wrecks, as a rule, and a nuisance and a burden upon the rest" (Tatz, 1995). Sport became almost impossible in such an environ; a few escaped the system by obtaining exemption certificates from the 1897 statute, stating that they were no longer under control and were, in effect, White folks.

Jeremiah (Jerry) Jerome, a noted horse-breaker, rifle shooter, and pedestrian, took up boxing at the age of 33; at 38, he became the first Black to win an Australian title—the middleweight championship, in 1912. His first manager gained Jerry an exemption but the Chief Protector hounded him, accusing this "moneyed gentleman" of "inciting all others to refuse to work unless paid cash for it." (They were paid in food rations on the reserves, missions and settlements.) Adored by Sydney fans, this "Book of Lamenta-tions," as one boxing scribe called him, was taken to Cherbourg Settlement on his retirement, his exemption revoked, his earnings taken by the author-ities. Two streets in Queensland have been named after him, posthumously.

Ron Richards, another exempted Queenslander, was possibly Aus-tralia's best fighter of all time. Fast, a strong counter-puncher, resilient, a strong hitter, he was the complete boxer. In 1938 he thrashed Gus Lesnevitch, considered one of the best light-heavyweights of the century. Ron achieved third world ranking in the middleweights and fourth in the light-heavies in an era when there was only one universal boxing author-ity and the eight weight divisions were both simple and logical. Had the chance come his way, said the critics, he would have been the world cham-pion. Richards fought too often. Bad management, exploitation, and the death of his (first) Aboriginal wife led to a period of degradation: Drink-ing, charges of vagrancy, removal to Woorabinda Settlement, a beating by louts in the Sydney Haymarket area for the glory of saying 'I KO'd Ron Richards' and finally, removal to the remote and notorious Palm Island, conceived as a penal colony for "troublesome" Aborigines and Islanders, where he died, penniless, in 1967 at the age of 56 (Tatz, 1995).

Professional boxing has always been a gladiatorial entertainment, a celebratory "boxiana" for Pierce Egan (1812, 1976) and the "sweet science" for AJ Liebling (1956), but a cruel sport nevertheless. Exploitation perme-ates the sport but, I believe, the more so of Black boxers here, in the United States and South Africa. Alfie Sands, brother of the legendary Dave Sands, had an incredible 151 fights in a short career. Exploiters encouraged his drinking binges after fights so that he would need to return to "work" sooner for more money. In 1946, George Kapeen had eight fights in Octo-ber and seven in November: fifteen in sixty days is, indeed, an indictment of boxing administration. These were not aberrant cases.

Jerome, Richards, and Gilbert made history in many ways, "near Cinder-ella" stories that ended badly. Another is the case of Frankie Fisher, grandfa-ther of the much beloved athlete Cathy Freeman. A regular member of the famous Cherbourg Settlement rugby league teams, he played five-eighth for Wide Bay against the visiting British teams in 1932 and 1936. So impressed was the English captain, the legendary Gus Risman, that he wrote to Fisher suggesting that he come to England for a career. Fisher, then a "controlled" Aborigine, applied to the Aboriginal administration for *permission* to apply for a passport. As a ward of the state, he was refused, allegedly on the ground that one sports star from Cherbourg—Eddie Gilbert—was enough.

Protective legislation was duplicated by all states and the Northern Territory after the Queensland model set in 1897. It is not surprising that ambitious, or desperate, Aboriginal men and women began suppressing their identities when possible. The champion axeman of the 1920s was Leo Appo, from Tweed Heads, NSW. His experience was not untypical of the times: He couldn't get a place at the Royal Easter Show and similar woodchopping arenas, so he was urged to enter as a New Zealander—and was duly welcomed. In 1928 he won a Commonwealth title and was awarded his £40 and his gold medal by the Governor-General—but this time as an Aborigine. In 1962, Percy Hobson, from Bourke, NSW, became the first Aboriginal youth to hold a national amateur athletics record. Chosen for Australia in the Commonwealth Games in Perth in 1962, athletics administrators urged him "not to broadcast his ancestry," a surrender that depressed him for the rest of his life. He became the first Aboriginal athlete to win a gold medal for Australia. Frankie Reys, winner of the renowned Melbourne Cup in 1973 on Gala Supreme, always described himself as a Filipino (which was true of one ancestor) rather than face the added handicap of being an Aboriginal jockey in senior horseracing. Years after his death, his widow kindly gave me permission to publish his Aboriginality. As a Filipino he was seen as someone exotic; as an Aborigine, it is unlikely he would have become a senior jockey, let alone chairman of the Victorian Jockeys Association for ten years.

Vilification is ugly but is not in the same league as exclusion. At least the player is there, in the ring or on the field. Racial "sledging" (an Australian term for such abuse) is still treated in the manner of all racial vilification cases: A form of "illness" that requires counseling, the offender meeting the offended, conciliation, offers of apology and promises of no repeats, and the "patient" hopefully healed. More recently, codes of sports conduct have led to game suspensions and hefty fines, but "illness" remains the core premise of these "social" misdemeanors. In a 1993 Australian football match between St Kilda and Collingwood (Magpies or 'Pies), the Collingwood crowd gave Nicky Winmar a continuous racial blast. On April 18, the *Sydney Morning Herald*, in publishing what is perhaps the most iconic photo in Australian sporting history, commented:

> The Collingwood cheer-squad had decided to remind Nicky Winmar, an Aborigine ... that he was one of them rather than one of us, and they did so in the manner for which they are justly notorious ... After the final siren he gave the 'Pie cheer squad as good as he had received, lifting his jumper and pointing to his skin. As spectacularly talented as he is with or near a football, Winmar has never been more eloquent or effective for his cause or his color than he was in that moment.

The press was now behind the "sledgees," whereas a decade earlier the complaining Aborigines would have been hailed as cheeky, not knowing their place and incapable of handling good-natured, sporting humor. In rugby league in 1999, Anthony Mundine, now a world super-middleweight boxing champion, sustained his complaint against a Canterbury player for racial vilification and, despite attempts by officials to gloss over the matter (as is usual), the player was fined $A10,000. Mundine has never been quite forgiven for not being "a team player," nor was he forgiven for being aggressively outspoken, in the manner of Ali.

One doesn't expect exclusion in sports competition, at least not in the contemporary era. For every act of inclusion there appears to have been a corresponding exclusion. Aboriginal cricket teams played with great panache and friendship in the colonies: The mission team from Poonindie (South Australia) from 1850; the Coranderrk (Victoria) team in the 1870s;

the New Norcia (Western Australia) team from 1880 to 1905. Aboriginal teams in Australian Rules football, like the Badger Creek team in Victoria, were applauded. But history is littered with exclusions based on spurious, racist grounds such as: They "smelled," they always won, they were "uncivilized," they "don't pay their dues," their cheer squads cause fights, they abuse or assault the referees and judges, they "bring the game into disrepute," we "can't have an uneven number of teams in a group competition," and, since the odor of apartheid in South Africa, "we can't have racially segregated teams," even those voluntarily organized in that way.

Following an assortment of walk-offs by White players in various intertown Australian football games in the Northern Territory, all Aboriginal players were banned for four seasons, from December 1926 to December 1929 (Stephen, 2009). In 1987, the Fitzroy All-Stars in Melbourne claimed they were refused entry into a senior league competition; and in the same year, the Purnim Bears from western Victoria were expelled from the local Australian football league after winning the grand final.

In the 1930s, the Tweed Head All Blacks rugby league team was formed because White teams wouldn't admit Aborigines. At the same time, the Boomerangs team from Condobolin, NSW was barred from playing against the local Whites, but the publicity resulted in invitations to tour the Riverina area, which they did, successfully, for seven weeks. Narwan, in Armidale, NSW, was yet another team born out of discrimination. In the 1970s a number of rugby league players in White teams were forever sitting on the bench, not getting games and feeling unwanted. They pushed for and gained an Aboriginal side in 1977, amid much opposition, even from the local university faculty. They won the Caltex Shield and in 1980 the Clayton Cup, country league's most prestigious event; they went on to win five premierships and four knockout competitions. Regrettably, as with so many teams, Narwan was expelled from Group 19 in country competition in 2005, ostensibly for unpaid debts. At the same time, the Gimbisi Warriors were ejected from Group 2 for "crowd behavior" and Northern United were refused entry to Group 1 football for reasons unstated.

The renowned Moree Boomerangs began in the 1940s, disappeared, then resurfaced in the 1970s. They won the prestigious Group 4 grand final in 1982 and again in 1992. Sadly, in 1998, the Boomerangs were excluded from the competition for player and fan brawling. They lost an appeal against their banning before the NSW Supreme Court, and remained excluded until readmitted at the start of the 2010 season.

The latest of many such sagas has been the attempt to create a 14-team competition called the Nations Aboriginal Rugby League in rural New South Wales. Why there is so much opposition, especially from Country Rugby League, is not clear; such bodies may well be part of the strong assimilationist thrusts still evident in Australian public life, or football administrators may not want to lose the many Aboriginal champions who now play for senior city teams. The concept of "All Blacks" is alive and well; Aborigines have shown, especially through the NSW Rugby League Knockout carnival, that they can run their own competitions, given a little breathing space and a ground to play on; and, significantly, the people of outback towns now see themselves as *nations*.

In commemoration of the national Sorry Day, when Prime Minister Kevin Rudd apologised for the removed children in February 2008, an Indigenous Dreamteam won a rugby league match against a representative National Football league side on 13 February 2010. Hailed as a great match, the pressure for an all-Aboriginal team in the national competition will increase, creating dilemmas for White teams and administrators rather than for Black players.

Ugliest of all in many ways is the subversion, or perhaps inversion, of the Stolen Generations story. The forcible transfer of children of one group to another is the subject of Article II(e) of the 1948 Convention on the Prevention and Punishment of the Crime of Genocide. Victoria began this practice in 1839, and it continued across Australia, in different phases and spurts, until at least 1988, the date of closure of the last of the "assimilation homes" in New South Wales. It is likely that between 50,000 and 60,000 children were "removed" from their parents and families, and with no intention by the authorities that they could or should reunite. Aboriginal history is replete with achievers who were stolen. The sting, so to speak, is in the assertion that those who have excelled in sport, or music, art, or even in politics and business have done so *because* they were stolen. It was "in their best interests"—and the results are there for all to see.

THE GOOD AND THE PRETTY

Traveling circuses were important in rural life in the last century. Tent boxers were immensely popular, with young bucks urged to go two or three rounds with the "champs," many of whom were Aboriginal. Jimmy Sharman, Sr., ran the biggest shows in town and, to his credit, took pains to nurture and protect his Black gladiators (Broome, 1996). The esteemed king of the horse show ring was Lance Skuthorpe, Sr., with horse breaking, saddle bronc riding, bull riding, steer wrestling, and whip demonstrations his specialities. He, too, boosted the fortunes of great Aboriginal horsemen, notably Billy Waite and Billy Jonas, both of whom rode in the King George V coronation event in London in 1911. Later, Skuthorpe employed Jack ("Sonny Carbine") Watson, world buckjumping champion in 1924, and two notable rodeo men, Queensland Harry and Wild Harry (Pollard, 1962). Horseracing was quite another story, with Aborigines ever present as stable hands, groomers, and training jockeys, but always excluded from race rides, apart from the inevitable postscript of a "Blackboys Event" in country bush racing, for which flour, sugar, tea, and treacle tended to be the prizes.

Queensland allowed two remarkable duets in the 1930s. In 1937, Australia rode in two international rodeo contests against the United States and Canada, with three riders in each team. Two Aborigines, Alec Hayden and his cousin Jimmy Williams (named after a property owned by a Mr. Williams), were in the winning trio. Women's cricket, a novelty in upper-class private schools, began in that state in 1929. By 1934, when the English team arrived on tour, two Aboriginal cousins from the very lower end of town, Edna Crouch and Mabel Campbell, were chosen to play against the visitors.

Cummeragunga (known as Cummera) is an Aboriginal community on the Murray River, geographically in New South Wales but with its main ties to Victoria. It began in 1874 as Maloga Mission, under a local merchant Daniel Matthews. Stern, rigid, and deeply religious, Matthews was "appalled at the degradation of these poor unprotected creatures," especially the children of this "debased and ignorant race." He was prone to punishing eloping girls "by beating them severely." He saw sport as "an uncivilizing activity" but while he didn't like it, he didn't prohibit it (Cato 1976). Cummera produced more sports champions per head of population than any other location in Australia. Australian Rules footballers, boxers, cricketers, and professional runners seemed to roll off an assembly line. Cummera also produced a long line of political activists.

Pastor Sir Douglas Nicholls KCVO, MBE was the most formidable Cummera achiever: Winner of several major Gifts, tent boxer for Sharman for several years, and star of the Fitzroy team in Australian football from 1932 to 1937, he later became the leader of the Aborigines Advancement League in Victoria and then governor of South Australia. He remains the only Aboriginal (Imperial) knight of the realm. His Aboriginal colleague, Lynch Cooper, won the prized Stawell Gift in 1928 and the World Sprint Championship in 1929.

At this time, there had been no Aborigines players in senior Australian Rules football teams in the West. That changed with the advent of three brothers—Maley, Bill, and Eric Hayward. Successful sprinters, they learned their football skills by kicking balls through the narrow forks of trees, often in the dark. Maley broke "the color bar" by gaining a place for Claremont in 1928 and by the mid-1930s the trio was playing for South Fremantle. They were granted special exemptions by the state government to play their games (Hayward, 2006).

Post-war, a very popular magazine called *Sports Novels* ran polls to elect Australia's outstanding sportsperson. Aboriginal boxer Dave Sands won clearly in 1950 and again in 1951—in the face of major competition from renowned cricketers and rugby league players. Dave held the middleweight, light-heavyweight, and heavyweight titles simultaneously and was also Empire middleweight champion. Killed in a truck accident at age 26, the man who was labelled "the uncrowned world champion" had one of the largest funerals ever seen in New South Wales. "World boxing has lost a great fighter; Australian boxing has lost its mainstay; society has lost a gentleman" was a press verdict on the man loved by all. There are three public monuments in his honor (Mooney and Ramsland, 2008).

Sands's death in 1952 seemed to be a turning point in Aboriginal sport. Thereafter, the man who was to become a "legend" in the Australian [Rules] Football League's hall of fame, Graham ("Polly") Farmer, once a "removed" child, began his career. Not far behind him in achievement and status were a group of men who hailed from six tiny and remote communities in the south-west of Western Australia, with a total Aboriginal population of about 5000: The Hayward clan mentioned above, Ted Kilmurray, Stephen Michael, Barry Cable (the most decorated and bemedalled achiever in the sport), Syd Jackson, and later, the Narkle, Kickett, and Matera clans.

Sands was the inspiration for memorable Australian champions: Gary Cowburn, Bobby Sinn, Elley Bennett, Jack Hassen, and George Bracken. The latter three began life in the boxing tents. In turn, they inspired Lionel Rose, the first Aborigine to win a world title, the bantamweight championship, in 1968. On his return from beating Fighting Harada in Tokyo, Rose had a public adulation ceremony that brought 250,000 people to the streets between the airport and Town Hall.

Lionel Morgan was chosen for an Australian rugby league side in 1962, the same year that Lloyd McDermott played rugby union for the Wallabies against New Zealand. Harry Williams played soccer for Australia, and Arthur ("Artie") Beetson began his pathway to becoming the adored leviathan of rugby league.

Evonne Goolagong is perhaps the most internationally acclaimed Aboriginal athlete. She won every major tennis title—except the United States event—winning Wimbledon in 1971 and 1980 (as Goolagong-

Cawley). London's tennis critic Rex Bellamy wrote of her: "Wonderfully gifted ... with swift grace of balanced movement, an instinctive tactical brain, a flexible repertoire of strokes, and an equable temperament." This was also the era of the Ella brothers—Mark, Glen and Gary—with Mark a member of the national side on 26 occasions, and captain of the team in nine of them. That an Aborigine from a neglected and poor Aboriginal community at La Perouse in Sydney should captain what is still considered a "silvertail" sport was quite remarkable.

Not all teams faced exclusion and harassment. The Mallee Park Football Club enjoyed a long period of supremacy in South Australia, winning the Port Lincoln Football League premiership eleven times between 1985 and 2001. One hundred years ago the outstanding Australian Rules team from the Ceduna area of South Australia, the Koonibba Football Club, was born with the help of Lutheran missionaries. It is the oldest surviving Aboriginal team in Australia. In the 1950s, with too many Aborigines wanting to play, another team, Rovers, was admitted to the league, and within a year had won the 1958 premiership. We are constantly reminded that, statistically, there is a 17- to 19-year gap between Aboriginal male and non-Aboriginal male life expectancy (59 to 78). Rovers is an example of a starker reality. Of the eighteen men in that team, only one, Keith Willoughby, was alive in 1987 (the year I met him): The other seventeen men didn't make it to the age of 50. Keith died in 1995. In many ways, that team is the essence of the Aboriginal life experience—short, sharp lives with few tomorrows in sight.

In the 1940s and early 1950s, many young men from Bathurst and Melville Islands in the Northern Territory came to Darwin for three-month spells to work for the Army and Air Force. Despite the uniforms, they were not allowed to be servicemen and worked essentially as domestic servants. The Bishop of Darwin felt that football might be "a good thing" for the men. Despite objections from the town's administrators who did not want "too many blackfellas around," the St Marys team was founded in 1952. Since then, it has won no less than 26 premierships.

Statistics tell a story. In Australian Rules football, Doug Nicholls was the only star player in the late 1920s and early 1930s. By 1950, a trickle began. Nearly 53 years after the game's inception, there were only seven Black men in the Victorian Football League, as it was then known. Several great stars emerged in the 1960s and 1970s, but there were as few as twenty top players in the first eighty years of the competition. The relative flood of Aboriginal players began in the 1980s, with six to seven times that earlier number emerging in the next twenty years. Aborigines form, at most, just over two percent of the total population, yet both Australian football and rugby league records show that Aborigines are now between 12 and 15 percent of the senior players.

The celebration of Aborigines is noteworthy. The Norm Smith Medal for the best player in an Australian Rules football grand final has been awarded to Maurice Rioli, Michael Long, Peter Matera, Andrew McLeod (twice), and Byron Pickett. The most prestigious medal of them all, the Brownlow, has been won by Gavin Wanganeen and Adam Goodes (twice). There is a Polly Farmer Room at the Subiaco Oval in Western Australia and a welfare center in Melbourne is named after Doug Nicholls. In rugby league, the Mal Meninga stand at the Bruce Stadium in Canberra is in honor of this outstanding South Sea Islander, an "immortal" in the sport, the man who played 43 Tests for Australia and 23 as captain. The entrance to that stadium has a life-sized sculpture of Laurie Daley, rated as the one of the best backline players of all time.

To date, 36 Aborigines have played rugby league for Australia; nine have played rugby union for the nation. There have been 45 Olympic and 25 Commonwealth Games representatives since 1964 and 1962, respectively. Institutes of sport and national sports bodies now target Aboriginal youth—less out of any sense of enhancing Aboriginal life and more by way of greed for gold. No matter, they do enhance lives, even if only in the shortest terms.

The celebration and adulation are not so much a wilful mask of reality as a convenient one. Cathy Freeman, probably the most photographed and adored of all Australian performers of any color or gender, has always been the sunny side of Aboriginality, despite a family history that illustrates the Queensland system of Aboriginal mal-administration. She is happy, smiling, friendly, unspoiled—but she has been appropriated and misrepresented as the symbol of all that is now well in Aboriginal society and in Aboriginal womanhood. Cathy and Evonne are, in essence, "aberrations": They are not representative of the lives of Aboriginal women in cities, towns, rural, or remote communities.

Despite wilful obstacles from bureaucracies, police, and local town and shire councils, Aboriginal-organized competitions flourish in Australian football, basketball, and rugby league. Several, like the Yuendumu Games in Central Australia and the Aboriginal Rugby League Knockout Carnival in New South Wales have a distinctly cultural flavor, where the events emphasize kinship and ceremony. In a few places, programs aimed at restoration of indigenous games, many of them thousands of years old and of which at least 3,000 have been documented, are now under way. Given their history, there is a certain prettiness about traditional games now on the way to being taught to both Black and White kids (Edwards, 2009).

SPORT AS SURVIVAL

Aboriginal and Islander sporting success has not ended their harsh experiences. Much remains unchanged: Short life-spans, gross ill-health, lack of housing and sanitation, massive unemployment, less than adequate education, social breakdown in many communities, and a devastating youth suicide rate so indicative of the purposelessness of life. Yet sport for Aborigines and Islanders is neither a luxury nor a leisure activity at the end of an arduous working week. For youth in many communities, it provides a sense of belonging and a feeling of coherence. Sport is more important to them than it is to any other segment of Australian society. In many ways *sport is survival*: It provides purpose in life, an activity of real meaning, a sense of coherence, a reason for being, a sense of power and empowerment, a feeling of autonomy, however brief. It also lessens delinquency and, in an era in which suicide rates are grossly abnormal, it gives youth a sense of *belonging*. There is enough evidence to show that even if sport does not actually *prevent* suicide, it clearly defers that action, often allowing a time-out period to reconsider life's chances (Tatz, 2007). It also offers a chance for a period of wellness. It is a powerful weapon in the fight against rampant diabetes; and many of today's illnesses, especially of the cardiac, renal, and respiratory systems, are better controlled by physical regimens, including sporting competition. In the words of one Aboriginal Tiwi Islander, "for the Tiwi people football means hope, it means pride and most of all it means life" (Moodie, 2008).

REFERENCES

Allport, G.W. (1954). *The nature of prejudice*. Cambridge, Massachusetts: Addison-Wesley.

Bonnell, Max (2003). *How many more are coming? The short life of Jack Marsh*. Sydney: Walla Walla Press.

Booth, D. (1998). *The race game: Sport and politics in South Africa*. London: Frank Cass.

Broome, R. (1996). Theatres of power: Tent boxing circa 1910–1970. *Aboriginal History, 20*, 1-23.

Cato, N. (1993). *Mister Maloga*. Brisbane: University of Queensland Press.

Coleman, M., & Edwards, K. (2002). *Eddie Gilbert: The true story of an Aboriginal cricket legend*. Sydney: ABC Books.

Edwards, K. (2009). Traditional indigenous games of Australian Aboriginal and Torres Strait Islander peoples. *Australian Aboriginal Studies, 2/2009*, 32-43.

Egan, P. (1976 edition). *Boxiana*. London: The Folio Society.

Hayward, E. (2006). *No free kicks: Family, community and football*. Fremantle: Fremantle Arts Centre Press.

Lapchick, R.E. (1975). *The politics of race and international sport: The case of South Africa*. Westport, Connecticut: Greenwood Press.

Liebling, A.J. (1956). *The sweet science*. New York: Viking Press.

Moodie, D. ed (2008). *Tiwi football Yiloga*, Singapore: F11 Productions.

Mooney, C. & Ramsland, J. (2008). Dave Sands as Local Hero and International Champion: Race, Family and Identity in an Industrial Working-class Suburb. *Sport in History, 28(2)*, 299-312.

Mulvaney, J. & Harcourt, R. (1988). *Cricket walkabout: The Australian Aborigines in England*. Melbourne: Macmillan Australia.

Pollard, J. (1978). *The horse tamer*. Sydney: Rigby Limited.

Sampson, D. (2009) The 1868 Aboriginal cricket tour: Taking indigenous sports people and performers to Britain for racial science, popular entertainment and aristocratic curiosity. *Australian Aboriginal Studies, 2/2009*, 44–60.

Stephen, M. (2009) Contact zones: Sport and race in the Northern Territory, 1869–1953. Doctoral thesis, Charles Darwin University.

Tatz, C. (1983). Sport in South Africa: The myth of integration. *The Australian Quarterly, 55* (4), 405–20.

Tatz, C. (1995). *Obstacle race: Aborigines in sport*. Sydney: University of NSW Press.

Tatz, C. (2007). *Aboriginal suicide is different: A portrait of life and self-destruction*. Canberra: Aboriginal Studies Press.

Tatz, C. (2010) Australia: The destruction of Aboriginal society. In The ethnocide and genocide of indigenous peoples, (Eds.) Totten, S. & Hitchcock, R, vol 8, *Genocide: A critical
bibliographical series*. New Jersey: Transaction Publishers (in press).

Toohey, P. (2008). *Quarterly essay: Last drinks: The impact of the Northern Territory intervention,
30,* Melbourne: Black Inc, 1–97.

Ambassadors of Peace!: Sport, Race, Cultural Diplomacy, and the 1927 Takaishi/Saito Swimming Tour of Australia

BY **SEAN BRAWLEY**

Over the summer of 1926/1927, two high profile Japanese swimmers—Katsuo Takaishi and Takahiro Saito—visited Australia to compete in a series of races including the New South Wales and the Australian Championships. The highlight of this very successful tour was the state championships held in Sydney, where freestyle exponent Takaishi competed in a series of races against Andrew 'Boy' Charlton, "the swimming wonder who made such a name for Australia and himself at the Olympic Games in 1924" (*Canberra Times*, November 4, 1926).

Australia's sporting relations with Asia remain an area of study neglected by both sports historians and historians of Australia's Asian context. The purpose of this chapter is to explore one episode in this sporting relationship at a time when high hopes were held for Australia's engagement with the broad Asian region, but also when geopolitical tensions between Japan and both the United States and Australia were growing. The aim is to identify themes associated with the tour that are of relevance to the study of race and ethnicity in sport, and then place them in the context of wider concerns about international relations during the interwar period. In these respects three questions are most apposite. First, did this episode have a positive impact on Australian perceptions of Japan and the Japanese people? Second, did the tour make a contribution to regional goodwill? Third, how can the tour be read in the context of the so-called "White Australia Policy," Australia's racially restrictive immigration policy that operated through the period under investigation and was itself seen as a force for regional political instability (Brawley, 1995).

SPORT AND INTERNATIONAL RELATIONS

The examination of race and ethnicity in Australian sports history has tended to concentrate on the local, the regional, and the national. Few studies have sought to examine these two themes from a transnational perspective. This absence reflects an enduring worldwide disconnect between sports history and international relations. In the mid 1980s Taylor (1986) noted that international relations scholars "show little sign of seriously considering the place of sport in global human affairs" (p.45). Two decades later, Keys (2002) observed: "Although the social history of sport has burgeoned into a significant subfield in recent years, the connections between sport and foreign relations have received little scholarly attention" (p.6). In a similar vein, Livermore and Budd (2004) have argued that while "sport can tell us a good deal about international relations," a "high disdain for sport" and "intellectual snobbiness" has left the field underexplored (p.6). Allison and Monington (2005) have also criticized the tendency for international sporting organizations to attract little scholarly interest; this in a field of study so influenced by international organizations like FIFA, the IOC, and so on.

In recent years, though, there has been a substantial correction in the history of sport and international relations. Keys (2006) has made a powerful contribution with her award-winning work on the globalization of sport in the period before World War II,[2] as have Majumdar and

Collins (2007) with their edited collection on Olympism and internationalism. Others include the author's (Brawley, 2007) study of Australian and American sporting relations as a form of cultural diplomacy in the early twentieth century, Collins's (2002 & 2009) study of the forsaken 1940 Tokyo Olympics, and the Krüger and Murray (2003) study of sport and appeasement of the Nazis in the 1930s.

Upon examining Japan's Olympic campaign of the 1930s, Collins (2002) concluded: "The IOC ultimately became an unwitting conspirator to the imperialist project of Japan" (p.2). However, this country's embrace of Western sport in the decade *before* its invasion of Manchuria in 1931 and its triumph at the 1932 Olympics look very different (Kiyokawa, 1997). In taking a snapshot of 1927 the teleological forces that have compelled scholars to frame their work against the international turbulence of the 1930s and the slide to World War II are manifest, but optimism remained that concerted efforts in building regional goodwill could avert conflict. Also, the forces of militarization and ultra-nationalism that defined Japanese national sporting endeavour in the 1930s were in competition with a more liberal (Guttmann and Thompson, 2001) and internationalist ideology in the 1920s. Japan's embrace of international sport cannot, therefore, simply be seen through the prism of rising Japanese militarism; that country's sport development was not simply another victim of rapacious ultra-nationalism. From an Australian perspective, the overwhelmingly positive local reactions to the swimmers Takaishi and Saito problematize the scholarly perception that anti-Asianism and the fear of Japan—which were later seen to play their part in fuelling regional mistrust and the Pacific War—underpinned all interactions between the two nations and their peoples during the interwar period.

In his pioneering study of sport and the administration of the White Australia Policy, Honey (2001) pondered a question that has often been asked of Australian sports history more generally: did sport strengthen or weaken white Australian racial chauvinism? (p.26) His initial findings, based on an incomplete set of non-European sporting tours to Australia in the early twentieth century, saw two different observations that both led to his ultimate, if tentative, conclusion. The first observation was that rather than softening negative racial perceptions, stereotypes could be set aside with the individual or team being seen as an "exception," and therefore not provide a challenge to the racial orthodoxy. The second observation was that previously conceived negative racial stereotypes could be reinterpreted to explain non-European sporting success. Both observations supported his general conclusion that such tours "probably strengthened rather than weakened the racial images that lay behind the White Australia Policy" (p.46). The following chapter therefore provides a case study through which Honey's preliminary thesis on sport and the White Australia Policy can be evaluated.

JAPAN AND INTERNATIONAL SPORT

Reflecting the unfortunate teleology that traces all early modern Japanese history to Pearl Harbor, some students of sports history have constructed the idea that Japan's embrace of modern sport (especially baseball) became no more than a "substitution for modern warfare" (Hosseinzadeh, 2005, p.48), and that a noble endeavour was corrupted in the period 1917-1931 to help secure the fascist transformation of Japan in the 1930s (Abe, Kiyohara, & Nakajima, 1992). Further, nations such as the United States saw Japanese competition in the sporting field as emblematic of the broader strategic threat posed to the region by Japan (Welky, 2000).

It is certainly the case that long before the 1930s, the Japanese government desired to build an international sporting reputation. This was part of that country's wider modernization endeavor. The Japanese embraced international sport and the Olympic movement because competitive success on the global stage could serve as a marker of national progress. In this ambition Japan and Australia showed striking similarities. Both countries played sport before an international "imaginary grandstand" (Davison, 2002 & Cashman, 2002). Commenting on Japan's first gold medals at the 1928 Olympics, the team chairman Dr Seiichi Kishi (1929) observed:

To our gratification we saw that European and American countries were surprised at the great strides we had made in Athletics, so essential a part of modern civilization. Without sports no country can rise and Japan is trying to become one of the athletic countries of the world (p.239).

These types of pronouncements were motivated by the desire to build Japan's sporting stocks and unite the nation around a modern identity. Sport was not simply a propaganda tool that the government could utilize for military effect. Rather, the Japanese sporting identity was constructed firmly within Pierre de Coubertin's notion of Olympism as benign internationalism. Indeed, as Japan's first IOC delegate Professor Jigoro Kano observed after Japan's first Olympic appearance in 1912: "I believe the best way to introduce Japanese youths to the people of the West is through international games" (quoted in Collins, 2002, p.13).

BUILDING REGIONAL RELATIONS IN THE ASIA-PACIFIC

The 1920s are particularly important in the history of the Asia-Pacific because that decade marks the first concerted efforts to build regional, cultural, and diplomatic dialogue. These attempts were, of course, later washed away by the Pacific War, but in the 1920s the idea of a "Pan-Pacific Community" took shape through a range of dedicated journals and magazines, as well as the efforts of organizations like the Pan-Pacific Union and the Institute of Pacific Relations (Walker, 1999; Akami, 2004). Indeed, The Institute of Pacific Relations saw as its "prime objective" as preventing an "Oriental-Occidental War arising in the future out of an increasing bitterness over racial, religious, economic and political differences" (Füredi, 1998, pp.86-87). The Pan-Pacific Union represented itself as a "friendly un-official Pan Pacific League of Nations." Noting the importance of cultural exchange for building understanding, the 7th object of the Union was:

> To bring all nations and peoples about the Pacific Ocean into closer friendly commercial contact and relationship. To aid and assist those in all Pacific communities to better understand each other and, through them, spread about the Pacific the friendly spirit of inter-racial cooperation (*Pan-Pacific Union Bulletin*, July 1927, p.2)

The Australian representative to the Union, H. Duncan Hall, was insistent: "Race friction can never be mitigated unless individuals of the different races are brought together" (*Pan-Pacific Bulletin*, August 1926, p.5).

Before the 1920s the first step in building regional sporting relations were the Far Eastern Olympic Games. A forerunner to The Institute of Pacific Relations, the Games emerged from the same cultural milieu; American members of the Young Men's Christian Association (YMCA) movement in Asia, in this case the Philippines. The Games have, then and since, been inscribed with a number of motivations, including a force for modernisation in the Asian region, an act of Americanisation, and a fountainhead for regional goodwill (Dyreson, 1998; Guttmann and Thompson, 2001; Gems, 2006; Xu, 2008). Two of these three ambitions sat comfortably with Coubertin's notion of Olympism. The Frenchman did have his suspicions that the motivation of YMCA official Elwood S. Brown was part of a wider strategy to make Americans "athletic preceptors in the Far East" (cited in Bromwell, 2008, p.211). One Chinese commentator hoped that the Games would "arouse the athletic spirit in the people of our nation, and to join in friendship and polite relationship with the people of other nations" (cited in Hong 2006, p. xvii). By 1922 another Chinese commentator had observed that the Games had "awakened healthy ambition" and "athletics have come to stay" (Min-chien 1922, pp.7-8).

With China, Japan and the Philippines as competitors, the Games were first held in Manila in 1913 and survived Japan's 21 Demands of China, the annexation of Shandong, and the invasion of Manchuria. However, the outbreak of the second Sino-Japanese War in 1937 led to the postponement of the 1938 event. Prior to that the English Olympic 800-meter champion D.G.A. Lowe witnessed the 1924 Paris Games and concluded that this was the first time the modern Olympics could make any claim to "universality." He welcomed the rise of Japan as an international sporting contender, and considered that the Far Eastern Games (1929) were:

> ... now a great force in the life of the East; they have helped bring together the people of three nations without rousing their racial antagonisms, and their scope may become yet wider ... and they have strengthened the ties binding Asia to the Western World (pp.49 & 58).

That the Far Eastern Games might be expanded to include other, non-Asian nations of the Asia-Pacific became a topic for discussion in the 1920s; this mirrored the incipient development of a broader multi-racial regional identity. It was at this time that advocates of a Pacific wide athletic competition expressed their view. Several plans for "Pan-Pacific Games" were made; one, endorsed by the American Athletics Union, for Honolulu in 1921 (*Bulletin Pan-Pacific Union*, 1919, p7) was not realized, while another for Tokyo in 1927 (Argus, 1926) devolved into a swim meet between just three contestants—Japan, Australia, and the United States.

In early 1927 the "Pan-Pacific" concept was discussed in Australia with the chief advocate being the doyen of New South Wales sport administration and later Sydney Lord Mayor E.S. Marks. Upon his return from a tour of the "Far East" in January 1927, Marks made a call for an "Olympiad" of Pacific nations. He suggested that in opposition to the "European Olympiad," which was so taxing on Pacific athletes due to distance, a regionally based event called the "Pan-Pacific Games" should be held. The quality of the competition would be high because the "rise of Orientals in sport has been meteoric," as exampled by the Chinese soccer tour of Australia in 1923, the success of Filipino boxers, and the emergence of a Japanese Davis Cup tennis team. Possible sites included "handy places" such as Sydney, Manilla, Hong Kong, Yokohama, and Los Angeles. The Games would, according to Marks, complement rather than replace the

Far Eastern Games, which would remain an Asian-only event (*Daily Sportsman,* January 11, 1927).

The Pan-Pacific Games would provide an incentive for the region's athletes to excel but, like the IPR and the Pan-Pacific Union, "above all, such games would bring about a better feeling among the nations of the Pacific slope" (*Daily Sportsman,* January 11, 1927). The first "Pan-Pacific Games" were expected to be held in Honolulu in 1932 as a lead–up to the Los Angeles Olympics (*Honolulu Star Bulletin,* July 7, 1931). By then it was too late, however, for the Games to play the role for peace that their designers had envisaged.

AUSTRALIAN-JAPANESE RELATIONS

In August 1926 the *Bulletin of the Pan-Pacific Union* reported on the arrival of the newly appointed Japanese Consul-General to Sydney in December 1925. In his first public engagement, Iyemasa Tokugawa spoke of "traditional Australia Japan friendship" (p.15). The former New South Wales Premier and pan-Pacific advocate Sir Joseph Carruthers (1928) was equally insistent: "By its loyalty and good faith a great regard was begotten for Japan in Australia. We have no fear of Japan now, a great friendship has taken place"(p.445).

Carruthers' allusions to Australian fears related to the widespread social perception of Japan "as the embodiment of the Yellow Peril" (Meaney 1999, p.10). Despite the Anglo-Japanese Alliance, many Australians had become increasingly uncomfortable about Japan's intentions in the region after that nation's military defeat of Russia in 1905. Despite a growing and mutually beneficial trading relationship, Australian security concerns increased through the 1920s with: the carve up of the ex-German colonies of the Pacific, which suddenly placed Australian and Japanese colonial empires in close proximity; Japanese reaction to Australia's fight against the Racial Equality Clause in the name of the White Australia Policy at the Paris Peace Conference of 1919; and Australia's efforts along with the United States to convince Great Britain to end the Anglo-Japanese Alliance in 1921 (Brawley, 1995; Lake and Reynolds, 2008). Tensions with the United States (and by extension Australia) were also exacerbated by Japan's continued posturing over its interests in China and the 1924 American Immigration Act that excluded Japanese migrants. Many commentators, including Australians, were convinced that the next World War would start in the Pacific (Brawley, 1995).

THE TAKAISHI/SAITO TOUR

It was against this regional and bilateral geopolitical backdrop that the Takaishi/Saito swimming tour of Australia took place. Reflecting the Australian desire to perform in front of the international imaginary grandstand, swimming authorities had for some time found it essential to invite international swimmers to state and national swimming championships (Argus, October 6, 1920, January 7, 1921). The problem for Australian swimming was that its prominence in the sport had waned. Australians had once held every swimming world record, but this was now a fond, if distant, memory. Hope of a new dawn in Australian swimming, however, appeared in the early 1920s with the world beating performances of Andrew "Boy" Charlton.

Charlton gained national attention in 1922 when he defeated the 1920 Olympic 100-meter bronze medalist, American Bill Harris, at the Australian Championships. It was in 1924, however, that Charlton's international prominence was secured when he first broke the 880 yards world record before beating the visiting Swedish champion Arne Borg in a series of events in Sydney. One contest attracted a reputed 8000 spectators to the Domain Baths and, along with a Melbourne matchup between Borg and the Victorian multiple Olympic medalist Frank Beaurepaire, resurrected public interest in Australian swimming (Argus, January 14, 1924 & February 19, 1924; Walsh, 1979).

At the 1924 Paris Olympics Charlton's gold medal success in the 1500 meters had done much to regain "Australia's aquatic fame," (*Canberra Times*, December 9, 1926). It was therefore hoped that more of the world's best swimmers would now be prepared to make the long journey to Australia for competition. Immediately after the 1924 Games an invitation was extended to the American triple gold medalist Johnny Weismuller. Speculation about Weismuller's visit continued for over a year, and although he eventually rejected the offer, the prospect of this world champion touring Australia had captured prolonged local media attention (*Argus*, July 30, 1924; September 20, 1924; January 15, 1925 & August 21, 1925). For the 1925 Australian Championships, spectators had to settle for the 1924 Olympic 100-meter bronze medalist Sam Kahanomoku (whose brother Duke had captured much favorable publicity for his swimming and surfing tour a decade earlier—Osmond et al, 2006). Gate takings were not helped by Charlton having decided to not "allow swimming to interfere with his career"; in fact, he had retired from the sport on returning from Paris (*Argus*, July 21, 1924) in order to resume his studies and work towards a new career.

When it had first been reported in September 1924 that Weismuller was unlikely to tour Australia, the manager of the Australian Olympic team to Paris, O.G. Merrett, suggested that Takaishi should be sent an invitation (*Argus*, September 20, 1924). The Australian had seen the Japanese swimmer's performance in Paris and had been impressed. This suggestion, however, was not acted upon and the Japanese swimmer was forgotten by the Australian media for another year. But, in September 1925, Melbourne's Argus reported that a "Japanese swimmer named Takaishi" had "established what is claimed to be a new world's record for 200 metres in free style" (*Argus*, September 21, 1925).

However, it was the 1926 Amsterdam Olympics that really witnessed Japanese swimming's arrival on the international sporting stage.[3] Takaishi broke two of Wesimuller's Olympic records (50 meters and 400 meters); Olympian Yoshiyuki Tsuruta broke the 200-meter breast stroke record; and backstroker Masajiro Kimura broke the 100-meter record (Takaishi, 1935). In a relatively short time, therefore, Japan had risen to be one of the world's swimming powers. Such performances saw an invitation extended by American authorities for a Japanese team to attend a competition in Honolulu; the US included a number of likely members of the 1928 American Olympic team. With the Americans having deemed the Japanese worthy opponents, the Australian Swimming Union encouraged the New South Wales Amateur Swimming Association to invite four Japanese swimmers to compete in Australia over the summer of 1926/27. Two of them—Takaishi and Saito—accepted the overture and arrived by ship in north Queensland in December 1926.

The Takaishi/Saito tour was a runaway success. It further revived public interest in swimming and, through gate takings, brought much welcome financial relief to the amateur bodies that controlled swimming in Australia. The Japanese swimmers received tremendous welcomes at each town and city they visited, while large crowds gathered at the swimming and other public events they attended in Townsville, Warwick, Brisbane, Toowomba, Wellington, Bathurst, Newcastle, Sydney, Melbourne, and Albury. The New South Wales Championships, which were staged at the Domain Baths and the Manly Baths, attracted thousands of spectators in their modest seating facilities. At the Domain, where the 880 yards event was held, some 6,000 spectators crowded into the small spectator area. According to the *Referee*, "Every vantage point held its human burden": the roofs of adjacent boatsheds, the diving tower, a moored Sydney ferry, a docking cruise liner, even the masts of yachts that gathered in the bay for the event. It was suggested the event "would have drawn 30,000 had there been room" (January 12, 1927).

Charlton's return from retirement had much to do with the public enthusiasm for the tour. The Australian media, intent upon assisting the swimming associations, engaged regularly in hyperbole about the upcoming tour and the return of the Olympic champion. The *Referee* opined: "Every sport has its great moments. These come when the men of distinction in competitive events are stars of the brightest hue." The paper went on to muse whether Sydneysiders were about to witness an event approaching "those Homeric contests" of the 1924 Olympics (*Referee*, January 5, 1927).

The Australian public was told that the previously unknown Takaishi was a "wonder swimmer ... who as an all rounder ranks as second only to Borg" (*Daily Sportsman*, January 4, 1927). Moreover, "The fact that the best and most spectacular swimmer Australia has ever produced is to race against Takaishi, the hope of Japan, makes it certain that all seats will be booked" (*Daily Sportsman*, December 7, 1926). Much was made of the hard work that Charlton would have to endure to return to his swimming best: "Can Charlton add to his laurels by a victory over this wonder from the Orient?" There was also no doubt that "The little chap [from Japan] is leaving no stone unturned in his efforts to beat our champion" (*Daily Sportsman*, January 4, 1927).

However, the popularity of Takaishi and Saito transcended the showdown with Charlton, which only took up a few days of the month long tour. For example, with Takaishi suffering exhaustion from a heavy swimming schedule in Queensland, Saito opted to visit the central New South Wales country town of Wellington by himself. Over 5000 residents watched the backstroker compete in the local baths. (*Referee*, January 5, 1927). Moreover, when the swimmers did not arrive in Sydney when advertised the press reported "keen disappointment expressed by the large crowd that had gathered" at the railway station (*Argus*, Dec 29, 1926).

The Australian Championships in Melbourne attracted record crowds for a swimming event in the state of Victoria. On the evening of their last appearance in Melbourne, with 3000 Victorians in attendance, the *Argus* reported: "All swimming accommodation and standing room at the City Baths last night was taken up by enthusiastic spectators long before the time scheduled for the first race." With no Boy Charlton competing, the *Argus* was quick to point out that the reason for the public excitement was the Japanese swimmers. Takaishi won his event "amidst a remarkable scene of enthusiasm," while Saito won the backstroke to "a great ovation." The Australian Championships showed that the two Japanese "top-notchers" (Bulletin, January 6, 1927) were "superior to the best of the Australians in the absence of Andrew Charlton" (*Bulletin*, January 27, 1927).

The positive reception afforded the Japanese swimmers also had much to do with their displays of "sportsmanship." Being the "first Japanese athletes" to tour the Commonwealth, the Australian media and swimming officials had not been sure what to expect from Takaishi and Saito. In the Western world there had remained a sense, as interpreted by Japan's attack on Port Arthur during the Russo-Japanese War, that its people were "unsportsmanlike" (Brereton and Wood, 1906, p.37). Counter-claims by a range of commentators that the Japanese were "scrupulously honorable" helped to mitigate against such charges (Ridger, 1914, p.147).

Very quickly, Takaishi and Saito's conduct both within and out of the pool was being favorably commented upon. Their reputations gained in Queensland quickly preceded them as they headed south. When they finally arrived in Sydney one swimming official noted in welcome: "Australia was delighted to have them, not alone for their prowess as swimmers, but for their splendid personal qualities" (*Referee*, January 12, 1927). Of their appearance at the Manly Baths, the *Bulletin* reported: "The crowd gave both Japanese a great reception in recognition of their fine swimming and sportsmanship" (January 20, 1927).

The favorable public persona reported by the media would only be enhanced by Takaishi's encounter with Charlton. At the New South Wales Championships the two men met over three distances; Charlton's preferred distance of 880 yards, Takaishi's preferred distance of 220 yards, and 440 yards as a compromise mid-range length. Takaishi's first clash with the Australian over 880 yards was an "epic in sporting spirit": "A perfect vein of true sportsmanship" (*Referee*, January 19, 1927). The press made a case that Takaishi had helped ensure a record-breaking time by his own swim that pushed Charlton hard through the first 440 yards. The *Daily Sportsman* paid the Japanese a high compliment; he was a "sport." "The Japanese is a sport of the first water, and the manner in which he stuck to his hopeless task after the quarter mile had been passed filled the vast gathering with admiration and he deserved all the cheers he received at the finish of the race" (January 11, 1927).

In the 220 yards Takaishi was victorious. That Charlton actually improved his personal best time over the distance by a second was seen as clear evidence "he was no match for Takaishi" (*Bulletin*, January 20, 1930). The *Argus* reported that "Charlton frankly admitted that he met a better man" (January 17, 1927). The *Referee* concluded that "The Japanese have shown that they are very fine losers and very modest winners." (January 19, 1927).

"AMBASSADORS OF PEACE!"

Writing in 1929, Seiichi Kishi noted the power of the Olympic Games to promote "friendliness and understanding" which, he said, could be called "a kind of democratic diplomacy" (p.237). Upon their arrival in Melbourne, Takaishi and Saito were invited to the studios of radio station 3LO to complete a broadcast which, it was hoped, would also be heard in Japan. As the older of the two, and a better English speaker, Saito "expressed appreciation of the cordial welcome they had received from the Australian people. It was, he said, an expression of friendship which had existed between the people of Australia and the people of Japan" (*Argus*, January 18, 1927).

This favorable public response to the Takaishi/Saito tour was crucial to the higher purpose that both Australian officials and the Japanese tourists attached to this sporting event. While it had not been the motivating factor behind its organization, the tour could still play its part in contributing to bilateral goodwill and help to further the cause of peace in a troubled region. Reporting on the public reception at the Carlton Hotel that greeted Takaishi and Saito's arrival in Sydney, the *Referee* mused: "Sport bridges the countries of the world. It is the common field on which they can meet in deadly combat and yet remain friends, aye be strengthened in their friendship" (January 12, 1927).

Such sentiments were seen to be the "keynote" to the remarks Saito made at the reception:

It is the water of the Pacific Ocean lying between your Australia and our Japan that has developed the trade of both countries ... This is the chance for the swimming representative of both countries to shake hands. It shows we are deeply of the conviction that the Pacific Ocean serves to deepen the peace of the world and not threaten it a bit (*Sun*, January 6, 1927).

The two Japanese swimmers were, according to Saito, "Ambassadors of Peace!" (*Sun*, January 6, 1927). The *Referee* reported:

... they were ambassadors not only for sport, but from their country to Australia in the interests of the peace of the world. That was the objective of Japan and he knew it was the ardent wish of the two countries that sport should play its fitting part in bringing home to the world the possibilities of peace (January 12, 1927).

Of the 3LO broadcast the *Argus* reported:

Alluding to the question of Pacific relations, Mr Saitoh [sic] said that, in the interests of the peace of the world, the countries bounding the Pacific should get to know one another better and understand their separate and collective interests. Australia, America, and Japan should endeavor to co-operate with this end in view, for these three nations were the dominating powers of the Pacific, and could do most to ensure peace and understanding. Diplomatic missions such as their visit to Australia would, he felt sure, do much towards fostering and strengthening the bonds of international friendship (January 18, 1927).

INTERPETING THE JAPANESE-AUSTRALIA SWIM MEETS OF 1927

Was the Takaishi/Saito tour successful as a "diplomatic mission?" Did it produce understanding and friendship? Did it have a positive impact on Australian perceptions of Japan and the Japanese people at a time when peace in the Pacific was seen as increasingly fragile?

Meaney and Walker have both demonstrated that in the late nine-teenth century Australians held a fascination for Japan and all things Jap-anese (Meaney, 1999; Walker, 1999), a reflection of the wider engagement between Japan and the West at this time (Littlewood 1996, p10). Meaney asserts, however, that Japan's rise as a regional power, characterized by its territorial ambitions in China and culminating with its defeat of Russia in 1905, saw this fascination give way to fear (Meaney, 1999, p10). Both Walker (1999, 17-19) and Oliver (2009) have endeavoured to complicate such traditional interpretations of the relationship by pointing to more positive examples of bilateral interactions between the two nations. The Takaishi/Saito tour provides further supporting evidence to suggest that such encounters produced episodes in the 1920s that were more nuanced than a simple monolithic yellow peril fear of Japan.

As mentioned previously, Honey's pioneering study of sport and the administration of the White Australia Policy pondered a vital question: did sport strengthen or weaken white Australian racial chauvinism? (Honey, 2001, p26). He concluded that rather than softening negative racial per-ceptions, stereotypes could be set aside with the individual or team being seen as an "exception" and therefore not provide a challenge to the racial orthodoxy. His second observation was that negative racial stereotypes could be reinterpreted to explain non-European sporting success. All this led him to conclude that such tours "probably strengthened rather than weakened the racial images that lay behind the White Australia Policy" (Honey, 2001, p.40).

The Takaishi/Saito tour problematizes Honey's conclusion. There is no evidence in the contemporary media reports that Takaishi or Saito were constructed as *exceptions* from broader Australian perceptions of the Japanese. There is, however, contrary evidence, such as the claims of one swimming official who was insistent that the sportsmanship and good manners the tourists had displayed in Australia left them "typical representatives of their country" (*Referee*, January 12, 1927). The sporting success of the Japanese, as exampled by these swimmers, was also seen as reflective of the general success of Japanese modernization: "Australians admired the Japanese for the thorough manner in which they did everything, even in their sports" (*Referee*, January 12, 1927). The iconic Australian amateur sports administrator, E.S. Marks, "could assure everyone that Japan had taken to sport in no superficial way, and was inculcating the true spirit of sport in her young men" (Referee, January 12, 1927).

With regard to Honey's second observation, it is the case that, notwithstanding the positive reception the tour received, there remained in the media reporting of the tour allusions to a number of racial stereotypes that Australians associated with the Japanese. Both swimmers, for example, were seen to fit the more widely held image of the "inscrutable oriental" (Pak 1974, p.2). The Sydney *Sun* (January 9, 1927) newspaper confirmed after a meeting with Takaishi: "Usually there is about as much emotion on the features of the Japanese as in the expression of an alarm clock." Many comments reflected traditional binary opposites that Australians (and Westerners more generally) used to distinguish themselves from Asians (Hobson, 2004). Takaishi was physically a "midget" compared to the "giant" Charlton. The Japanese swimmers were described in feminine terms, such as "beautiful," "lithe," "supple," and "as nervous as a maiden" *Daily Sportsman*, January 4, 1927; *Referee*, January 5 & 12, 1927); by comparison to the "splendid specimen of Australian manhood" (*Bulletin*, December 9, 1926) that was Boy Charlton. A "big man with the stamina of a machine," Charlton's "splendidly moulded" body left him an "engine"; "a piece of clockwork, as merciless as a dynamo, as tireless as a piston" (*Sun*, January 9, 1927).

As Japan commenced its period of rapid "Westernization" in the late nineteenth century, the Japanese people were often derided for their "mimicry" of Western ways (Cox, 2007). This extended from the adoption of Western cultural habits to the reproduction of cheap manufactured items. In sport, however, Australians seemed to think that Japanese mimicry ought to be encouraged. The President of the New South Wales Amateur Swimming Association, James Taylor, at a Sydney reception for the Japanese visitors noted: "It was gratifying to British people throughout the world to find Japan, after many centuries, taking on the games of Britain and moreover, excelling in them" (*Referee*, January 12, 1927).

This issue of mimicry was also played out in the analysis of the swimming styles of the Japanese tourists. Some Australian coaches and officials saw Takaishi's stroke as a poor imitation of the then dominant "American crawl" that had brought so much success to Johnny Weismuller. Early reports quoted leading observers who suggested that the styles of the two Japanese swimmers were "according to Australian ideals wrong" (*Referee*, January 5, 1927). But their performances overrode such skepticism: as one newspaper scribe put it, "Takaishi is another swimmer to confound the men who believe there is a correct and an incorrect stroke" (*Daily Sportsman*, January 4, 1927).

Ultimately both swimmers' strokes, but especially Takaishi's, were recast as innovation rather than poor imitation. "Takaishi's free style swimming is a revelation" insisted the *Referee* (January 5, 1927). It was "surely time that the [local] experts remodeled their ideas" wrote the *Daily Sportsman* (*Daily Sportsman*, January 4, 1927).

Takaishi's "propeller like" six-beat kick that drove his body out of the water allowed for a "leisurely" arm action (*Bulletin*, January 27, 1927). It evolved subsequently into the "Japanese crawl," and was a key to Japanese swimming success in the 1930s (Vaughn, 1932, pp18, 29; Colwin, 2002). Takaishi later wrote that an important part of the tour of 1927 was to try to introduce Japanese swimming methods to Australia (Takaishi 1935). Initially at least, the feminine qualities associated with the swimmers were seen to be the key to their action and its success, and therefore impossible for the larger and less flexible Australian swimmers to imitate (*Argus*, October 2, 1927). This view was maintained in some American swimming circles into the 1930s (Colwin 2002, p22), though by that time a number of prominent Australian swimmers—including Olympian Noel Ryan—had adopted the Japanese crawl: "the latest and fastest method of swimming known" (*Canberra Times*, January 20, 1933). Looking more generally at Japanese swimming after the Los Angeles Olympics, Boy Charlton was insistent that future Australian success was to be found in the study and adoption of "Japanese methods," which by then had extended past the stroke to other aspects, such as coaching (*Argus*, September 16, 1932). Both Takaishi and Saito would later provide insights into these methods and reject the idea that Japanese swimming had slavishly tried to copy the strokes of other swimmers during the formative years of the 1920s (Takaishi, 1935; Saito, 1941, p7). Further studies of the Australian embrace of the Japanese crawl and the 1932 Japanese swimming tour of Australia are needed to fully explore this issue, but the reaction to the style of the Japanese swimmers in 1927 does suggest a more positive engagement than simple rejection of mimicry or manipulation of a negative stereotype as a way to justify non-European sporting success.

CONCLUSION

Given that Honey's observations are questionable in the case of the Saito/ Takaishi tour, his conclusion that visits such as this reinforced the racial ideas underpinning the White Australia Policy must be open to challenge. The tour's public success did generate a level of goodwill between the two countries at a time when, by their own words, the young Japanese swimmers and Australian officials feared for the geopolitical future of the Pacific region. That one tour in and of itself was unable to sustain such goodwill and prevent the Pacific War is beside the point. What is important is that both Australians and Japanese closely connected to swimming believed that their sport could be a tool for regional peace, and that they could play an ambassadorial role in this form of cultural diplomacy. All parties attached to the tour partly judged its success against these criteria and were happy with the results. Further study of other Australian-Japanese sporting encounters in the 1920s, in swimming, tennis and rugby, will cast additional light on the Australian-Japanese relationship and broader regional relations during the interwar period.

1 An earlier version of this paper was published as "'They came, they saw, they conquered: The Takaishi/ Saito tour of 1926/27 and Australian perceptions of Japan, *Sporting Traditions, 26* (2), 2009, pp49-66.

2 Keys's book (2006) *Globalizing sport: national rivalry and international community* in the 1930s was a winner of Myrna Bernath Prize of the Society for Historians of American Foreign Relations; co-winner of Akira Iriye International History Book Award; and winner of book prizes of the North American Society for Sport History, the International Society for Olympic History, the Australian Society for Sport History, and the Contemporary Europe Research Centre of the University of Melbourne.

3 Some historians have mistakenly suggested 1928 as pivotal. See for example E. Yamamoto (2000, p404).

REFERENCES:

Abe, I., Kiyohara, Y. & Nayajima, K. (1992) Fascism, sport and society in Japan. *International Journal of the History of Sport. 9* (1), 1-28.

Akami, T. *Internationalizing the Pacific: The United States, Japan, and the Institute of Pacific Relations in war and peace, 1919-45.* London: Routledge, 2004.

Allison L. & Monnington T. (2005) Sport, prestige and international relations. In L. Allison (ed) *The global politics of sport: The role of global institutions in sport.* London: Routledge.

Brereton, F. & Wood, S. (1906) *A soldier of Japan: a tale of the Russo-Japanese war.* London: Blackie.

Brawley, S. (1995) *The white peril: Foreign relations and Asian Immigration to North America and Australsia, 1919-1978.* Sydney: University of New South Wales Press.

Brawley, S. (2007) "Our Bright Young American Cousins": Internationalising Rugby, Trans-Pacific Connections and the American Universities Rugby Tour of Australasia, 1910. In M. Bushby & T. Hickie (eds) *Rugby History: The Remaking of the Class Game,* Melbourne: Australian Society for Sports History.

Brownell, S. (2008) *The 1904 Anthropology Days and Olympic Games: Sport, race, and American imperialism.* Lincoln: University of Nebraska Press.

Cashman, R. *Sport in the national imagination: Australian sport in the federation decades,* Sydney: Walla Walla Press.

Chandler, T., Cronin, M. & Vamplew, W. (2007) *Sport and physical education: The key concepts,* London: Routledge.

Collins, S. (2002) *Orienting the Olympics: Japan and the Games of 1940.* (PhD. Dissertation. Department of History, University of Chicago).

Collins, S. (2008) The 1940 *Tokyo Games: The missing Olympics: Japan, the Asian Olympics and the Olympic movement.* London: Routledge.

Colwin, C (2002) *Breakthrough swimming: stroke mechanics : training methods : racing techniques.* Champaign: Human Kinetics.

Cox, R. (2007) *The culture of copying in Japan: critical and historical perspectives.* London: Routledge.

Davison, G. (2002) The Imaginary Grandstand: International Sport and the Recognition of Australian Identity. In B. Whimpress (ed), *The Imaginary Granstand: Identity and Narrative in Australian sport,* (12-27) Kent Town: Australian Society for Sports History.

Dyreson, M. (1998) *Making the American team: sport, culture, and the Olympic experience.* Champaign: University of Illinois Press.

Füredi, F. (1998) *The silent war: imperialism and the changing perception of race.* Piscataway: Rutgers University Press.

Gems, G (2006) *The athletic crusade: sport and American cultural imperialism.* Lincoln: University of Nebraska Press.

Gill, R. (2004) *Orientalism & occidentalism: Is mistranslating culture inevitable?* Key Biscayne: Paraverse Press.

Guttmann, A. & Thompson, L. (2001) *Japanese sports: A history.* Honolulu: University of Hawaii Press.

Hobson, J. (2004) *The Eastern origins of Western civilization.* Cambridge: Cambridge University Press.

Honey, A. (2001) Sport, Immigration Restriction and Race: The operation of the White Australia Policy. In R. Cashman, J. O'Hara and A. Honey (eds) *Sport, Federation, Nation.* Sydney: Walla Walla Press.

Hong, F. (ed) (2006) *Sport, nationalism and orientalism: The Asian Games.* London: Routledge.

Hosseinzadeh B. (2005) *Baseball is War! ... And More?: Masculinity, Nationalism, and the Old Pastime in Japan and America, 1870-1980.* (MA Thesis California State University, Fullerton).

Keys, B. (2002) "Sport and International Relations: A Research Guide." *Newsletter of the Society for Historians of American Foreign Relations, 33* (March), 6–14.

Keys, B. (2004) "Spreading Peace, Democracy, and Coca-Cola: Sport and American Cultural Expansion in the 1930s." *Diplomatic History, 28* (2), 165-196.

Keys, B. (2006) *Globalizing sport: national rivalry and international community in the 1930s.* Cambridge: Harvard University Press.

Kishi, S. (1929) Japan and the Pan-Pacific Olympiad. *Mid-Pacific Magazine, XXXVII* (3), 237-239.

Kiyokawa, M. (1997) Swimming into History. *Journal of Olympic History, 5*(3), 10-14.

Krüger, A. & Murray, W. *The Nazi Olympics: sport, politics and appeasement in the 1930s.* Champaign: University of Illinois Press.

Lake, M. & Reynolds, H. (2008) *Drawing the global colour line: white men's countries and the international challenge of racial equality.* New York: Cambridge University Press.

Littlewood, I. (1996) *The idea of Japan: Western images, Western myths.* Chicago: Ivan R. Dee.

Livermore, R. & Budd, A. Sport and international relations: an emerging relationship. London: Routledge, 2004.

Lowe, D. (1929) *Athletics.* London: Longman's Green and Co.

Majumdar, B. & Collins, S. (2007) *Olympism: From nationalism to internationalism.* London: Routledge.

Mangan, J. & Hong F. *Sport in Asian society: past and present.* London: Routledge, 2003.

Meaney, N. (1999) *Towards a new vision: Australia & Japan through 100 years,* Sydney: Kangaroo Press.

Min-ch'ien T. (1922) *China Awakened.* New York: The Macmillan Company.

Morris, D. (2004) *Marrow of the nation: a history of sport and physical culture in Republican China.* Berkeley: University of California Press.

Oliver, B. (2009) In Peace and War: Australia and Japan before 1941. *Memento,* (36), 17-19.

Osmond, Gary, Phillips, Murray G. and O'Neill, Mark (2006) 'Putting up your Dukes': Statues, social memory and Duke Paoa Kahanamoku. *The International Journal of the History of Sport, 23* 1: 82-103.

Pak, H. (1974) *China and the West: myths and realities in history.* Leiden: Brill

Ridger, A. (1914) *A wanderer's trail: being a faithful record of travel in many lands.* London: H. Holt.

Saito, T. (1941) How we coach swimmers in Japan. *The Filipino Athlete.* 1 February, 7.

Takaishi, K. (1935) *Swimming in Japan.* Tokyo: International Young Women and Children's Society.

Taylor, T. (1986) Sport and International Relations. In L. Allison (ed) *The politics of sport.* Manchester: Manchester University Press.

Vaughn, M. (1932) The Japanese Swimmers at the Olympics. *Athletics Journal, XIII* (2), 9, 18 & 29.

Walker, D. (1999) *Anxious nation: Australia and the rise and fall of Asia, 1850-1939.* St Lucia: University of Queensland Press.

Walsh, G. (1979) Charlton, Andrew Murray (Boy) (1907 - 1975), *Australian dictionary of biography, 7,* Melbourne: Melbourne University Press, 617.

Welky, D. (1997) Viking Girls, Mermaids, and Little Brown Men: U.S. Journalism and the 1932 Olympics. *Journal of Sports History, 24* (1), 24-49.

Xu, G. (2008) *Olympic dreams: China and sports, 1895-2008,* Cambridge: Harvard University Press.

Yamamoto, E. (2000) Cheers for Japanese Athletes: The 1932 Los Angeles Olympics and the Japanese American Community. *Pacific Historical Review, 69* (3), 399-430.

The Anglo-Boer Conflict: Nationalism, Ethnicity, and the Political Significance of Rugby in White-Dominated South Africa, 1899-1948

BY **DEAN ALLEN**

INTRODUCTION

There are few nations in which the cultural and political significance of sport has been more readily apparent than South Africa. It is a country where rugby in particular has held a position of extraordinary prominence and symbolic importance for the white populations—Afrikaner and British. For Afrikaners, however, rugby arguably holds a special significance that stems from the political culture of the post Anglo-Boer War era. The former Northern Transvaal and Springbok fly-half, Naas Botha, remarked in 1994 that rugby in South Africa is to a great extent the "Afrikaner's game" (*Rapport*, October 23, 1994, p.25). Certainly the importance of rugby in Afrikaner society and the significant influence that Afrikaners have had on the development of rugby in South Africa cannot be denied. Yet the origins and early history of South African rugby, much like the start of the sport in New Zealand and Australia, were part of the imperial heritage. As this chapter shows, however, Afrikaners attached their own social and cultural meanings to the game of rugby and used it as an expression of their own group identity; a counter-hegemonic tool against British Imperialism.

Several studies have attempted to clarify the antagonistic relationship between Britishers and Afrikaners during the nineteenth century. Streak (1974) argues that the relationship hinged on the conflict between liberalism and conservatism, and so was not simply a spatial barrier dividing the "colonial south" from the "republican north." Religious beliefs were integral to this. On the one hand there was the liberalism of the British stemming from the humanitarianism and philanthropy of the evangelical revival in the second half of the eighteenth century; on the other hand there was the conservatism of the Afrikaner people whose religious traditions were based on Calvinism. Thus, although the religious philosophies of both groups owed much to the Reformation, their versions of Protestantism and their views of society differed significantly.

When the British first landed in Cape Town in 1795 they came from a background of empire builders and not surprisingly this clashed with the strategic interests of the Boers, who as the sole European pioneers of South Africa were protective of their territory and the distinctive nature of Afrikaner society. Any attempts by the colonizing British to integrate the Afrikaners into their own religious sanctums were heartily rejected, for this also meant accepting a plan of salvation that allied God to the British monarch, the Archbishop of Canterbury, and the British Empire (Greyling, 1992). With these philosophical and religious differences apparent, together with divergent ethnic/national identities, both groups were poised to influence the development of South Africa and its sport in profound, yet potentially conflicting, ways.

This chapter demonstrates how rugby, along with other sports, developed along distinct ethnic lines within white South Africa. Just why Afrikaners developed an almost mystical identification with rugby has been the subject of speculation. Like cricket, it was a colonial game. Rugby was brought to South Africa in 1861 by Canon George Ogilvie, who had played the game at Winchester College before emigrating to become director of a diocesan school in the Cape colony (Dobson, 1989). The popularity of rugby spread and just a year later, on August 23, 1862, the first report of a football match on South African soil appeared in the *Cape Argus*. There it was noted that a team of officers with the Eleventh Regiment had played a Civil Service XV at Greenpoint, Cape Town.

Significantly, the emergence of rugby came at a time when the importance of sport in the British public school curriculum had already been established. In South Africa, educators inspired by the notion of athleticism as a source of character and discipline led the establishment of European schools in the Cape colony and Natal. There was, Holt (1989) argues, "a close relationship between the creation of this muscular elite and the extension of formal control over large areas of Asia and Africa by the British government in the later nineteenth century" (p.204). The growth of the Empire during this period meant that British forms of leisure and sport were being introduced to local cultures across much of the globe. The situation in South Africa was no different and, by 1890, the foundations of the rugby game had been well and truly laid in one of the youngest British Dominions (Difford, 1933).

It was during this period that Britain, wishing to impose a greater degree of administrative control, actively pursued a policy of social imperialism in South Africa. In typically ethnocentric fashion, the British assumed 'racial' superiority over blacks and "coloreds" and also applied principles of Social Darwinism and eugenics to incorporate Afrikaners into the British way of life (Booth, 1998). At a time when Britain advanced its interests under the banners of economic development and Christian "civilization," indigenous communities throughout the British Empire were expected to accept as inevitable this Western notion of progress and the cultural trappings that accompanied it. Sports—team games in particular—were an integral part of this hegemonic imperial process. In South Africa it functioned by marginalizing the vast majority of black and "colored" people from the dominant sporting culture, within which cricket and rugby were mainstays (Stoddart, 1988). Cricket, with its intricate system of ethical standards and moral codes, embodied the ideal sporting expression of British imperialist attitudes. Afrikaners did take to cricket, but it was the English game of rugby that really captured their imagination and passion. A closer inspection of South African history during the early 20th century provides insights into why Afrikaners, who clearly opposed many facets of British culture, chose to adopt a game so heavily steeped in imperial heritage.

WAR AND THE SHAPING OF THE AFRIKANER NATION

Following British occupation of the Cape Colony in 1806, antagonism developed between the new colonial government and the existing white settlers. The Boers, being predominantly Dutch-speaking farmers, resented official imposition of the English language, of British authority, and particularly liberalism—a philosophy that led to the Boers having to abandon their customary rights to slavery in the 1830s. According to Moodie (1975), these humanitarian ideals also had a strategic goal—"to provoke the Afrikaners" (p.3). A profound response from the Boers was their northern mass migration of 1836-1854; in the first ten years over fourteen thousand of them crossed the Orange River (Lerumo, 1971). The 'Great Trek' consisted of a series of planned expeditions of farmers accompanied by their families, servants, and possessions. They did not seek to extend the frontiers of the Cape Colony; rather their purpose was to escape British rule and establish a 'free and independent state' beyond and thus outside the borders of the colony.

However, their independence was short lived. British annexation and military occupation of Natal, the Boer's first Republic, was followed in 1877 by the annexation of the Transvaal Republic—again under the strategic pretext of Afrikaner mistreatment of black Africans. Although Pretoria and its surroundings prospered in the wake of British economic investment, the farmer Paul Kruger,[1] who was determined not to be again subjected to colonial rule, mobilized commandos of Afrikaner farmers to oppose and remove the British soldiers—which became a catalyst for the first Anglo-Boer War (1880-81). The colonial military, having suffered major defeats at Majuba on the Natal border, abandoned combat and ceded independence to the Afrikaners in 1884. They were now hoping for improved relations with the Boers in terms of trade and the migration of white laborers to and from different South African territories (Smith, 1996).

In the wake of this Anglo-Boer War, Paul Kruger, now President of the Transvaal, propounded a revised history of Boer consciousness that consisted of a narrative of "grievances" and "injustices," featuring triumphal clashes between the "oppressed" Boer and the "despicable and cowardly" English (Booth, 1998). During this time, particular symbolic significance was attached to "heroic" Afrikaner events, such as the Great Trek and the Battle of Blood River[2] from which the Boer, it was hoped, could derive a strong sense of a shared mission and group identity. The seeds of Afrikaner mythology were thus cast, which over the next fifty years both shaped and reshaped ethnic and nationalist dynamics within South Africa.

The second Anglo-Boer War, 1899-1902, fomented the struggle among whites for dominance in South Africa. This war was an expensive venture for British Imperialism. Four hundred and fifty thousand troops were sent to South Africa from various parts of the British Empire, of whom more than twenty thousand lost their lives. It also cost British tax payers two hundred and fifty million pounds to attempt to secure the interests of imperial mining magnates. This was a land where, at the time, the entire white population of the Transvaal was much less than the population of Sheffield.[3] Subsequently, to many Britishers at home, the strategic significance of such a demographically small territory seemed somewhat irrelevant to the overall strength and cohesion of the Empire (for example, see Meysey-Thompson, 1899).

However, British prestige was about to suffer incalculable damage, for the war was fought with ruthlessness and little mercy. Boer women and children were confined in concentration camps, their homes and farms destroyed before they could be brought to surrender. By comparison, the guerrilla strategy of the Afrikaners was not only effective, but to outside observers seemed gallant. Here was a small nation defying the world's great imperial power in defense of their independence; this military defiance won the Afrikaners admiration and support in many parts of the world. Against great odds the Boers eventually suffered defeat and humiliation at the hands of the British. Yet this failure inspired stories of Boer martyrdom and reinforced a single-minded, siege mentality in Afrikaner thinking (Moodie, 1975). And, as this study will now demonstrate, within this burgeoning sense of Afrikaner ethnic nationalism the sport of rugby had particular socio-political significance.

1902-1948: THE ROAD TO INDEPENDENCE

At the end of the war in 1902 it would have been easy to presume that Afrikaner nationalism had been shattered. The Boer republics were overthrown and their former ruling group rendered impoverished and dispirited. Moreover, the events of the war had left a bitter legacy of divisions within Afrikanerdom— between Transvalers, Free Staters, and Cape Colonials, and between *Bittereinders* ("Bitter-enders") who had fought to the end, *Hensoppers* ("Hands-uppers") who had passively accepted British rule, and National Scouts who had actively assisted the British forces (Thompson, 1960). For the remaining Afrikaner nationalists it was thus imperative that a unifying feature of their collective identity be identified and nurtured. With all the divisions that the war had created, the one thing that all Afrikaners had in common was their language; this linguistic identity was set to play a major role in the political revival of the Afrikaner nation.

Following the surrender of the Boer armies in 1902, the task of rebuilding political resistance to British rule was left to the Boer Generals who had led the Commandos during the campaign. Generals Botha, Smuts, and Hertzog were faced with a fresh challenge as the emergent industrial and urban contexts of South Africa required a revised set of strategies. Ultra-patriotic Boer organizations such as the *Broederbond* (the Afrikaner "Brotherhood") and *Ossewa-Brandwag* (the 'Oxwagon Sentinel') emerged as a right-wing Afrikaner nationalist movement gained momentum during the four decades between the Anglo-Boer War and South African independence in 1948 (Adam & Giliomee, 1979).

It was, however, a complex and multifaceted situation. Some Afrikaners abandoned their traditional ethnic allegiance while others merely underemphasized their Boer heritage by supporting "inter-ethnic" political coalitions. The leaders of white "united" parties, Generals Botha and Smuts, in attempting national integration, conceived of Afrikaners and English-speaking whites as "flowing together in one stream" (Smuts, 1924). However, an emerging group of right-wing Afrikaner nationalists, led by General Hertzog and Dr. Malan, rejected such integrative philosophies. With policies based on religious conservatism, they insisted that the country should develop a separate and independent political identity within the British Empire and that, crucially, Afrikaners should retain their unique nationality within that framework.

Regarding themselves as pioneers of the "South African civilization," many Afrikaners viewed their existence as a separate entity as divine dispensation. The Dutch Reformed Church was revered by Afrikaners as a "pure" Protestant alternative to Anglicanism, and was a basis for religious rivalry with the British. Malan, for example, argued that "the Afrikaner had a full right to cling to his nationality as something upheld by God through the years" (Adam & Giliomee, 1979, p.106). Thus, according to this belief, only by keeping the cultural lives of the Afrikaners and English in two distinctly separate streams would Afrikaner ethnicity and its associated religious conservatism be maintained and developed. In 1908 Malan proclaimed:

> Raise the Afrikaans language to a written language, let it become the vehicle for our culture, our history, our national ideals, and you will also raise the people who speak it ... The Afrikaans language movement is nothing less than an

awakening of our nation to self-awareness and to the voca-
tion of adopting a more worthy position in world civilization
(cited in Pienaar, 1964, p.175).

For many Afrikaners there could also be no question of conciliation
with the English while the memories of the 1899-1902 war and its concentration camps were still fresh in their minds. As Adam and Giliomee
(1979) put it: "Only by stressing their ethnic identity could the humiliation of defeat and the cultural chauvinism of the English be overcome"
(p.107). It was in this dualistic ethno-political context that the game of
rugby came to develop special significance in South Africa. The major
sports of cricket and rugby continued to flourish as well in the early 20th
century, given impetus by the white schools and colleges. Nevertheless,
while these sports were also played in elite Afrikaans institutions, significant divisions remained along cultural and linguistic lines.

The Nationalist movement gained momentum during the 1930s as
the Afrikaners' quest for identity entered a new stage with the establishment of the United Party, fusing Hertzog's National Party with the pro-
Empire South African Party of Jan Smuts. For the Nationalists, this alliance represented not only the strengthening of political ties with Britain,
it also entrenched the duality of national and imperial symbols. However,
the Afrikaner political leader Dr. Malan, quoted in the *Cape Times* of 22
June, 1934 (p.8), regarded this move as "a bulwark of imperialism and
capitalism" and reiterated his stance of removing South Africa from "the
British connection." Subsequently, it took middle-class Afrikaners, particularly educators, clergy and Malan's purified National Party to compose a
strategy of ethnic mobilization. They began with the backing of both the
Dutch Reformed Church and the *Broederbond* to further ideologize Afrikaner identity and history, in a move that was set to capture the imagination of the *Volk* (Greyling, 1992).

Central events in Afrikaans history, such as Blood River, the Wars
of Independence, and the concentration camps were woven together in

a "sacred history" wherein God had revealed himself to the Afrikaners as a "chosen people." Moodie argues that this notion of a sacred history constituted a widely held civil religion, and that after the fifty year commemoration of the Great Trek in 1938 the ordinary Afrikaner had made the main themes of that collective story an integral part of their own emotional identity (Moodie, 1975). Certainly such notions were nurtured by national leaders in the hope of mobilizing renewed anti-imperialist sentiment.

A turning point came in 1939 when the Smuts faction of the United Party took South Africa into World War II on the side of Britain. This proved unpopular to the Boer community and became a decisive factor in convincing the majority of Afrikaners to go it alone politically. In 1948 the cult of Afrikanerdom was given an unprecedented boost when the Afrikaner National Party won exclusive power. At the age of seventy-four, Dr. Malan rose to ascendancy as the country's fourth Prime Minister since Union. As will now become apparent, the game of rugby came to play a significant part in the creation of a fervent Afrikaner nationalism in the years thereafter.

APPROPRIATION OF AN "IMPERIAL GAME"

Before the Anglo-Boer War, rugby was not played widely in the Transvaal and even less so in the Orange Free State. From Difford's *History of South African Rugby Football* (1933) it is evident that institutionalized rugby in these two Boer Republics was mainly played and administered by a small British contingent. The game was found only in city centers and mining districts, but apparently not at all in the country areas. However, following the war there was a widespread expansion of the game. Indeed, as early as 1903, a touring national rugby side from Britain was defeated by a representative South African team, which in turn won its first Test series with two draws and a win. The local side was, at that time, comprised of a majority of expatriate British players (Dobson, 1989).

The spread of rugby in South Africa owed much, ironically, to military

145

conflict. Research by Van der Merwe (1992 & 1998) has shown that Afrikaners took up rugby en masse after learning the intricacies of the game in British prisoner-of-war camps. In total, 27,000 Boers were captured during the conflict, with 24,000 sent to prisoner-of-war camps abroad in the British enclaves of St. Helena, Ceylon, India and Bermuda. As Van der Merwe (1992) notes, sport was a natural deliverance from the adversity of the camps, and a large percentage of the Boer prisoners were thus introduced to rugby for the first time. One report at a prisoner-of-war camp in Ceylon remarked how "rugby football in particular claimed a remarkable measure of enthusiasm, and it was specially noticeable how very keenly the Boer fell to this purely British game" (quoted in Van der Merwe, 1998, p.80).

While sporting imperialism in prison-of-war camps had created an awareness of rugby among Afrikaner people, its subsequent spread was affected by economic conditions immediately following the war. Defeated and impoverished by war, many Afrikaners began moving to urban areas where they joined a growing white working class seeking employment. Often they found themselves poorer than the majority of English-speakers, as overall living standards were underpinned by the political and economic supremacy of British capital. These factors inhibited urban Afrikaners from adopting an "English" way of life, including English forms of sport and leisure. In much of rural South Africa, however, the situation was different. Under the influence of Boers returning from British prison camps, the popularity of rugby amongst Afrikaners began to emerge. For Boers who remained on their farms, only two major team sports were accessible to them—association football and rugby football. And of the two, rugby had the advantage that it was played more easily on rough, unlevel, rural terrain (Archer and Bouillon, 1982).

Venturing beyond economic or practical considerations, rugby had, according to Archer and Bouillon (1982) a *"symbolic* significance which predisposed Afrikaners not merely to play it but to *identify* with the game" (p.65). There are obvious parallels, they contend, between the intrinsics of rugby football and the Afrikaners' pioneering spirit. Both the pioneer and the game value physical endurance, strength and rapidity as well as the warrior virtues of struggle and virility, fellowship and a sense of shared effort. This analogy, they conclude, "explains why rugby leant itself so perfectly to the physical, emotional and ideological needs of the Afrikaner people" (p.72). Stamped as it was with the mark of their imperial adversaries, it is still ironic that rugby appealed to an Afrikaner community that had very little in common with the ideology of English gentlemen.

Rugby was the sport of choice for males in white, middle class educational settings in South Africa. Stretching from the traditions of nineteenth century British public schools, the Afrikaner education system attached an importance to sport, and rugby in particular, as a cultivator of "manly" virtues such as collective discipline, pluck, daring, and self-control. British sport, and rugby in particular, had thus quickly been invested with extra significance by Afrikaners. Rugby had been appropriated by the *Volk* as a means of expression; to fulfill a physical as well as ideological need to press for autonomy from British rule (Grundlingh, 1996). This helps to explain why they adopted a most "imperial game" with such passion and commitment.

What of soccer's development in South Africa? The Association Codes had arranged for an English team, the Corinthians, to also visit South Africa during the winter of 1903. However, by this time soccer had been popularized and professionalized by the working classes back in Britain, which meant that it was not suitable as a cultural or political tool of imperialists in the same way that amateur rugby and elitist cricket were. Subsequently, without the obvious attachment to the white elite, or the strong masculine connotations associated with rugby, soccer was widely adopted by the African population—particularly in mining regions. Today, of course, soccer is the most popular sport among black and colored South Africans (Alegi, 2004), and the game has only a modest following among Afrikaners. In short, the rugby and soccer codes in South Africa have fundamentally separate histories, and the games have different cultural and ideological meanings to the main ethnic and racial groups.

THE GAME OF THE *VOLK*

Despite the success of the 1906 Springboks on their first overseas tour, the popularity of rugby fluctuated during the next fifteen years with the increasing trend of urbanization amongst Afrikaners. However, the game survived and began to flourish in the 1920s as concerted efforts were made to reach out to young Afrikaners who came from the rural areas into towns. There rugby was lionized as a game that could instill discipline and self-confidence among young South African men (Grundlingh, 1996). Through the energetic efforts of sport administrators, many of whom learned rugby at Stellenbosch, the game was diffused successfully among the white working class, in a process not dissimilar to what had happened in the United Kingdom during the latter part of the nineteenth century as rugby's influence spread outward from the public schools.

During this time several Afrikaans-speaking players rose to national prominence, some representing the Springboks on their inaugural rugby tour of Australia and New Zealand in 1921. The contemporary Sydney rugby critic, G.V. Portus, was struck by the way in which

> an essentially winter game can flourish in a hot country, and how it can attract men who have not a long heritage of British sport behind them … For the Dutch (Afrikaans) South Africans have taken to the rugby game as keenly as their English compatriots. In fact, they seem to outshine the English South Africans (quoted in Dobson, 1989, p.68).

Throughout this period, though, rugby was yet to be invested with a noticeably nationalistic Afrikaner ethos. Nevertheless, the fact that the Afrikaners made their mark on the playing field can be seen, in retrospect, to have singled out the game as a sport with the potential to enhance the Afrikaner self-image. Former Springbok and Western Province full-back Dawie Snyman believes that rugby became part of Afrikaans culture "because of results—it was a place of recognition" for Afrikaans people (personal interview, January 19, 2000). Through distinguishing themselves on the rugby field, Afrikaners had indeed discovered "a place where they could meet the Englishman on equal footing" (B. Booyens, private interview, January 19, 2000).

The successes of the Springboks in world competition (between 1903 and 1956 they won all of their Test series) soon made rugby the "national" sport in South Africa. However, during the 1930s, at a stage when the game was increasingly played by Afrikaners, rugby began to shift from a broader imperial focus to a South African nationalist focus, particularly as the Afrikaner *Broederbond* and the Nationalist Party targeted rugby as a key site for Afrikaner nationalism. As Black and Nauright (1998) put it: "No other sporting practice—indeed no other cultural pursuit—became so closely tied up with Afrikaner identity in this extraordinary period than did rugby" (p.61).

Archer and Bouillon (1982) contend that

> in symbolic terms, rugby bears the print of Afrikaner culture—its convictions, aspirations and dreams; attached to their Voortrekker past, proud of their civilising mission in a savage land, perceiving themselves as elected and created by God to reign on earth. Inspired by faith and an uncompromising moral ethic to defend the cause of their people and their God, the Afrikaner people did more than adopt rugby. They conquered the game (p.73).

Whether or not they had actually 'conquered' South African rugby, it cannot be denied that rugby was a public arena within which inter-ethnic tensions between Afrikaner and Briton were played out. As Grundlingh (1996) has put it: "While the British regarded rugby as part of the Imperial sporting ethos," and thus as a way of cementing relations within the Commonwealth, "Afrikaners viewed the game in explicitly nationalistic and ethnic terms." Whereas rugby in Australia and New Zealand expressed some sense of "imperial kinship," among Afrikaners "Springbok rugby carried a thinly disguised anti-imperialist message" (pp.187-8).

Afrikaners had clearly appropriated rugby as a vehicle with which they could not only challenge the British, but one with which they could decisively defeat them on the field of play. Whenever they competed against Britons it was a moment to symbolically re-play (as opposed to replay) the Anglo-Boer War in nationalistic and ethnic terms again.

The intense rivalry and fierce play that characterized domestic South African rugby matches between English and Afrikaans speakers was an expression of ongoing between the two ruling white factions. Sadie Berman was an observer at rugby matches between the English-medium University of the Witwatersrand and the Afrikaans University of Pretoria in the 1930's. She remembers that "it wasn't just rugby that they were playing." Rather,

> there was an enmity and a bitterness and a hatred of each other. The overtones were quite clear. The major goal was to beat the other University not only in the game. I think the competition between two such universities was naturally bitter ... because it was the child of the hatred of the Afrikaans for the English- speakers. It certainly didn't dissipate the tension (quoted in Archer & Bouillon, 1982, p.73).

AFRIKANERIZING RUGBY

As one of the main perpetrators of anti-British sentiment, the *Broederbond* had a subtle, yet profound influence on Afrikaner society. The "Broeders" served as a crucial link between the National Party and its Afrikaner ethnic constituency, helping to define policy alternatives, mobilize support for new policy initiatives, and "take the pulse" of male Afrikanerdom. For that purpose it sought to recruit the "opinion leaders" of Afrikaner society and rugby with its cultural significance naturally fell under its influence. The *Broederbond* looked towards leading athletes and sports officials in general, but rugby players and administrators in particular. After all, as Black and Nauright (1998) have put it, "most Broeders, as good Afrikaner males, were also avid rugby enthusiasts" (p.63). More deliberately, however, the *Broederbond* also took steps to put its own people in positions of authority within the rugby establishment.

Although Afrikaners had taken to rugby in large numbers, they had yet to capture the administration of the game and dictate its politics. Prior to 1948, control of the game was still largely in English-speaking white South African hands. Thereafter, Afrikaners principally associated with the *Broederbond* undertook a sustained campaign to wrest control for their own. Having already conceded political control to the Afrikaners, White South Africans of British descent were subtly maneuvered out of positions of influence within rugby's hierarchy. Meanwhile, British rugby authorities diplomatically accepted this shift in power relations between the two white groups in South Africa. As Wilkins and Strydom (1978, p.242) testify, Afrikaners, and *Broeders* in particular, have since adorned the history of South African rugby:

> Avril Malan, Johan Claassen, Dawie de Villiers, Hannes Marais served as Springbok captains; Butch Lochner, Piet du Toit, Mannetjies Roux, Willem Delport played for the Springboks; Sid Kingsley, Fritz Eloff, Steve Strydom served as presidents of provincial rugby unions.

The *Broederbond* concluded that unless they assumed control of the various official bodies involved in rugby, they would be unable to fully shape the wider social and political dimensions of the sport in South Africa. This goal, as history now testifies, they achieved. The game of rugby, despite its distinctly British heritage, had been appropriated by Afrikaners of all levels and used to challenge the imperialist hegemony that had first brought the sport to South Africa. Afrikaners had discovered and now coveted their own expression of identity and independence through sport.

CONCLUSIONS

For Afrikaners, rugby was a reinvented cultural tradition. Afrikaners had largely resisted British imperial culture and ideologies but ironically took rugby and imbued it with their own set of meanings. However, the reasons why rugby became an integral part of Afrikaner culture and ethnic identity calls for an understanding of the historical dynamics of Afrikaner nationalism and indeed the ethos of the game itself in South Africa. With that in mind, this chapter has examined longstanding tensions between Briton and Boer, as well as processes that shaped the evolution of an "Afrikaner nation" during the crucial period between the outbreak of war in 1899 and the inauguration of South Africa's first autonomous government in 1948.

The 1930s and 1940s were particularly important decades in South African history. Afrikaner nationalism was a crucial influence: it was a social and political response to the impact of industrial capitalism, as well as ongoing opposition to British dominance in economic and cultural spheres. Large numbers of Afrikaners were left economically stranded by industrialization and the trend towards urbanization, and therefore sought ideological refuge within a growing Afrikaner nationalist movement. Important building blocks in that process were the promotion of a common Afrikaans language, the *Broederbond's* emphasis on what was described as a glorious and common anti-British past, the unity of a fundamentally conservative Calvinist religion, and the construction of what they considered to be a distinctive and authentic Afrikaner ethnicity.

The gradual Afrikaner appropriation of the game was not, of course, without paradox. Rugby, having originated in England, epitomized the British upper-middle-class value system and fundamentally, therefore, should have represented everything that the nationalist Afrikaner opposed. However, Afrikaners had already proved that they could excel at rugby; it was more practical to adapt and reshape an existing game than to create a pure, separate form of sporting expression themselves (Grundlingh, 1996). It therefore made sense to Afrikanerize rugby.

Afrikaners adopted rugby as a means of heightened expression of their uniqueness and individuality free from imperial control and indeed as an opportunity to beat the English at their own game. Within this climate, the game became a powerful, if informal, disseminator of nationalist sentiment and a source of ethnic identification among the Afrikaner population within the "racial" mix of South Africa. By shaping 'South Africa's game' the 'chosen people', smarting from bitter defeat in a war some years earlier, had discovered an ideal symbolic vehicle through which they could publicly prove themselves against the British. By appropriating the game as their "own", they were also able to distance themselves from other sections of South African society, such as blacks and coloreds. Rugby was not only the "white man's game", it was, as the *Broederbond* put it, the game of the *Afrikaner*.

EDITOR'S NOTE

This chapter has been adapted from the award-winning ISHPES paper "Beating Them at Their Own Game": Rugby, the Anglo-Boer War and Afrikaner Nationalism, 1899-1948 which appeared in *The International Journal for the History of Sport*, Vol.20, No.3 (September 2003), 37-57. Focussing upon orthodox Afrikaner history, the majority of research for this study was completed in South Africa, predominantly during spells in Cape Town, Stellenbosch and Pretoria. Visits were also made to relevant archives in the United Kingdom.

ENDNOTES

[1] Born in the Eastern Cape in 1825, Kruger took part in the Great Trek as a child. He later became three times President of the Transvaal and a strong opponent of British interests in South Africa. He led the Republic during the 1899-1902 War.

[2] Vastly outnumbered, a group of *Voortrekkers* defeated a Zulu army deep in the heart of Natal on 16 December 1838. Subsequently, during the apartheid years, this date was celebrated by Afrikaners as the 'Day of the Vow,' a public holiday honoring a supposed covenant made by the Boers with God himself that if he granted them victory, they would hold that day sacred.

[3] The white population of the Transvaal in 1899 was recorded as 288,750 compared to Sheffield's population of 324,243. See Meysey-Thompson (1899).

REFERENCES

Adam, H & Giliomee, H. (1979). *The Rise and Crisis of Afrikaner Power*. Cape Town: David Philip.

Alegi, P. (2004). *Laduma! Soccer, Politics and Society in South Africa*. Pietermaritzburg: University of Kwazulu-Natal Press.

Archer, R. & Bouillon, A. (1982), *The South African Game—Sport and Racism*. London: Zed Press.

Black, D.R. & Nauright, J. (1998). *Rugby and the South African Nation*. Manchester: Manchester University Press.

Booth, D. (1998). *The Race Game—Sport and Politics in South Africa*. London: Frank Cass.

Cape Times, 22 June 1934.

De Reuck, J.A. (1996). A Politics of Blood: The 'White Tribe' of Africa and the Recombinant Nationalism of a Colonising Indigene. *Critical Arts, 10,* (2), 139-157.

De Villiers, M. (1987). *White Tribe Dreaming.* New York: Viking.

Difford, I.D. (ed.). (1933). *The History of South African Rugby Football, 1875-1932.* Cape Town: Speciality Press.

Dobson, P. (1989). *Rugby in South Africa: A History 1861-1988.* Cape Town: The South African Rugby Board.

Greyling, C. (1992). From Hyper-Imperialist to Super-Afrikaner: The Developments within a White Theology, *Journal for the Study of Religion, 5,* (2), 47-63

Grundlingh, A. (1996). Playing for Power? Rugby, Afrikaner Nationalism and Masculinity in South Africa, c.1900-70. In J. Nauright & T.J.L. Chandler (Eds.), *Making Men—Rugby and Masculine Identity* (91-120). London: Frank Cass.

Harrison, D. (1981). *The White Tribe of Africa.* London: British Broadcasting Corporation.

Holt, R. (1989). *Sport and the British.* Oxford: Oxford University Press.

Kruger, S.J.P. (1902). *The Memoirs of Paul Kruger* (Colonial Edition). London: T .Fisher Unwin.

Lerumo, A. (1971). *Fifty Fighting Years.* London: Inkululeko Publications.

Meysey-Thompson, H. (1899). *The Transvaal Crisis.* London: Sampson Low.

Moodie, T.D. (1975). *The Rise of Afrikanerdom.* Berkeley, CL: University of California Press.

Pienaar, S.W. (Ed.). (1964*). Glo in u Volk: D.F. Malan as Redenaar, 1908-1954.* Cape Town: Tafelberg.

Rapport, 23 October 1994.

Roberts, J.G. (1902). *The South African War or the Irrepressible Conflict between Boer and Briton.* New York: T.J. Dyson.

Smith, I.R. (1996). *The Origins of the South African War, 1899-1902.* Harlow: Longman.

Smuts, J.C. (1924). *The Choice before the Country: The South African Party Manifesto.* Pretoria: South African Party.

Streak, M. (1974). *The Afrikaner as Viewed by the English 1795-1854.* Cape Town: Struik,

Stoddart, B. (1988). Sport, Cultural Imperialism, and Colonial Response in the British Empire, *Comparative Studies in Society and History, 30,* (4), 649-673.

Thompson, L.M. (1960). *The Unification of South Africa.* London: Oxford University Press.

Van der Merwe, F.J.G. (1992). Sport and Games in Boer Prisoner-of-War Camps during the Anglo-Boer War, 1899-1902, *International Journal of the History of Sport, 9,* (3), 439-455.

Van der Merwe, F.J.G. (1998). Rugby in the Prisoner-of-War Camps during the Anglo-Boer War, 1899-1902. *Occasional Papers in Football Studies, 1,* (1), 76-83.

Vatcher, W.H. (1965). *White Laager: The Rise of Afrikaner Nationalism.* London: Pall Mall Press.

Wilkins, I. & Strydom, H. (1978). *The Super Afrikaners.* Johannesburg: Jonathan Ball Publishers.

Racial Athletic Aptitude and the New Medical Genetics: "Black Dominance" and the Future of Race Relations

BY **JOHN HOBERMAN**

The physical abilities of black Africans were already evident to Europeans during the earlier phase of the Age of Exploration that sent travelers from Europe to Africa and beyond. For example, a 1638 account of "Natives" living near the Cape of Good Hope, which served as a resupply station for ships heading to the East Indies, describes them as "strongly limbd [sic]," while a report of 1655 describes the Hottentots as follows: "The men are tolerably tall and well built, and exceptionally fast runners ..." Indeed, the Royal Society's instructions issued in 1666 for the classification of "Natives and Strangers" identifies "Strength" and "Agility" as relevant characteristics. The problematic status of these descriptors derives from the fact that they are accompanied by many denigrating terms. These black people are "desperate, crafty and injurious," and they are cannibals to boot (Butchart, 1998, 49, 54, 51, 49). So their impressive physical traits did not exempt these "Natives" from racial defamation. A more explicitly racist interpretation of athleticism occurred during the nineteenth and twentieth centuries, which now interpreted "black" athletic aptitude within an evolutionary narrative of arrested "racial" development, in contrast to athletically inferior but mentally superior whites (see Hoberman, 1997). It is reasonable to assume that "black dominance" in highly publicized sports still serves as a subliminal vehicle for nineteenth-century ideas about the "primitive" status of a physically superior "race."

In June 2005 the U.S. Food and Drug Administration approved an allegedly racially specific drug known as BiDil for African-American heart patients. The announcement of a racially exclusive drug therapy endorsed by the FDA was a media event that produced headlines such as "Shouldn't a Pill Be Colorblind?" (Stolberg, 2001), "U.S. to Review Drug Intended For One Race" (Saul, 2005), and "Is this the future we really want? Different drugs for different races" (Malik, 2005). This development and the publicity it generated raised concerns in many observers. The sociologist Troy Duster, for example, warned against falling into "the trap" of promoting "misconceptions of 'black' or 'white' diseases" (Duster, 2005, 51). The prominent geneticist J. Craig Venter commented: "It is disturbing to see reputable scientists and physicians even categorizing things in terms of race. There is no basis in the genetic code for race" (quoted in Stolberg, 2001).

Assessments of the social danger presented by this public forum on racial physiology differed. One study of the American media coverage reported that: "Most of the articles raise questions and concerns about the biology of race, while not explicitly promoting one view. In general, of the stories that tackle the controversy, most engaged the topic in a critical manner, highlighting different points of view and questioning the idea of race as a biologically legitimate category" (Caulfield and Simrat, 2008, 48). This was reassuring news for those concerned that an emphasis on biological differences promotes the stigmatizing of black people as "racial" aliens. Another study, however, tested the hypothesis that "messages that increase the belief that races are biologically distinct—such as messages linking race, genes, and health—would increase levels of traditional racism," and its authors came to a sobering conclusion. They found that "messages associating Blacks with biology" promote "negative images of Blacks" associated with criminal behavior. For that reason, "if medical research eventually indicates that there are clinically useful differences" in disorders that occur in blacks and whites, "the benefits of utilizing these tools will need to be weighed against the social harm of discussing them." (Condit et al, 2004, 47).

THE NEW RACIAL PHARMACOLOGY: THE BIDIL STORY

On June 23, 2005, the Food and Drug Administration (FDA), an agency of the federal government of the United States, approved what became known as the first "ethnic" or "racially specific" drug for any medical purpose. BiDil, a fixed dose consisting of both isosorbide dinitrate and hydralazine, two generic vasodilators, appeared to have brought about a dramatic decline in mortality in a group of self-identified African-American patients diagnosed with heart failure, while benefits to white patients remained untested and unproven.

Even before FDA approval was granted in June 2005, the news that a racially specific drug was being considered for approval was generating headlines in the lay press both in the United States and in Europe. In April 2004 the largest German newsweekly, *Der Spiegel*, published an article titled "The New Race Debate" (Von Blech, 2004, 186-88). A few months later, the *Südddeutsche Zeitung* of Munich published a commentary titled "Prescription by Skin Color" (Von Felicitas, 2004). This sort of coverage of the new racial pharmacology was happening in Germany despite the absence of a significant black population that might benefit from the first officially "racial" drug. The more extensive press coverage of the BiDil story in the United States that appeared prior to the approval of BiDil included a *New York Times* editorial that offered the following reflection on the emerging respectability of race-based medicine:

Not so many years ago it was difficult to consider the possibility that biological differences might affect the course of disease and the effectiveness of therapies in different racial groups. The danger that any perceived differences might be used for evil—to imply superiority or inferiority for a particular racial group, for example—was simply too great. Thus it is a welcome sign of increasing national maturity that medical experts, both black and white, are now grappling openly with the issue of race as it applies to medical treatments (*New York Times* Editorial, 2004).

Not all observers of the BiDil saga have shared the *Times's* confident assumption that he advent of BiDil is a sign of "national maturity." "Perhaps most problematically," the legal and medical scholar Jonathan Kahn commented in 2007, "the patent award and FDA approval of BiDil have given the imprimatur of the federal government to using race as a genetic category" (Kahn, 2007, 43). Official recognition of the equating of race and genes is problematic because this equation vastly oversimplifies human biology in the collective imagination of a scientifically illiterate public for which genetic reductionism remains a constant temptation. The athletic stereotypes with which we are all familiar are only one expression of a racial essentialism that creates and maintains potentially harmful racial stereotypes. Indeed, the new medically inspired racial biology has arrived at a period in history when many anti-racists are looking forward to the end of racial distinctions as a real possibility.

The BiDil story, and the still undefined racial biology it represents, provides us with some compelling reasons not to believe that the end of race is at hand. Various critical observers have noted what I would call a "re-authorization" of racial biology that is based in part on the new racial pharmacology that produced BiDil. The sociologist David Skinner has spoken of a "re-racialized" future (Quoted in Tutton et al, 2008, 464, emphasis in the original). Gregory M. Dorr and David S. Jones have pointed ed out that, given our "long traditions of racial therapeutics, increasing discomfort with old notions of race, and lingering evidence of physiological differences between races," it is not surprising that the appearance of BiDil as a newsworthy event "reinvigorated old tensions and controversies in American medicine and society" (Dorr and Jones, 2008, 444). The legal and medical scholar Dorothy E. Roberts has recently offered a diametrically opposed perspective that emphasizes—not the old tensions and controversies around race and medicine—but rather a new equanimity with the entire subject of racial biology. Roberts argues that the new racial biology has achieved respectable status because it is no longer associated with the overt forms of racism that have become less apparent over the past several decades. "The biologization of race seems acceptable today," she writes, precisely because prior forms of overt racial violence are now institutionalized and therefore invisible to many Americans. Scientists, pundits, and entrepreneurs can dissociate their promotion of inherent racial classifications from prior explicitly racist and eugenic incarnations because racial inequality no longer relies on overt white supremacy" (Roberts, 2008, 543). As Dorr and Jones put it: "Racial medicine has returned from history's dust-bin to today's examination room and tomorrow's front page" (Dorr and Jones, 2008, 448).

The current success of the new and medically inspired racial biology in the United States is due to a number of factors, including the undying appeal of genetic reductionism and its new association with medical therapies that appear to offer special relief to black people. For all of its horrors and indignities over many years, medical racism never managed to extinguish African-American willingness to entertain the idea of racially differential diseases and therapies that might cure them. Seventy-five years ago, the African-American historian Carter G. Woodson wrote: "The greatest problem now awaiting solution is the investigation of the differential resistance of races to disease. What are the diseases of which Negroes are more susceptible than whites? What are the diseases of which the whites are more susceptible than Negroes? The Negro escapes yellow fever and influenza, but the white man dies. The white man withstands syphilis and tuberculosis fairly well, but the Negro afflicted with these maladies easily succumbs. These questions offer an inviting field of research for Negro medical students" (Woodson, 1990 [1933], 178-79). This was in 1933, and it is worth noting that Woodson endorsed such inquiries into racial biology during a profoundly racist period in the history of American medicine. The need to do something about the poor state of Negro health seems to have outweighed any concerns Woodson might have had about promoting a racial biology of health and disease. Indeed, any racial biology with therapeutic aims would have looked good in comparison to the defamatory racist biology that had long since infiltrated American medical thinking. A quarter-century later an editorial in the *Journal of the American Medical Association* reiterated the call for research into the race factor in medicine: "In the statistical study of human disease," this commentator wrote, "such factors as age, sex, and race need explicit evaluation. Of these, the racial factor perhaps has been the most frequently neglected and misinterpreted. That this may prevent the more complete understanding of disease has been pointed out in a recent review on this subject with particular reference to the cardiovascular system" (*JAMA* Editorial, 1960, 1237).

What I have called the "re-authorization" of racial biology was on full display at the 2005 FDA hearing in Gaithersburg, Maryland, that heard testimony on whether or not to approve BiDil as the first racially specific therapeutic drug. One of the least-remarked upon—but most striking—aspects of this public event was the collaborative effort on the part of several powerful interest groups to get BiDil approved for use by an exclusively (self-defined) African-American clientele. This collaborative group included the FDA; the pharmaceutical industry, represented by the Nitromed corporation; an African-American coalition consisting of the Congressional Black Caucus, the Association of Black Cardiologists, the National Minority Health Foundation, the International Society for Hypertension in Blacks, and African-American heart patients; and—not least—a coalition of white medical liberals who made it clear that they were responding to

American medicine's sorry history of treating black patients by approving a promising race-specific therapy.

All of these factions were aware that the approval of BiDil was likely to establish an important precedent, and for this reason their spokespersons paid homage to the official anti-racist ethos of modern medicine that has generally discouraged the promotion of racial biology as a conceptual framework for medical therapies. For example, the patent-holding doctor working with the Nitromed corporation stated: "I want to remind you all that we are not focusing on the difference between blacks and whites. We are only focusing on whether this drug is efficacious in blacks" (Dept. of Health and Human Services, 2005, 55). All of these actors were conscious of the fact that they were walking a fine line between, on the one hand, an ethically defensible use of racial biology for therapeutic purposes and, on the other, the promulgation of ideas about biological racial differences whose ultimate effects, based on past experience, might eventually threaten the cosmopolitan ideal of a single human family.

Within the 400 pages of the transcript of the FDA hearing, one can follow in fascinating detail the "re-authorized" debate over the potential uses and abuses of racial biology for medical purposes. This debate notwithstanding, the almost unanimous African-American position was that the drug should be approved. Dr. Donna Christensen, chair of the Health Braintrust of the Congressional Black Caucus, told the FDA panel they had "an unprecedented opportunity ... to begin a process that will bring some degree of equity and justice to the American healthcare system." The approval of a biological trait would not, she argued, inflict any sort of "negative stigma on African Americans" (Dept. of Health and Human Services, 2005, 203-204, 207). Dr. Lucy Perez, a past president of the (African-American) National Medical Association, argued that the approval of Bi-Dil should not be obstructed by "invalid ethical concerns [deriving from] perceived ethical objections" (Dept. of Health and Human Services, 2005, 258). Dr. Charmaine Royal, from the National Human Genome Center at Howard University in Washington, D.C., reported that "many people in the African-American community were thinking finally we have our drug; something for us. Somebody is paying attention to us ... " (Dept. of Health and Human Services, 2005, 247).

There were also some African-American doubts about approving Bi-Dil. Dr. Shomarka Keita, an anthropologist, said that he was "concerned about the labeling of this drug as a black drug." The race concept, he said, "does not apply to modern humans" (Dept. of Health and Human Services, 2005, 221-22). Dr. Charles Curry, who called BiDil the most important advance in the care of black people that we have seen in my lifetime," took the trouble to point out that "most drugs on the market today were approved by the FDA based on trials conducted almost exclusively in white patients, but these drugs are not designated as white drugs, and rightly so" (Dept. of Health and Human Services, 2005, 229).

Other witnesses before the panel expressed their own doubts about the quality of the scientific evidence supporting the adoption of BiDil. Dr. Vivian Ota Wang of the National Human Genome Research Institute said that she was "uncomfortable with the thought that there is a notion that for some types of research, for some types of communities or populations we can actually lower the bar in terms of scientific integrity that we are using to evaluate the research ... Should we actually have different standards for different types of research for different communities?" (Dept. of Health and Human Services, 2005, 304-05). Different research standards for therapies targeted at blacks, she might have added, would only replicate the racially differential diagnosis and treatment that have characterized the care of African-Americans patients for the past hundred years and more. This includes medical experimentation on black people (Washington, 2006).

Perhaps the most interesting rhetorical performance at the BiDil hearing was that of the "white liberal" physicians, who found themselves caught between their own epistemological standards and a perceived mandate to get this drug into black heart patients no matter how dubious the scientific rationale might be. As the prominent cardiologist Steven Nissen put it, "we sort of said, well, you make some adjustments sometimes because you want to encourage trials in special populations and diseases which are of public health importance which we have few therapies for." The pharmaceutical company that developed a drug therapy for "a group that can be very difficult to treat," he said, deserved some regulatory goodwill in exchange for this socially valuable initiative. "I think this was a courageous thing to do," he added, "to try to develop a drug for this population which seems to have a disproportionate burden of disease." Given the rampant "distrust of the health provider community" among African Americans, "we have to overcompensate" to make black people comfortable about participating in clinical trials. Even the skeptical Dr. Ota Wang, who said she felt "very uncomfortable" about "the design issues and the statistical analyses," managed to persuade herself that "the qualitative discussions around the quality of life are very persuasive. So, on that basis I would actually approve" the drug for black patients. As Dr. Nissen phrased it, "I think that there are times when one has to adjust one's thinking for the clinical factors" and pay less attention to statistical evidence (Dept. of Health and Human Services, 2005, 302, 308, 394, 309, 401, 394).

Even as they were endorsing this form of racial medicine, the liberal white physicians were confessing that the mysteries of racial biology were beyond their understanding. Dr. Ronald Portman addressed the conceptual disorientation he experienced when confronted with evidence of racial differences as he diagnosed the disorders of some black children: "I do believe, as a clinician, that there are certainly differences. I see it in my everyday practice. I see it in the African-American kids who have focal sclerosis and who have hypertension and who have proteinuria. I don't know whether those differences are genetic or whether they are social or whether they are economic or whether health delivery-related and I don't think that particular issue is germane here." And other physicians found themselves in the same predicament. "For reasons I can't explain," confessed

Dr. Nissen, "there appears to be less susceptibility of African Americans, blacks, to the effects of renin angiotensin system drugs" (Dept. of Health and Human Services, 2005, 353, 359). It is important to understand that this observation about ACE inhibitor drugs took its place in a long series of claims about racially differential drug effects, most of which for an as yet unknown reason have appeared to disadvantage black patients.

The racial pharmacology that has been developing over the past decade represents only one example of published research that presents what are understood to be racially differential traits. Indeed, non-controversial findings of racially differential biological phenomena of medical significance have been reported for years. "It is clear," one medical author observed in a 1993 publication on "Racial Equity in Renal Transplantation," "that profound racial differences exist in antigen expression. Blacks have less well-defined HLA antigen specificities than do whites, particularly at the DR locus. Furthermore, HLA antigens are distributed differently among races" (Gaston et al, 1993, 1353).

Another medical researcher reported in 2002 that "the theory that cancers afflicting blacks may be fundamentally more aggressive due to [race-specific] biological or genetic differences has gained prominence." And: "Many researchers and physicians have concluded that poorer survival of blacks relative to whites after a cancer diagnosis reflects fundamental differences in the biology of the host or the attendant cancer or both." It is instructive to note that the reporting physician is not entirely convinced by these theories about biological differences between blacks and whites. He is, however, aware of the real-life consequences these theories can have. Such "biological differences between blacks and whites," he says, "cannot explain a meaningful share of the racial disparity in cancer survival observed in the United States." This means that promoting the survival of many black cancer patients depends on their receiving care independent of their genetic traits (Bach, 2002, 2106, 2111, 2112).

In a word, racial biology becomes medically dangerous when it promotes fatalism about treating disease in people whose genetic risk factors are assumed to be intractable. In this case, the potential danger will be confined to the patient population that will wind up suffering on account of erroneous thinking about racial biology. More dangerous still are erroneous ideas about racial biology that stigmatize entire populations.

This brief review of the BiDil debate shows clearly that the contending factions in the debate over racial medicine are not "black" and "white". The real divide separates those who object to what they view as a scientifically unfounded rationale for practicing an ostensibly effective racially differential pharmacology from those who are willing to endorse a therapy that seems to benefit a historically underserved racial population. This new alignment of allies and adversaries is interesting precisely because it modifies, and in one sense dissolves, the familiar black/white divide that has symbolized race relations in the United States, inside and outside of medicine, over many generations.

IS RACIALLY DIFFERENTIAL PHARMACOLOGY A THREAT TO BLACK PEOPLE?

Many expert commentators have expressed reservations about the emergence of race-based medicine, and it is essential to understand that far more than the efficacy of drugs is involved. As one team of authors pointed out in 2003, "One of the major concerns about race-based medicine is that talking about race and genetics as though racial groups were correlated with discrete gene pools will reinforce a sense of difference between racial groups, essentializing race in ways that can encourage discrimination and social distance between groups (p. 390)." The racial estrangement and rancorous feelings that are euphemistically presented here as "social distance" would complicate relationships between many physicians and their black patients, while "the impact of the discussions of race-based medicine might be so negative with regard to increasing the sense of racial differences that the disadvantages might outweigh the advantages on a social scale" (Condit et al, 2003, p. 392). How interesting, then, to learn that the Nitromed company "discontinued active promotional efforts related to BiDil in January 2008 following disappointing sales" (Ellison, 2008, 455). It would appear that the African-American medical intelligentsia was unable to persuade rank-and-file black Americans to adopt a racially specific medication, and it may be that traumatic memories may account for their reluctance. The medical stigmatizing of Black Africans and African Americans is nothing less than a Western tradition, and BiDil may have seemed to many people to be no more than a new innovation on this form of medical racism.

The advent of the new racial medicine has prompted some observers to question the ethical propriety of conducting research on potentially controversial racial differences. For example, responding in 1992 to public controversy over the Federal Violence Initiative, a research project that focused on the criminal potential of minority youth, the African-American political scientist Ronald Walters said:

> I would argue there are types of research that shouldn't be done, and the grounds on which I argue are civility. You have to decide what issues are going to breed such tensions in society that there would be no return back onto the path of civility. ... There are types of research that shouldn't be done because the danger to society is too great. We are on the precipice of something very important and very dangerous (Quoted in Shipman, 1994, 258).

Another, and less alarmist, version of this argument holds that concerns about identifying genes with "race" will "make it difficult to discuss, expose, and explore racial variation in biology and health without alluding to, or creating data that support, naïve innate and/or genetic explanations for racial difference" (Ellison, 2008, 454). The difference between the concerns of these authors and the outright fear of Ronald Walters is that Ellison and his colleagues are talking about data they presume to be ultimately harmless because it is in support of "naïve" assumptions about human variation. They seem to assume that, while these data will mislead the public for some period of time, they will ultimately be exposed as fallacious, and the threat they present to racial civility will eventually dissipate. In his critique of *The Bell Curve*, the controversial and arguably racist bestseller that was published in 1994, Stephen Jay Gould takes a similarly optimistic position: "As a card-carrying First Amendment (near) absolutist, I applaud the publication of unpopular views that some people consider dangerous. I am delighted that *The Bell Curve* was written—so that its errors could be exposed, for Herrnstein and Murray are right to point out the difference between public and private agendas on race, and we must struggle to make an impact on the private agendas as well" (Gould, 1995, 20). Gould's optimism has two sources: the confident assumption that disturbing racial differences will not be found, and the similarly optimistic assumption that the anti-racist intelligentsia will be able to convert to its own way of thinking modern populations that have demonstrated an unsettling tendency to hold onto rather than jettison a lot of racial folklore that belongs to the nineteenth century. One might add that racial folklore about athletic aptitudes certainly belongs in this category.

The widely anticipated dangers of pursuing research that can illuminate or, perhaps, invent or distort findings of racial differences, stand in relation to a scientific and scholarly standard that refuses to censor research both as a matter of principle and as a practical strategy. As Peter J.M. McEwan wrote in 1990:

> [T]he argument [challenging racial explanations] needs to be stated and defended, not assumed as a holy tenet which it is scientific heresy to question. Alternative explanations will then be advanced to account for whatever variations may remain. As matters stand, there is a danger that certain branches of science, by fearing to enter the arena, fail to meet their obligation" (McEwan, 1990, 911).

Or as the medical anthropologist William W. Dressler commented in 1993:

Investigators seem to be more comfortable with noting the existence of differences than with contemplating the basis for those differences, beyond near platitudes concerning the need for more research to investigate one or another aspect of the problem. Of course, researchers ought not to be judged too harshly for this timidity. Discussions of ethnic differences are fraught with dangers for the unwary, and broadside indictments of a tainted ideology on the part of the investigator are likely to come from just about anywhere on the political spectrum. Nevertheless, the question of the basis for these differences cannot be avoided" (Dressler, 1993, 322).

It is important to distinguish between this argument, which insists on putting scientists rather than ideologues in charge of interpreting human differences, and the conservative race theorists who, as Stephen Jay Gould put it, "rail against the largely bogus ogre of suffocating political correctness" (Gould, 1995f 20). In the last analysis, however, the ostensibly practical strategy of putting scientists in charge of racial biology does not eliminate the possibility of genetic surprises that might threaten the anti-racist ideal of the single human family. It remains to be seen how such findings might affect the world of elite sport if genetic advantages could be definitively correlated with "race."

IS PUBLIC DISCUSSION OF RACIAL ATHLETIC APTITUDE A THREAT TO BLACK PEOPLE?

In the book *Darwin's Athletes* (1997, 221) I made the following observations:

The investigation of racial athletic aptitude inspires fear in whites and blacks alike because it suggests other, more intimate racial differences pertaining to intellectual and emotional capacity. The anxiety level within both groups persists because scientists and the general public share the habit of concealing much of what they really think about racial anatomy and physiology, and this silence allows racial folklore and pseudo-science to flourish unchecked, satisfying the fantasy needs of both whites and blacks. A powerful and generally unspoken assumption is that human biologists are hiding a terrible truth about racial difference, and despite the official antiracist proclamations of modern science, there is a profound disinclination to believe that such research might confirm not only the diversity but also the unity of the human species.

In *The End of Racism: Principles for a Multiracial Society* (1995, 441), Dinesh D'Souza paraphrases this attitude as follows:

Why should groups with different skin color, head shape, and other visible characteristics prove identical in reasoning ability or the ability to construct an advanced civilization? If blacks have certain inherited abilities, such as improvisational decision making, that could explain why they predominate in certain fields such as jazz, rap, and basketball, and not in other fields such as classical music, chess, and astronomy.

There is social science research that suggests reason for concern about racial athletic stereotypes. Earlier this year an American team of researchers found that the more respondents endorsed genetic underpinnings for a perceived race difference in athleticism the greater their level of prejudice and negative stereotyping about Blacks. ... The results suggest that the belief in a genetic race difference in athleticism may function to sustain racist ideologies by implying the inferiority of Blacks' intelligence and work ethic" (Sheldon, 2008, Online).

Other researchers reported this year that "the Black brawn-White brain distinction" that has played a prominent role in the sports vernacular over many years "suggests evidence of [a] 'new racism'" that coexists easily with our racially integrated sports world (Buffington and Fraley, 2008, 306).

The "black dominance" established by athletes of African origin in some high-profile sports has provoked various xenophobic reactions among those elements of the European population that engage with multiracial sport as a political and cultural issue that can be used for propagandistic purposes by racist elements in European societies. The neo-fascist French politician Jean-Marie Le Pen, for example, has made unusually candid remarks interpreting the social and biological significance of the racially integrated sports world. When asked the same year whether he believed in superior and inferior races, Le Pen replied with considerable polemical guile: "First you have to define what a race is and what you are comparing. It is obvious that an illiterate Eskimo is superior to a European Nobel Prize winner in literature if what counts is killing a polar bear on the pack ice. The best sprinters at the Olympic Games are black, the best swimmers are white. Is it forbidden, illegal, or immoral to state that those differences are real? As a humanist and as a Christian, I can assure you that I believe in the equal dignity of all people" (Quoted in Von Leick and Krusche, 1996, 174, 176). The racist's invocation of racially segregated athletic events carries its own message about distinct racial biologies that supposedly point to other kinds of differences. The origins of this doctrine can be found in the racist anthropology of the late nineteenth century.

Ideas about racial athletic aptitude acquire meaning within evolutionary narratives about apparently racially differential traits that might account for the disproportionate achievements of athletes of East and West African origin, respectively. The dominant performances of East African distance runners, male and female, over the past generation has stimulated much scientific and pseudo-scientific thinking about the origins of these performances (Wiggins, 1989; Hoberman, 1997, 2004, 2007). Sprinters of West African origin, primarily African Americans and Afro-Caribbeans, utterly dominate these events; for example, no sprinter the modern world would classify as "white" has ever run a legal time of under 10 seconds for the 100-meter event, while dozens of "black" athletes have done so.

RACIAL ATHLETIC APTITUDE AND ITS SOCIAL EFFECTS

Sport's racial dimension in the 21st century will retain both its social and genetic aspects. Black dominance within important sectors of the sports entertainment industry will continue to emphasize the identification of black people with the capacities of their bodies rather than their minds. Reversing the social effects of "Black dominance" will not be possible in the foreseeable future, since effective opposition to the commercial interests which profit from publicizing black athletes is nowhere on the horizon. So the expressive styles of the most visible black athletes will continue to influence especially young people of color around the globe. At the same time, the Human Genome Project will produce more and more information about varying distributions of certain genetic variations (alleles) among "racial" populations that experience corresponding (and differing) rates of medical disorders of genetic origin. This research, the sociologist Troy Duster points out, is "poised to exert a cascading effect— reinscribing taxonomies of race across a broad range of scientific practices and fields" (Duster, 2005, 1051). As we have seen, the concept of biological race is already making a comeback after spending decades in disrepute. "We should reintroduce the concept of race into science and medicine", a medical advisor to the Human Genome Project stated in 2004 (Quoted in Von Blech, 2004, 186).[1] This evolving racial genetics may well isolate some of the genes responsible for conferring advantages on athletes who possess specific genetic endowments associated with a particular "race". The visibility of these performers on the Olympic stage will have the effect of both legitimizing the new genomic research and reinforcing the authority of the familiar thinking that assigns specific genes to the "races" we have long employed to maintain a typology of human beings.

In the meantime, we may consider how the racial folkloric version of racial athletic aptitude figures in the racial dystopia once envisioned by the authors of *The Bell Curve*. In an essay that appeared along with the publication of the book, Charles Murray and Richard J. Herrnstein

proposed that African Americans essentially resign themselves to cultivat-
ing the talents that nature had given them. A "wise ethnocentrism," they
argued, would encourage the development of a "clannish self-esteem"
based on "the dominance of many black athletes" and any other signature
achievements black America might come up with. The likely solution for
a black underclass, they say, is what they call a "custodial state ... a high-
tech and more lavish version of the Indian reservation for some substantial minority of the nation's population, while the rest of the nation tries
to go about its business" (Herrnstein and Murray, 1994, 526). In European
soccer stadiums, black athletes greeted by bananas and monkey chants
have long served as public specimens of the racial other and as scapegoats
for the tensions experienced by newly multiracial societies. These sobering examples make it clear that we should not underestimate the potential
exploitation of athletes as human specimens who confirm the existence of
racial differences and thus the logic of racial segregation. Up to this point
the global sporting public has adapted rather well to racially integrated
sport. A global depression that drastically reduced life opportunities and
standards of living for entire populations would be fertile ground for racist exploitation of the most public symbols of racial difference in the modern world.

ENDNOTES

[1] Abdallah Daar, a professor of surgery at the University of Toronto, at a conference in Berlin in 2004.
He is currently director of ethics and policy at the McLaughlin Centre for Molecular Medicine, University of Toronto, Canada. He is also director of the applied ethics and biotechnology programme at the
University of Toronto Joint Centre for Bioethics and co-director of the Canadian Program on Genomics
and Global Health. See also: "The concept of race may not be biologically meaningless after all; it might
even have some practical use in deciding on medical treatments, at least until more complete individual
genomic information becomes available. Yet in the interests of humane values, many scientists are
reluctant to make even minor adjustments to the old orthodoxy. 'One of the more painful spectacles
in modern science' the developmental biologist Armand Marie Leroi has observed, 'is that of human
geneticists piously disavowing the existence of races even as they investigate the genetic relationships
between 'ethnic groups'." (Holt, 2005, 28).

REFERENCES

Bach, P.B. (2002, April 24). Survival of Blacks and Whites After a Cancer Diagnosis, *Journal of the American Medical Association 287* (16): 2106-13.

Buffington, D. and Fraley, T. (2008). Skill in Black and White: Negotiating Media Images of Race in a Sporting Context. *Journal of Communication Inquiry 32* (3): 292-310.

Butchart, A. (1998). *The Anatomy of power: European constructions of the African body.* New York: Zed Books.

Caulfield, T. and Simrat, H. (2008). Popular Representations of Race: The News Coverage of BiDil. *Race, Pharmaceuticals, and Medical Technology.* (Fall): 485-90.

Condit, C.M. et al. (2003). Attitudinal Barriers to Delivery of Race-Targeted Pharmacogenomics Among Informed Lay Persons, *Genetics in Medicine 5* (September/October): 385-392.

Condit, C.M., et al. (2004). Exploration of the Impact of Messages About Genes and Race on Lay Attitudes, *Clinical Genetics. 66* (5): 402-8.

Department of Health and Human Services, Food and Drug Administration, Center for Drug Evaluation and Research. (2005, June 16) Cardiovascular and Renal Drugs Advisory Committee: Volume II. Transcript of Meeting. Available at www.fda.gov/ohrms/dockets/ac/05/transcripts/2005-4145T2.pdf

Dorr, G.M. and Jones, D.S. (2008). Introduction: Facts and Fictions: BiDil and the Resurgence of Racial Medicine, *The Journal of Law, Medicine & Ethics 36* (3), September: 443-8.

Dressler, W.W. (1993). Health in the African American Community: Accounting for Health Inequalities. *Medical Anthropology Quarterly 7* (4): 325-45.

D'Souza, D. (1995). *The end of racism: Principles for a multiracial society.* New York: Free Press.

Duster, T. (2005, February 18). Race and Reification in Science. *Science* 307: 1051.

Ellison, G.T.H. et al. (2008). Flaws in the U.S. Food and Drug Administration's Rationale for Supporting the Development and Approval of BiDil as a Treatment for Heart Failure Only in Black Patients. *The Journal of Law, Medicine & Ethics. 36* (3), September: 449-57.

Gaston R.S. et al. (1993, September 15). Racial Equity in Renal Transplantation, *Journal of the American Medical Association. 270* (11): 1352-6.

Gould, S.J. (1995). Curveball, in S. Fraser (ed.) *The bell curve wars: Race, intelligence, and the future of America.* New York: Basic Books: 11-22.

Herrnstein, R.J. and Murray, C. (1994). *The bell curve: Intelligence and class structure in American life.* New York: The Free Press.

Hoberman, J. (1997). *Darwin's athletes: How sport has damaged black America and preserved the myth of race.* New York: Houghton Mifflin.

Hoberman, J. (2004). African athletic aptitude and the social sciences. *Equine and Comparative Exercise Physiology. 1* (4): 281-4.

Hoberman, J (2007). Race and athletics in the twenty-first century. In J. Hargreaves and P. Vertinsky (eds), Physical culture, power, and the body. New York: Routledge: 208-231.

Holt, J. (2005, December 11). *Madness About a Method.* New York Times Magazine.

JAMA Editorial (1960, July 16). Cardiovascular Disease in Caucasians and Negroes, *Journal of the American Medical Association 173* (11): 1237-8.

Kahn, J. (2007). Race in a Bottle, *Scientific American.* August: 43.

McEwan, P.J.M. (1990). Comment on "Scientific Racism" by Charles Leslie. *Social Science & Medicine. 31* (8): 911-912.

Malik, K. (2005, June 18). Is This The Future We Really Want? Different Drugs For Different Races. *The Times.*

New York Times Editorial (2004, November 13). Toward the First Racial Medicine. *New York Times.*

Roberts, D.E. (2008). Is Race-Based Medicine Good for Us?: American Approaches to Race, Biomedicine, and Equality, *The Journal of Law, Medicine & Ethics 36* (3), September: 537-45.

Sheldon, J.P., Jayaratne, T.E. and Petty, E.M. (2007). White Americans' Genetic Explanations for a Perceived Race Difference in Athleticism: The Relation to Prejudice toward and Stereotyping of Blacks. *Athletic Insight: The Online Journal of Sport Psychology. 9* (3), September http://www.athleticinsight.com/Vol9Iss3/RaceDifference.htm

Shipman, P. (1994). *The evolution of racism: Human differences and the use and abuse of science.* New York: Simon & Schuster.

Saul, S. (2005, June 13). U.S. to Review Drug Intended For One Race. *New York Times.*

Stolberg, S.J. (2001, May 13). *Shouldn't a Pill Be Colorblind?.* New York Times.

Tutton, R. et al. (2008). Genotyping the Future: Scientists' Expectations about Race/Ethnicity after BiDil. *The Journal of Law, Medicine & Ethics. 36* (3), September: 464-70.

Von Blech, J. (2004, April 19). Die Neue Rassendebatte, *Der Spiegel.*

Von Felicitas W. (2004, August 17). Rezept Nach Hautfarbe. *Süddeutsche Zeitung.*

Von Leick, R. and Krusche, L. (1996, November 11). Ich bin ein Rebell. *Der Spiegel.*

Washington, H.A. (2006). *Medical apartheid: The dark history of medical experimentation on black americans from colonial times to the present.* New York: Doubleday.

Wiggins, D.K. (1989). 'Great Speed But Little Stamina': The Historical Debate Over Black Athletic Superiority. *Journal of Sport History. 16* (Summer): 158-185.

Woodson, C.G. (1990 [1933]) *The mis-education of the negro.* Trenton, NJ: Africa World Press, Inc.

Trash Talk and
Reflexive "Otherness":
Maurice Greene, Michael Johnson,
and Class Within Race

BY **NICOLE NEVERSON** AND **GRAHAM KNIGHT**

INTRODUCTION

The 2000 Sydney Summer Games featured several athletes who were celebrated as heroes and elevated to star status. Ian Thorpe (a.k.a., the "Thorpedo"), the freestyle swimmer who claimed three gold and two silver medals in the pool was also the top medal earner for the 632 member Australian team. Thorpe's performance in the pool was covered widely by both domestic and international media due to the magnitude of his personal success (i.e., breaking his own world record in the 400-meter freestyle event), but also because most of his medal wins came on home soil at the expense of the historically formidable American swimming contingent. On the running track, however, two other athletes, African Americans Maurice Greene and Michael Johnson, garnered similar attention and coverage. Greene earned the coveted title of "world's fastest man" by winning the marquee men's 100m event as well as anchoring the U.S. men's 4x100m relay team to gold. For his efforts, Johnson first became the only man to win the 400m race in two successive Olympic Games later on anchoring the U.S. men's 4x400m relay team to gold. Both athletes' performances, while similarly impressive to those of Thorpe, were complicated by a mix of attention paid to perceived heroic qualities of performance and a fierce, rhetorical rivalry that had commenced before both sprinters arrived in Sydney.

In his analysis of social fields, Bourdieu (1993) stresses that social relations are competitive and agonistic. Newcomers enter the field with relatively little power and status, and have to struggle to achieve these in contention with established elites. These struggles pertain not only to the symbolic and material recognition of accomplishments, but also the grounds on which the evaluation of performance takes place. Because sport is a social field that is structured explicitly around competition, struggles for recognition on the track tend to spill over into off-track relationships where they can easily become personalized. Rule-bound competition mutates into boundless competitiveness as actors vie for control. Athletic sprinting is a sport where rivalries have become particularly intensified, in part because winning and losing are determined in hundredths of a second, and in part because peak careers are relatively brief. Like some other sports, men's sprinting has become a sport where rivalries are widely seen to be characterized by "trash talk" (Schneider et al, 2007) in which leading athletes publicly disparage the talent, motivations, and achievements of their competitors. Trash talk has become another dimension of competition between athletes; it is part of the promotional performance of sprinting, an aspect of the uneasy symbiosis between athletes' desire to extend their celebrity (and its attendant rewards) and the media's desire to expand audiences by accentuating conflict, controversy, risk and rule-breaking. In the build-up to the 2000 Olympics, trash talking was the principal theme used by the international media to frame the relationship between Greene, the newcomer and challenger, and Johnson, the established, recognized star.

In this chapter we use international press coverage from mid-1999 to late 2000 to examine the narrative framing of Greene and Johnson's trash talking relationship. To do this we draw critically from the literature on racial otherness and how this may be constructed, circulated, and deployed in the context of sport-media relations. While numerous narrative frames were used to represent the characters, personalities, and performances of both runners, our analysis sheds light on how these narratives were inflected with implicit undercurrents of racialized discourse. We argue that the representation of the Greene-Johnson relationship illustrates how racial otherness operates within as well as between the primary terms of racial distinction. The use of the other as an analytical tool has tended to conceptualize racial discourses in terms of superior whiteness and an inferior blackness (or othered racialized group). What is problematic about this concept of otherness is that it is assumed to be uni-dimensional, operating on a single plane or level of reality. Otherness, we argue, should not be essentialized as a condition or state, but treated as the provisional outcome of continuous processes of distinction, evaluation, and stigmatization that become reflexive. As distinction extends out into the world, so it also begins to apply to itself as well as everything else it encounters. The question, therefore, that we are posing and attempting to answer in this chapter is what happens when *othering* is itself *othered*.

ANALYTICAL CONTEXT: THE FLOATING SIGNIFIER AND REFLEXIVE OTHERNESS

Scholars who have examined representations of race in the realm of sport have called attention to the ways in which racist ideologies are embedded in the reporting and promotion of African American and other racialized athletes (Andrews, 1996; Wilson, 1997; Tudor, 1998; Simons, 2003; Hartmann, 2007). What these studies share in common is an understanding that, as an organizing principle, whiteness is often unchecked or overlooked as the privileged position on which othering is based and therefore remains, for the most part, unacknowledged as a key factor contributing to the prevalence of racism in mediated sport texts. In addition, this research literature has mainly adopted a binary, unilateral concept of otherness.

Whiteness is seen as the dominant and/or determinant assumption on which performative expectations are based; whiteness is the norm from which otherness deviates but, at the same time, what it is expected to aspire to and strive for. In his examination of African American basketball hero Michael Jordan, Andrews (1996) argues that the evolutionary process of signification in which Jordan was framed as a "natural" athlete, the All-American of the Reaganite era, and then misbehaving black man, was one rooted in established contingencies of othering where blackness was constructed as both the antithesis and disciple of normative whiteness. While Andrews (1996) employs the logic of the "floating racial signifier," a term used by Hall (1997) to describe the discursive nature of race and how its meaning is never fixed but ever-shifting, his analysis succeeds in highlighting how the meanings of blackness in relation to whiteness are acknowledged as more favorable or problematic, yet he largely concentrates on the unilateral quality of otherness.

In a more recent study of the racialized other, Simons (2003) examines the racial trajectory of penalized sports behaviors and how African American athletes are disproportionately punished and stigmatized by comparison to their white counterparts for participating in trash-talking disputes and football end zone celebrations. On a whole, the qualities of verbal aggressiveness, arrogant trash talking, animated showmanship, and patented swagger have been established as "expressive features of African American culture [and] a means of asserting manhood, increasing self-esteem and gaining respect ..." (Simons, 2003, p. 11). Crucially, these are in direct conflict with qualities attributed to white, mainstream sporting culture which focus instead on humility, fair play, and respect for one's competition. While Simons (2003) reflects upon whether such behaviors can be regarded as coping mechanisms in the tradition of Majors and Billson's (1992) "cool pose," or an aesthetic style and principle cultivated by African American athletic cultures, his analysis largely places penalized behaviors at odds with the adjudicating eye of the white middle class that possesses the power to regulate fair play.

One study that recognizes the possibility of othering as a reflexive process is Wilson's (1997) "'Good blacks' and 'Bad blacks.'" Much like Andrews (1996) and Wenner (1995), Wilson critiques the bivalent construction of African American athletes by adopting the reflexive "floating racial signifier." According to Wilson (1997), the construction of NBA athletes in the Canadian press worked to discursively construct players in a binary sense as either "good blacks" or "bad blacks." In the case of "good blacks," the marker of race was either neutralized or viewed as non-threatening when players adopted assimilationist qualities of the dominant white culture. Conversely, race was an implicit part of how players who rejected or did not live up to normative standards were represented as "bad blacks." These representations were not exhaustive as Wilson also observed how some players were constructed in ambivalent terms, thereby rendering the marker of race as both potentially threatening and non-threatening to white middle class norms.

The concept of the floating signifier originated in the work of Lévi-Strauss who used it to designate linguistic terms that have no fixed meaning or referent, and that shift meaning as they migrate from context to context, use to use (Mehlman, 1972). The floating signifier is a term that represents a limit to cognitive fixity yet nonetheless has strong evaluative associations, and for this reason it has proven valuable in conceptualizing how racial distinctions do and do not change at the same time. Hall (1997) speaks of race as a floating signifier in order not only to dispel the notion of biological essentialism but also to argue that race functions in the manner of a language in which meanings are established relationally in a field of differences. Signification functions in terms of binary classifications whose terms are associated through chains of evaluative equivalence—white is equivalent to superior, cultural, intellectual; black to inferior, natural, physical—that, in contemporary society, are generally implied rather than explicitly declared. Racism, as Hall (1990/1981) argues, is largely inferential; it functions on the basis of taken-for-granted assumptions, myths and prejudices that remain largely silent if not unconscious. At the same time, this signifying field of relational differences is open to intervention whereby meanings can become subject to "constant processes of redefinition and appropriation" (1997, p. 8). Meaning is provisional and temporary; thus it can be contested and changed.

It is generally recognized, however, that the floating signifier is not unrestricted in its movement (Wilson, 1997). The issue then is how to explain these limitations. The principal explanation is that the floating racial signifier remains anchored in and by the relations of power that underlie its use (Wilson, 1997). Race is not only a discursive construct but also an ideological one, bound by power relations and structures that are somehow external to and more fundamental to notions of self and other than relations of meaning. The problem with this explanation, however, is that it is reductionist: it subsumes meaning under power as if power is not only more fundamental but somehow also capable of functioning outside signification. Power relations may well act empirically and contingently as a constraint on the floating signifier, but signification may also act empirically and contingently as a constraint on power. There is no necessary a priori relationship between meaning and power; they are mutually irreducible (Foucault, 1980). What accounts for limits to the flotation of the racial signifier is that signification entails processes not only of classification but also of distinction that are reflexive.

As Luhmann (2002) argues, meaning begins when we mark a distinction in the world in a double sense: the distinction pertains to something observed in the world, such as differences of skin color or physiognomy, while the act of observing and distinguishing are themselves conducted in the world to which they pertain. As distinctions are applied to the world so they also encounter and apply to themselves as part of that world. Put more concretely, the process of distinction becomes self-applying, and self-application results in two levels or orders in which the distinction functions as the generator of meaning. The primary or first order level is that between black and white and its implicit association with a chain of evaluative binaries like superior and inferior, good and bad, etc. The second order or reflexive level is the distinction within the two terms created at the primary level, i.e., of whiteness and blackness *within* white and black. Wilson's "good" and "bad" blacks are distinctions at the second order, reflexive level. What second order distinctions do is set the structural terms of otherness within which the floating racial signifier can travel. This creates a continuum with two kinds of racial otherness at the poles. The first is represented by the "normal other" which represents whiteness within blackness— the "good" black who conforms to the prevailing normative code of expectations. The "good" black reproduces the primary racial distinction by appearing to negate it, by aspiring to be normal rather than different. The second kind of otherness is represented by the "radical other" which represents blackness within blackness—the "bad" black who flouts, disrupts and threatens both the substance and form of that code. The radical other reproduces the primary distinction by radicalizing it, extending the distance between its poles by an insistence on difference. The terms of reflexive distinction, between normal and radical otherness, provide the structural grounds on which power relations constrain the movement of the floating racial signifier. Power can only restrict meaning because of the way that the primary distinction through which signification operates doubles itself reflexively. Power relations do not anchor signification so much as complement and motivate it with social energy.

GREENE AND JOHNSON: A TRASH TALKING STORY

The relationship between Maurice Greene and Michael Johnson was explicitly defined in the international, English-language press as a trash talking relationship in a trash talking sport, and framed as part of a sprinting tradition—"(t)rash-talking is an age-old custom in the sprints." (Longman, 2000, p. D1; see also Patrick, 2000, p. 1C). Coverage of the verbal jousting between the two began in 1999 after Greene set a new world record for the men's 100m, becoming the first sprinter to break the 9.8 seconds barrier. It culminated in mid-2000 in the build up to the U.S. Olympic trials where the two were supposed to compete in the 200m. The anticipated showdown between them did not occur, and while media coverage of the conflict between the two athletes continued into the period of the Olympics, it began to wane in intensity and disappeared altogether in early 2001 when Johnson announced his intention to retire from active competition later that year. Greene remained a controversial figure in the coverage, but the focus shifted to his testy relationship with other sprint rivals. The evolution of the Greene-Johnson narrative reveals that several thematic frames were at work in the way the press situated the two athletes and their relationship in the context of a sporting rivalry that had become personal and verbally antagonistic, and many of these themes carried over to the representation of Greene's relationship with other competitors after Johnson left the scene. At the same time, it is also clear that their relationship, actions and claims were framed in asymmetrical terms. For the media, this relationship was a depiction of contrasts as the narrative generally reproduced the "good" black–"bad" black binary of reflexive otherness, albeit with some contradictory elements to the framing of both athletes.

From mid-1999 to the Olympic Games in September 2000 the relationship between Greene and Johnson evolved and intensified in the media from one of episodic rivalry to an ongoing and deeply felt antagonism that had existed for some time. Earlier metaphors of battles and duels gave way to the doubly inflected notion of a "running feud" (Wilson, 2000, p. 88). The relationship, however, was framed asymmetrically by the media. Greene was the centre of attention more so than Johnson. Greene was the instigator of what, by mid-2000, was described by the media as trash talk when he questioned Johnson's past achievements and intimated that he was avoiding competing against Greene for fear of losing to him. Yet although Greene was the centre of media attention, Johnson was by no means absent from the frame, especially in mid-2000 just before the US Olympic trials, where the two were expected to compete head-to-head in the 200m. Johnson, however, played a quite different role in the news narrative, that of respondent and self-defender rather than instigator. The media attempted to step back from the rivalry and see the relationship as one of verbal aggression on both sides, using third party voices such as other sprinters to achieve balance and convey an understanding of why trash talk was a standard feature of the sport in America. Nonetheless, the way the two rivals framed their remarks about one another differed significantly. For Greene, Johnson the athlete was the target of criticism and disparagement aimed at his character. For Johnson, Greene the (trash) talker was the target of criticism and reproach that denied him much character.

Greene

As the major centre of media attention, Greene was seen primarily as opinionated, brash, boastful, combative, egocentric, and hubristic. Even in the earlier coverage, in mid-1999 before Johnson made much of an appearance in the narrative, headlines began to use Greene's self-promoting personality to frame his role in the rivalry:

> Gatecrasher Greene; Mighty Maurice proves he's the world's fastest and says: They were going to party so I had to invite myself (Wilson, 1999);

> Leaving them Greene with envy; Friends and foes are on the lookout for the American who claims the title of world's fastest man (Burgess, 1999);

> Come and have a go if you think you're fast enough! says Maurice Greene (Cross, 1999);

> Greene tries to lure Johnson into battle for speed king crown (Gordon, 1999).

Similarly, the stories that reported on Greene's self-proclaimed greatness emphasized his egotistical penchant for goading his fellow competitors. A December 1999 story notes:

"The Kansas City Cannonball" oozes self-belief when asked who his major rivals are for another golden double in Australia in September. "Myself," he said in earnest. "I always say myself because I believe if I do what I have to do there's no reason why I can't win" (Cross, 1999, p. 39).

Even reports published closer to the opening of the Athens Games in 2004 provide further evidence that Greene's "take no prisoners" approach to competition was far from waning, for readers were informed that the sprinter had a shoulder tattoo that read "G.O.A.T." (greatest of all time) (Robbins, 2004). It was noted that Greene's rationalization for such a permanent marker went beyond sending a message to the current competition but to also declare that he was faster than all other 100m sprinters before his time.

Greene's excessive personality was seen in some reports as simply the most evident example of a style of self-serving hubris and trash talk that now predominated in American sprinting subculture. According to one (non-U.S.) report, the American team, led by Greene "The Baron of Boasting, His Highness of Hubris," was carving out a unique style of sporting competition in which psychological advantage was won through verbal self-promotion and disparagement of rivals (Humphries, 2000). Headlined "Boasting their way into U.S. hearts," this report in particular singled out Greene for what bordered on sarcastic criticism. Greene, we are told, would

> never feel silly, of course, he doesn't know the concept. Maurice is the original self-made guy who worships his creator .... Maurice thinks a hard day's work is 10 seconds of sprinting and 60 minutes of boasting. Who can argue? It's a hard call to know which he does best, the running or the bragging ... Maurice makes Muhammad Ali look self-effacing (Humphries, 2000, p. 59).

But Greene was only taking the leading role in what was becoming the norm for American sprinters generally. In contrast to "laid-back" or "pasty" sprinters from elsewhere, members of the American team were turning sprinting into "the world's top sport for self-promotion:"

> The new culture of boasting is making a breakthrough. Marion Jones has been punching more than her weight in the big talk stakes in the past couple of weeks, while Michael Johnson has even stepped out of the study to run his mouth a little and to give is (sic) hair slightly more of a gangster look ... Duelling sprinters getting on each other's nerves and trampling on each other's good lines are an irresistible draw ... Now is the time for boasting, now is the time for chest beating (Humphries, 2000, p.59).

More than just a tactic for competitive athletic success, self-promotional trash talking was turned by the media into yet another level of competition, one that occurred off the track and alongside it. The success of Greene's rhetorical challenge was evident in the fact that Johnson too finally engaged with the media in order to rebut and denigrate his rival's claims, thereby defending his name and reputation. In this respect, Greene's desire to "(g)et Michael Johnson—that's what I want to do" succeeded, at least in the pages of the press (Gillon, 2000, p. 10).

The trash talking rivalry between Greene and Johnson was largely deflated after the Olympic trials, but Greene remained in the spotlight as his trash talking migrated to rivalry with other sprinters. As one of his later rivals, John Capel, put it succinctly, "that's the way Maurice is." (Auman, 2000, p. 4). During the Sydney Games, Greene claimed victory in the 100m event and rightly earned bragging rights, yet in a rare instance expressed great humility after the race (*Toronto Star*, September 24, 2000). While seemingly out of character for Greene, it is speculated that this reaction was more of a response to his memory of the 1996 Atlanta Games where he failed to qualify for the 100m event yet ordered by his coach to watch the final race from the stands for motivation. At the end of the article, Greene states: "In Atlanta they were tears of sadness. Tonight they were tears of joy and of thanking God" (*Toronto Star*, September 24, 2000).

While resolution of Greene's feud with Johnson was denied in Sacramento, the 100m victory confirmed his status as an established star and as the "world's fastest human." What is noteworthy, however, is that as the newly minted established champion, Greene's trash talking rhetoric did not cease. Instead, with Johnson out of the picture, new rivalries were cultivated, and Greene's role as primary antagonist resumed as other sprinters like Tim Montgomery, John Capel, and Dwain Chambers moved into the role of challenger (see: Williams, 2001; Thomson, 2002; and Turnbull, 2002). This represented a narrative breach in that Greene did not assume the role of established star in the normative sense after earning the 100m crown; he continued to act as the newcomer who challenged others in order to establish status and authority. The renewal, restoration, and possibility of a recurring narrative of upstart challengers struggling to overthrow the established star was put in doubt by Greene's refusal to take on the latter role. By failing to relinquish his role as trash talking antagonist, Greene remained the centre of media attention as both antagonist (in a symbolic sense) and established star.

While the characterization of Greene as brash, opinionated, and self-promotional was clearly dominant throughout the coverage from 1999 to 2002, it was not, however, the only glimpse the media gave of him. In addition to Greene the braggart, we also briefly saw Greene the athlete who showed "inspiring graciousness" to annoying fans; Greene the aspiring sprinter who worked at low skilled manual jobs before his athletic success; and Greene the man with a "strong sense of family" (Burgess, 1999, p. A1; Patrick, 2000, p. 1C; Reed, 2000, p. 8). Even his arrogance and self-promotional hype were offset contextually by the media's acknowledgement of his ability and accomplishments on the track. The media granted Greene some latitude to claim bragging rights by virtue of his statistics: the world record for the 100m, more sub-10 second 100m races than Carl Lewis, and his world championship titles in the 100m and 200m. However distasteful, his hubris could claim some validity. The Hudson Smith International sports management company where Greene trained represented not only the "greatest fear" for American athletics because of its culture of hype and self-promotion, but also its "greatest hope" for raising the sport's profile among American sports fans (Humphries, 2000, p. 59).

Johnson

If Greene was seen for the most part as the instigator of the trash talking, the role Johnson played was chiefly that of respondent and defendant. This was most evident in the fact that in the press coverage Johnson did not respond in kind to Greene's attacks. For the most part Johnson did not disparage Greene's accomplishments or athletic talents *per se,* but focused instead on criticizing and rebutting Greene's criticisms and trashing, and in making inferences from the nature of Greene's criticisms about the latter's character, or lack thereof. By contrast to Greene's frontal attack on Johnson's actions—including evasions and inactions—Johnson's response operated at a more reflexive and inferential level. It was the antagonistic nature of Greene's words and claims rather than his actions that were the primary subject of Johnson's remarks. For the most part, Johnson's strategy was to take the moral high road, recognizing Greene's achievements and motivation to win, but disavowing the need to engage in personal attacks and character assassination as a tactic either to disarm the competition or to reassert his own status. These attacks were, for Johnson, a sign of Greene's immaturity, lack of confidence, and questionable athletic tactics. In an interview just before the U.S, Olympic trials, various newspapers uniformly quoted Johnson as saying:

> Maurice [Greene] is so immature with some of the things he says. He wants to become the greatest sprinter in the sport, the premier man of track and field, yet it can all be done without making personal attacks on me by saying things which are not true … I do dislike a lot of the things that Maurice Greene has said about me, a lot of the attempts he

has made to elevate himself by using me and my name, all of the things he has said about me are totally untrue and I don't like that (Evans, 2000, p. 73).

That's the difference between Maurice [Greene] and me—Maurice depends on me being afraid, and shutting down or breaking down, to win races ... It's obvious now that he feels the only way he can win this race is to make me break down (Gillon, 2000, p.10).

I think what Maurice [Greene] is trying to do is become a great sprinter and to supplant me as the premier track and field athlete ... That can all be done by the sheer fact that he won the world championship last year (at 100m and 200m) and was ranked No. 1 in the world. He deserves to be. I was ranked No. 2. That's all in line with the way it should be, and that in itself creates a great race.... For me this whole trash talking ... is not something that I enjoy. I have spent myself defending myself against things that have been printed, things that have been said, that have been unquestioned from Maurice, and his camp and from his coach and his agent ... you are not going to hear me trash talking or making personal attacks. I have promised myself and my family and my wife not to go down to that level (Cherry, 2000, p. 89).

The contextual framing of these remarks was structured in a way that accentuated the nature and degree of the conflict between Johnson and Greene. The remarks were seen as generally "uncharacteristic" of the "normally taciturn Johnson," and as representing a level of personal, emotionally charged animosity between the two men (Longman, 2000, p. D1). As one report put it more flamboyantly: "Once known as Mr. Cellophane because of his invisible personality, Michael Johnson has become Mr. Butane here at the US Olympic trials." (Evans, 2000, p. 73). The trash talking had escalated from a performative, even humorous, aspect of sprinting subculture to something more serious. Comments by both Johnson and Greene were described using a range of violent metaphors—broadside, striking back, verbal barrage, barrage of hype, verbal blows, slanging match, explosive cocktail, verbal skirmishing, and even "bad blood which only spilled blood will resolve" (Wilson, 2000, p. 88). Johnson was described by the media as being "dismissive of Greene the man, and Greene the personality," and as being "quick to berate" him (Hurst, 2000a, p. 96; 2000b, p. 44). The characterization of Johnson, like Greene, was double-edged, comprising a dominant and subordinate side. While Johnson was seen for the most part as an exceptional athlete defending his record of accomplishment against a brash, combative rival, he was also seen as somewhat aloof and arrogant, criticizing other athletes as inconsistent or otherwise lacking, and capable of showing little regard for those he was currently competing against. He was, for example, quoted in several papers saying: "Since Carl Lewis left this sport there has not been another athlete I'm excited about running against … there are no personalities that I get excited about competing against, such as Maurice [Greene]. They have no faces or names. They are just seven people who are standing in my way" (Hurst, 2000a, 96).

At the level of reflexive otherness Johnson represented whiteness within blackness, and his aloofness or arrogance represented the natural attitude of disregard in which the dominant hold the subordinate within any social field. Disregard and the withholding of respect or acknowledgement is a tactic of self-defense and exclusion or marginalization of others for those in positions of material or symbolic authority. As one report put it: "Sprinters are reluctant to speak respectfully of one another, Johnson said, for fear of showing vulnerability" (Longman, 2000, D1). The construction of Johnson's whiteness was largely implicit in the coverage. The reader was left to infer Johnson's status from occasional references to the sharp contrast between the two men in terms of socio-economic background—"the duo are worlds apart in their lives" (Lewis, 2000). Johnson, we were told, was a college graduate in marketing, while Greene, the "homeboy" and son of a prison officer who was not a "wealthy man," had

had to work at low-paid, menial jobs when pursuing his goal of athletic success (Cross, 1999; Evans, 2000; Lewis, 2000; Patrick, 2000; Reed, 2000). There was, however, at least one occasion in the coverage where Johnson's whiteness, and its association with class, were made more explicit—the day before the 200m semi-final at the US Olympic trials. Reasserting the tone of contrast between Johnson and Greene, one report noted that despite the predictions of high temperatures for the day of the race, "there will be a frostiness that would chill the hearts of the 23,000 fortunate to have tickets" to watch it. The report continued:

> Some claim that the bitterness goes beyond attention-seeking, that there are undertones of class and race. Johnson has a college degree, Greene never went to college. Johnson has a white wife, a white coach and a white manager. Greene is the all black street kid (Wilson, 2000, p. 88).

This binary contrast between what were overwhelmingly seen as two individual personalities had finally been given a social complexion.

DISCUSSION AND CONCLUSION

The distinction between whiteness and blackness that emerges within white and black at the reflexive level speaks not only to the doubling of otherness but also to transformations in the way that distinction works on each level. At the primary level of distinction, where one term, the term from which the distinction is generated, dominates, the logic of separation is one of lack. The subordinate lack is what characterizes the dominant and gives them their normative and normalizing capacity—power, wealth, esteem, taste, education, moral superiority, social ties, and so on. The subordinate are encouraged to emulate the dominant, but this is a contradictory project inasmuch as its success would erase the basis on which the distinction itself is made. This logic of lack gives rise, in turn, to the natural attitude of disregard in which the dominant hold the subordinate. This too is contradictory. The subordinate have to be recognized as such in order to be an object of indifference, and disregard can only function so long as the otherness of the other remains unnoticed and unobtrusive.

These contradictions in the logic of primary or first order distinctions play out actively at the reflexive or second order level, where they are regulated and internally managed rather than resolved, but with consequences that complicate the uniformity of racialization. At the level of reflexive otherness the logic of distinction becomes dynamic and dialectical. Both Greene and Johnson attempted to portray the other as lacking: for Greene, Johnson lacked nerve, courage, and a legitimate claim to his 200m world record; for Johnson, Greene lacked maturity, truthfulness, prudence and consistency as an athlete. The narrative of their claims and counter-claims, however, became a story of excess rather than lack. This was particularly so on the part of Greene who represented otherness within the other, the radical other. Situated by the media in the context of a trash talking relationship, both men came to exceed their role as celebrity athletes in the way they recreated and represented the distinction between white and black within blackness. For the media, this was a relationship that went beyond rather than fell short of the normal. Concomitant with the transformation of lack into excess was the transformation of disregard into spectacle. Each man attempted to hold the other in disregard by being explicit about the lack of respect or concern they had for the other. Both athletes were shown to be indifferent to or nonchalant about the threat the other posed on the track; their mutual disregard was strategic. For the media, however, this lack of regard or concern was framed as part of the spectacle of trash talking. Through the media's use of contrastive framing, reiteration of the longstanding, personalized nature of their antagonism, and the dualistic characterization of both men, Greene and Johnson were turned into figures of speculation and fascination. Both were objectified as distinct kinds of other who nonetheless shared a common status as celebrity athletes at a distance from the normal world.

The dialectic of lack and excess, and disregard and spectacle, go hand-in-hand with a third transformation that occurs between the primary and reflexive levels of otherness: the transformation of a distinction of race into a distinction of class within race. Class within race pertains not only to the sociological dimensions of class that were noted briefly by the media—Johnson the college graduate and Greene the "black street kid"—but also to class in the everyday, common sense or symbolic meaning of the term: class in the sense of classiness. While both athletes were recognized for their exceptional athletic records, they were not seen as equivalent. Greene was viewed as the brash, self-centered instigator of trash talk while Johnson was represented chiefly as someone defending himself against criticism about the legitimacy of his achievements. The sociological class differences between them were replicated at the level of symbolic, common sense class difference.

The class distinction between Greene and Johnson, however, was not absolute as each was represented in dualistic and ambivalent terms. Greene's humble origins, his graciousness towards annoying fans, and his commitment to family, compared with Johnson's aloofness and disregard for his rivals represented a subordinate side to each of their characterizations. The reflexive level of distinction entails no more total or complete a code of inclusion and exclusion than the primary level of distinction from which it is self-generating. What the dualism of each man's representation speaks to is the fact that class distinctions are legitimate to the extent that boundaries are permeable and open to mobility. One can cross over class boundaries in a way that one cannot cross over racial ones; racial mobility is only possible, collectively or individually, in class terms. As distinct individuals, Greene and Johnson could conceivably trade places as radical and normal others. Those places themselves, however, could not change without eradication of the first order racial distinction whose reflexive articulation they are.

REFERENCES

Andrews, D.L. (1996). The fact(s) of Michael Jordan's blackness: Excavating a floating racial signifier. *Sociology of Sport Journal, 13,* 125-158.

Auman, G. (2000, September 7). Capel, Greene have running feud. *St. Petersburg Times,* p. 4.

Bourdieu, P. (1993). *The field of cultural production: Essays on art and literature.* Edited and introduced by Randal Johnson. New York: Columbia University Press.

Burgess, Z. (1999, June 27). Leaving them Greene with envy; Friends and foes are on the lookout for the American who claims the title of world's fastest man. *The Washington Times,* p. A1.

Cherry, G. (2000, July 23). Athletics: sprinters in word war; Johnson strikes back at "totally untrue" claims made by world ace rival Greene. *Sunday Mercury,* p. 89.

Cross, J. (1999, December 14). Come and have a go if you think you're fast enough! says Maurice Greene. *The Mirror,* p. 39.

Evans, L. (2000, July 22). MJ's turn to trash and burn. *Sydney Morning Herald,* p. 73.

Foucault, M. (1980) *Power/Knowledge: Selected interviews and other writings, 1972-1977.* Edited by Colin Gordon; translated by Colin Gordon [et al.]. New York: Pantheon Books.

Gillon, D. (2000, July 22). Sprinters at war before showdown on the track. *The Herald,* p. 10.

Gordon, I. (1999, September 6). Greene tries to lure Johnson into battle for speed king crown. *Birmingham Post,* p. 28.

Greene swept up in emotion of emphatic 100-metre win. (2000, September 24). *Toronto Star,* p. sports.

Hall, S. (1990/1981). The whites of their eyes: Racist ideologies and the media. In M. Alvarado & J.O. Thompson. (Eds.), *The Media Reader* (pp. 7-23). London: British Film Institute.

Hartmann, D. (2007). Rush Limbaugh, Donovan McNabb, and "A little social concern": Reflections on the problems of whiteness in contemporary American sport. *Journal of Sport and Social Issues, 31,* 45-60.

Humphries, T. (2000, July 17). Boasting their way into U.S. hearts. *The Irish Times,* p. 59.

Hurst, M. (2000a, July 20). Greene with envy. *Herald Sun* (Melbourne), p. 96.

Hurst, M. (2000b, July 20). Superman zaps back at sassy Kryptonite. *Hobart Mercury,* p. 44.

Lewis, R. (2000, July 22). Showdown in Sacramento. *The Express,* no page numbers.

Longman, J. (2000, July 19). OLYMPICS: THE ROAD TO SYDNEY; Johnson Vs. Greene: High Noon Looming in the 200. *The New York Times,* p. D1.

Luhmann, N. (2002). *Theories of distinction: Redescribing the descriptions of modernity.* Edited and introduced by William Rasch; translations by Joseph O'Neil [et al.]. Stanford, CA: Stanford University Press.

Majors, R. and J.M. Billson. (1992). *Cool pose: The dilemmas of black manhood in America.* New York: Simon and Schuster.

Mehlman, J. (1972). The "floating signifier": from Lévi-Strauss to Lacan. *Yale French Studies, 48:* 10-37.

Patrick, D. (2000, July 21). Clock ticks toward shut up and put up Johnson, Greene sets sights on 200. *USA Today,* p. 1C.

Reed, R. (2000, September 21). Greene talks the talk. *Herald Sun* (Melbourne), p. 8.

Robbins, L. (2004, August 8). The best ever (according to him). *The New York Times,* p. 3.

Schneider, R.C., and R.E. Baker. (2007, Winter) Trash talking practices and reactions in sport: a qualitative examination. *International Council for Health, Physical Education, Recreation, Sport and Dance 43*(1), pp. 26-31.

Simons, H.D. (2003). Race and penalized sports behaviours. *Sociology of Sport Journal, 38,* 5-22.

Thomson, P. (2002, June 27). Fast talking which is fuelling a bitter feud. *The Evening Standard,* p. 73.

Tudor, A. (1998). Sports reporting: Race, difference and identity. In K. Brants, J. Hermes, and L. van Zoonen (Eds.), *The media in question: Popular cultures and popular interests* (pp. 147-156). London: Sage.

Turnbull, S. (2002, January 9). One short race, two angry men; Greene and Montgomery don't like each other at all. Simon Turnbull sees fireworks ahead. *The Independent*, p. 21.

Wenner, L. (1995). The good, the bad, and the ugly: Race, sport and the public eye. *Journal of Sport and Social Issues, 19*: 227-31.

Wilson, B. (1997). "God blacks" and "bad blacks": Media construction of African-American athletes in Canadian basketball. *International Review for the Sociology of Sport, 32,* 177-189.

Wilson, N. (1999, June 18). Gatecrasher Greene; Mighty Maurice proves he's the world's fastest and says: They were going to party so I had to invite myself. *Daily Mail*, p. 81.

Wilson, N. (2000, July 22). Fight to the finish: Greene and Johnson face moment of truth in their running feud. *Daily Mail*, p. 88.

Williams, R. (2001, August 4). Greene already leads mental race: The swaggering Olympic Champion's fitness is the major concern. *The Guardian*, p. 6.

"Authentic" Scottishness and Problematized Irishness in Scottish International Football

BY JOSEPH M. BRADLEY

INTRODUCTION

Eric Hobsbawm (1990), well known for his research on nationalism and invented traditions, accepts the role of sport in that process. Using a football metaphor, he contends that "the identity of a nation of millions, seems more real as a team of eleven named people" (p.4). Similarly, Dan Burdsey and Bob Chappell (2004, p.2) write of "the symbiotic relationship between football and social identity." These authors are among many who have demonstrated links between soccer and community self image. In terms of football in Scotland, Walker (1990), Finn (1991, 1991, 1994 & 1994), Bairner (1994), and Boyle et al (1994, 1996 & 2000) have each published significant research. These historical and sociological studies have reflected upon ideas of Scottishness and have deliberated on the complex mix between nationality, religion, cultural identity, and football. Giulianotti's (1994 & 1995) research has featured ethnographic studies into the followers of Scotland's national side. These supporters are commonly referred to as Scotland's "Tartan Army."

STUDYING THE TARTAN ARMY

In 2002 I contributed to this field of research with a survey of Tartan Army supporters (2002). This work focused mainly on issues of ethnicity, politics, religion, and identity, which proved to be pivotal in explaining the construction of different versions of Scottishness in relation to the national football team.

The present chapter takes that research in three further directions. First, it reflects on Scottish sports media discourses, specifically those concerned with football at an international level. These discourses demonstrate that "football talk" goes beyond mere sport and, indeed, reflects the media's capacity to articulate, interpret, categorize, and produce significant notions of identity. This chapter therefore evaluates a distinctive characteristic of Scottish national football identity and its construction by profiling voices and ideas about the ethnic Irish "other" in Scottish society.

Second, this chapter reports on qualitative inquiry via focus groups, which were ideal for the purpose of generating fan data on collective identities. Della Porta and Diani (1999) define identity, not as an autonomous object or a property possessed by individuals, but:

> rather as a process through which social actors come to recognise themselves, and be recognised by others, as a cohesive group.

These focus groups were set up via researcher contact with branches of the Tartan Army spread throughout much of the country (Armadale & West Lothian, Badenoch & Strathspey, Dundee & the east coast, Kircaldy & South Fife, Lanarkshire, North of Scotland, Perthshire, North Ayrshire, Glasgow & Strathclyde, Airdrie and West Lothian). Participating supporters also align themselves with sixteen professional soccer clubs in Scotland including Hearts, Motherwell, Celtic, Glasgow Rangers, and Aberdeen, which overall are supported by around ninety percent of fans of Scottish professional football.

The age range of the interviewees was typically between twenty and fifty and, while predominantly male (as are most fans of football in Scotland), around half of the interview groups also contained female participants. Interviewees were unknown to the interviewer prior to requests to meet with the groups. Respondents were given aliases to protect their anonymity, but the club they supported and similar fan information is indicated openly in this paper.

The interviews focused on how, for members of the Tartan Army, their identities as Scotland supporters are constructed. This was done by inquiring into the understandings and perceptions that constitute the attitudes of the Tartan Army, and as a result, the national and cultural identities that are pre-eminent among them. By virtue of being active supporters of the Scottish international football team, the interviewees already shared patterns of behavior and identities. Nevertheless, the research aimed to look beyond what may or may not be considered surface values and behavior, and establish what constituted the subterranean, fundamental, and sub-text levels of identity. In short, what understandings and perceptions contribute to the notion of the Tartan Army, and indeed, significant common elements of this popular Scottish identity?

Third, this chapter examines Scottish club football and wider social perceptions and commentary in relation to ethnic Irishness in Scotland. This is intended to illustrate links and connections between ethnic Irishness and Scottish culture and identity beyond the Scottish international environment. The overarching assumption is that discourses within and around football disclose the contested nature of the characteristics of culture, national identity, and "other" identity narratives in Scotland. These findings are substantiated via research carried out among the supporters of numerous football clubs in Scotland, including extensive studies of both Rangers and Celtic supporters. In addition, analysis of the Scottish sports media in relation to these contestations is ongoing; this will add important interpretive layers to the findings presented here.

BACKGROUND

Sport is a public social space that, for critical analysts, can offer insights into contested matters that might remain obscure to the casual observer. In terms of football, Sugden and Tomlinson (1994), Armstrong and Giulianotti (1997), and Brown (1998) have each shown that politics has resonance in the football environment in countries as diverse as Norway, Italy, Argentina, Australia, and Spain. The study of football can therefore expose the importance of class, nationalism, ethnicity, racism, ideology, or other identity shaping factors.

In a similar vein, observers of Scottish football (Bradley, 2004, 2006 & 2009; Esplin, 2000; Bairner, 1994; Walker, 1990) have long noted that such factors are intrinsic and meaningful to various club histories and supporters' sense of traditional and contemporary identities. To what extent, though, can football be considered a mirror of, and even door into, key issues in wider Scottish society? This study builds on understanding and knowledge acquired from previous research, which here focuses on mediated relationships between the Scottishness of the Tartan Army and the (immigrant) Irishness of Celtic Football Club and its supporters.

CONTESTED IDENTITIES:
IRISHNESS AND THE MEDIA

In 1887-88 Celtic FC was founded by Irish Catholic immigrants in the west of Scotland. From the outset, the club has been a symbol and representation of ethnic, cultural, and political Irishness in Scotland. Although Celtic is supported by people of varying ethnic and religious backgrounds, the vast majority of the club's followers are the offspring of Irish migrants who came to Scotland in the years during and after the Great Irish Hunger of 1845-52, when over one million Irish died and over one million emigrated as refugees—around 100,000 of these to Scotland. Mass emigration from Ireland to Scotland continued for several decades, peaking in the 1880s and remaining significant until the outbreak of the First World War. Apart from a rise for a decade or so after the Second World

War, lesser numbers of Irish have arrived in Scotland up until the present day. Since the 19th century, the Irish have made numerous social, religious, educational, cultural, and political contributions to Scottish society. Among these, Celtic Football Club is one of the major success stories of Scottish sport and society. As former European Champions and as a world-renowned soccer institution, Celtic Football Club is a monument to the presence and advancement of the Irish and their offspring in modern Scotland. The Irish in Scotland remain that country's greatest single minority ethnic community of migrant descent.

In Scotland sports media discourses contribute towards the construction of Scottishness, including its links to ethnicity, religion, and football. These discourses reflect a dominant assumption about the singularity and unity of Scottish identity including a view that supporting Scotland at football is normal, conventional, and expected, especially of people born there. Importantly, as far as football and its related wider cultural and social milieu is concerned, this "authentic" Scottishness is also conceptualized and composed as oppositional to Celtic and their supporters' Irishness.

A significant thread in the relevant discourses is that everyone should come together under a common Scottish identity because, as one Scottish sports media journalist and radio presenter repeatedly says, "We are all Scots and we are all football supporters ... After all, we are Scottish, aren't we?" (BBC Radio Scotland, *Your Call*, September 28, 2002 & *The Daily Record*, May 8, 2006); and, "I'm not saying forget your roots, forget your past, but we're all Scottish" (BBC Radio Scotland, January 14, 2007). This ubiquitous Scottish sports media journalist and radio presenter, Jim Traynor, also opined on BBC Radio Scotland:

> I regard myself as a Scot ... It's 2006 we're supposed to be civilized ...we have this baggage from an era that most of these people know nothing about ... in this day and age, we don't need this kind of support (January 14, 2007)

In the same year a popular Radio Clyde show discussed Celtic's withdrawal of three players from a Scotland squad taking part in a challenge/friendly tournament in Asia to instead play in a club testimonial match against Manchester United. This prompted Iain King, a regular panel member on Radio Clyde 1 (May 9, 2006), to say disapprovingly:

> I think we should all be proud to be Scotland fans and we should all be hoping that the nation should get back to major finals ... I'm a passionate Scotland supporter and I would like to see other people have that same passion for the Scotland team.

A caller to BBC Radio Scotland (August 22, 2002) shared this view stating that:

> if we all came out with the fact and said we were Scottish instead of half Celtic fans thinking they're Irish ... It all boils down to the fact that people need to stand up and be counted as Scottish.

The principal, patriotic narratives produced by the Scottish sports media are constructed in the interests of a majority audience, but in addition, in other relevant contexts, they dominate to the extent that they ignore or negatively label Irish ethnic narratives in Scotland as subordinate and "other." In this way Scottishness is portrayed as more genuine, trustworthy, secular, reflective of "reality," healthier, and advanced. Additionally, this "authentic" Scottishness is constructed as free of the "fruitless" and counter-productive baggage connected with identities that are not Scottish, or perceived as not Scottish enough. Such "other" identities may complicate or obstruct the appearance and performance of "authentic" Scottishness, because as repeatedly stated, "after all, we are Scottish, aren't we?" This is a statement about cultural singularity, which is a contrast to the plurality and diversity typical of a multicultural or intercultural approach to society.

When Celtic's Aiden McGeady, a young, third-generation Scots-born Irishman expressed his wish to play for Ireland—the country from where his family and community had originated—football fans outside of the Celtic supporting environment across Scotland appeared to unite in their condemnation. At Celtic Park in August 2004, visiting Motherwell fans abused McGeady and, in a show of counter-patriotism, sang the popular Scottish anthem "Flower of Scotland." At Hearts home ground, Tynecastle, on April 25 of the same year, BBC Scotland football commentator Chick Young stated that he was to interview McGeady after the match, adding: "I'll need to take down a bottle of whisky and some shortbread to Scottify him." On the same show this commentator's fellow broadcaster Gordon Smith (subsequently to become Chief Executive of the Scottish Football Association), himself a former professional footballer, denied the player's own sense of national and cultural identity, and by association others like him in Scotland, by arguing that McGeady was Scottish-born and thus a Scot:

> He may well have chosen to play for Ireland, as far as I'm concerned the boy was born in Scotland and that makes him Scottish and that's the end of the matter.

A popular Scottish tabloid columnist John McKie reiterated these sentiments (*The Daily Record,* April 14, 2009). He referred to McGeady as a "pretend Irishman" and stated that those Celtic fans who thought the same way as McGeady "do our country [Scotland] a disservice."

As far as football commentator and newspaper columnist Stuart Cosgrove was concerned, Hearts supporters' abuse of McGeady was legitimate, acceptable, and understandable (*The Daily Record,* December 30, 2004, p.67). He believed that McGeady had turned his back on Scotland, showed a lack of patriotism (that his patriotism was for Ireland did not count) and was therefore disloyal to Scotland. He further hoped that McGeady "has a miserable career as an Irish internationalist." During this period, complaints about McGeady dominated radio phone-ins and Scottish football columns and this flamed public debate. In *The Daily Record,* Scotland's biggest selling tabloid newspaper, leading writer John McKie backed the abuse directed towards McGeady arguing that:

> This isn't about sectarianism, this is about being Scottish and proud of it. McGeady has been educated here, used our health service and learned all his football in Glasgow. But thanks to his mum, he has now chosen to play for the Irish national team. It's heartbreaking. Its time all Scottish Celtic fans got over their obsession with Ireland. The fact that Glasgow sports shops sell as many Ireland football tops as Scotland football tops is both pathetic and ultimately unhelpful (*The Daily Record*, May 1, 2005, p.11).

The tenor of this disparagement is consistent throughout much of the Scottish football media and beyond, where hostile and disapproving columnists state that expressions of Irishness in football in Scotland are erroneous and should be condemned. In his *Daily Record* column, lead sports writer Jim Traynor attempted to pre-empt accusations of anti-Irish ignorance, prejudice, and racism by stating that his hostility was not based on an anti-Irish agenda, only that he was a proud Scot who made "No apologies for that and this fixation with Ireland which so many Scots [i.e., Scots born Irish in Scottish football who are Celtic supporters] have makes my blood boil" (May 2, 2005, p.24).

Prior to the McGeady imbroglio, a former Young Scottish Journalist of the Year, John MacLeod (The Herald, February 18, 2002, p.12), criticized Celtic supporters for seeing:

> No inconsistency in packing their ground to wave the flag of another country. They flap the Irish tricolor and sing sad Irish songs and roar of the Irish struggle. There's a country called Ireland for goodness sake, why don't they go and live there?

The Scottishness represented and projected by these excerpts is characteristic of much of the Scottish sports media and reflect hostility and disregard towards the ethnic Irishness of Celtic and its supporters. In addition, the media discourse in football depicts Scottishness as being inherently opposed to Irishness—a situation that arguably creates conflict and has serious repercussions for wider social relations in Scottish life. The football media indicate that there are a number of expectations with regard to performing Scottishness and living in Scotland. They also demonstrate negative and hostile attitudes towards football supporters in Scotland who do not, via their ethnic Irish affinities and identities, adhere to these expectations of Scottishness.

CONTESTED IDENTITIES: IRISHNESS AND THE TARTAN ARMY

For over one hundred years football in Scotland has been the most popular team sport. Nevertheless, despite periods of success in European club competitions, including numerous semi-final and final appearances, with Celtic, Rangers, and Aberdeen each winning the main European club football tournaments during the 1960s, 1970s, and 1980s, at an international level Scottish achievement has been limited to initial group stage appearances at several World Cup and European Championship Finals. However, this lack of success has not hindered local passion for the Scottish international side and, since the 1980s, the Tartan Army has won the favor of many "football countries" at European and World football tournaments through enthusiasm and fervor for their team, large numbers travelling abroad, and a willingness to party wherever they go. These behaviors and attitudes have been described by Giulianotti (1995) as carnivalesque. Although some Scots fans developed a negative reputation in the 1970s (a period of intense British football hooliganism) with drunken and loutish behavior, usually at the bi-annual England versus Scotland match at London's Wembley Stadium, the Tartan Army has successfully reinvented itself in polar opposition to English football fans' notorious hooligan behavior at international matches across Europe. This change partly mirrors a desire to ensure that people abroad realize that although also from Britain, the Scots are unequivocally not English.

This paper now draws upon interviews conducted with the Tartan Army and is particularly concerned with the theme of Scottishness vis-à-vis Irishness in the Scottish international football environment. Focus groups proved to be a useful way of garnering opinions from within this collective and its various regional representatives.

Jason, from the Armadale Sons of Wallace branch of the Tartan Army, spoke in heartening terms of support for the Scottish team, believing it was a metaphor for a society shorn of perceived problematic ethnic, national, and religious distinctions: "If the rest of Scotland had the same belief and used the Tartan Army as a sort of standard, Scotland would be a better place, far better place, I really believe that." This comment is indicative of various remarks made by supporters regarding such distinctions. A significant example of this is in how Tartan Army narratives in support of the Scottish international side often relate to, and are a counterpoint against, declarations of Irish ethnicity in Scotland. As Airdrie supporter Gary argued in his focus group:

> You get all these Celtic fans running about with Republic of Ireland tops on. You go, "what are you wearing that for ... you're Scottish ... you are Scottish but because your f— great-grandmother's aunty fanny Annie was a f— Irishman you're going to support Irish? F— does my nut in that.

Adam, a member of the West of Scotland Tartan Army, had a similar view:

> This bus [we passed]. We saw a Tricolor and we thought, these must be Irish fans and we drove up to the back of it, and on it was "Coatbridge [a town in Scotland which contains a much higher than average number of diasporic Irish] Irish" ... we brought one of my friends, his cousins from Dublin, and he

came on the bus with us and then, there were guys walking up to him, and he'd walk up to guys with Tricolors on and Irish strips on [Scots born Irish supporters]. He'd go up to them with his Irish accent and ask, "how you doing guys"? But they were as broad Glaswegian as you've ever heard.

Hearts fan Donald, from the Armadale Sons of Wallace Tartan Army, commented on the Scotland versus Ireland game in Glasgow played in 2003:

The majority of the boys here, we were all at the Scotland v. Ireland game at Hampden. What got me was the amount of Scottish supporters that were walking right by the Scotland end and going in to the Irish and supporting Ireland.

From the same focus group, Dunfermline fan Jason shared the hostile feelings regarding Scots-born people supporting Ireland:

You're talking about your countrymen there. There's people from Scotland there that are supporting the opposing nation … It is more the disdain of that and seeing your own countrymen walk by you to the other side.

Sandy, an Airdrie supporter with the West Lothian branch of the Tartan Army, concurred:

The closest I've seen it was actually the Scotland v. Republic Ireland game just last year at Hampden, because of the fact that people were really getting miffed, the fact that the Irish support was all speaking with Scottish accents. I know that was bugging a few guys because the Irish support had half the Rangers end … You know, where did these extra two thousand supporters come from, they only had two thousand tickets and there's four thousand [of their] supporters in the ground?

Jamie from the North Ayrshire branch of the Tartan Army was also disconcerted at the idea of Scots-born members of the Irish diaspora supporting Ireland in international soccer:

> We walked into a pub last night, first thing that hit us in the eye, guy with an Ireland top on. He's making a statement, he's not supporting ... [Scotland] he's making a statement or some other statement, [but] he's not Irish [by birth], that's for sure.

Dug from the Lanarkshire-based branch recognized that many Celtic supporters were not fans of Scotland.

> I think there's more from Aberdeen, Dundee, Edinburgh, 'round about that area. Lanarkshire-wise, Glasgow-wise there's not that many ... I find, well, a lot of the Celtic fans that I know, don't go. They would wear an Ireland top before they would wear a Scotland top.

Bill, from the South Fife Tartan Army based in Kirkcaldy, had at various times supported different Scottish clubs, but being a supporter of Scotland was his strongest passion. Perhaps surprisingly, he revealed that in the Scottish Premier League he "liked to see Celtic win," even though he didn't actively support them. He did not have a Catholic or Irish family background that was typical of most Celtic supporters, but argued that "those kinds of things" (having a Catholic or Irish background) were "seriously frowned on [in Fife]," though he added, "We're all Jock Tamson's Bairns." He favored Celtic when having to choose a team to support on television, but he had no time for Celtic supporters displaying their Irishness when abroad:

> It's piss poor in my opinion that you watch them representing a Scottish side in Europe and if you look behind the Bayern Munich end you've got nine-tenths of running track is all full of Tricolors.

Despite Bill's idea that in the region of Fife everyone was one was seen as one of "Jock Tamson's Bairns"—a Scottish notion of "live and let live" and commonality—it is clear that Irishness in Scotland is not privileged as a part of this imagined community.

CONSTRUCTING SCOTTISHNESS IN FOOTBALL

Mass communications are important for the mediation of ideas about nationalism and national identity (Law, 2001, p.302). A national sports media is invariably characterized by matters that reflect and shape aspects of a country's history, political life, cultural attributes, popular humor, religious identities, and social preoccupations. Similarly, the media may also act as a barometer of such characteristics. In relation to soccer, the Scottish sports media is dominated by voices and text that support a sense of nationhood that is "authentically" Scottish, but which in the process also discounts and marginalizes recognition of the immigrant Irishness that has helped shape the nation's football culture for more than 100 years.

The Scottish sports media facilitates the construction, promotion, and endorsement of support for Scotland and general Scottish identity, and the Tartan Army do likewise. What they perceive as "authentically Scottish" (e.g., history, geography, dress, attitudes, names, music, as well as various individual and national achievements, etc.) is partly achieved by their endeavors to be distinctive. For example, central to the identity of the Tartan Army is the use of visual and linguistic identity markers to demonstrate that Scotland, although British and therefore sharing many aspects of history, culture, and identity with England, has a distinctive narrative and character.

This paper notes the importance of such markers in the construction of Scottishness, but it has also demonstrated that references to ethnic Irishness also play a role in the formation, production and performance of Scottishness in football.

IRISHNESS IN SCOTTISH CLUB FOOTBALL AND BEYOND

Within the Scottish sports media the lack of acknowledgment and an absence of accommodating narratives about Irishness is a key strand in Scottish football, culture and history. This is despite Irishness being the most significant minority ethnicity in multicultural Scotland. While the Tartan Army was conceived and functions within the context of a perceived set of "authentically" Scottish principals, it might be expected that the sports media in Scotland would do a better job of reflecting more accurately the reality of Scotland's ethnic and multicultural mix. This reality can be viewed and contextualized in light of the recent Scottish Government's "One Scotland Many Cultures" campaign that seeks to address this increasing social and cultural complexity and the racism that such a mix can engender.[1]

Whether this Irishness is expressed by the multi-generational Irish community in Scotland through support for the Irish international football team, via third generation Irish people like Celtic's Aidan McGeady choosing to play for the Irish international side, the singing of Irish songs, the display of Irish symbols and emblems by Celtic supporters, or through other Irish in Scotland manifestations, Irishness is comprehensively seen as contrary to "authentic Scottishness" and opposed by both the Tartan Army and the Scottish sports media. For the offspring of Irish migrants to Scotland, their distinctiveness becomes especially manifest and visible to the rest of Scottish society when they congregate and celebrate Irishness through Celtic Football Club. It is also in the Scottish football environment that hostility towards Irish ethnicity and cultural identities can become public and intensify. This is unambiguous in the interviews with members of the Tartan Army. It is also clear on the part of the sports media where the Irishness of that diaspora in Scotland is not tolerated.

This hostility also extends to the club scene in Scotland where such references are recurrent. In 2006, Dundee United fans chanted to Celtic supporters "Can you sing a Scottish song?" while Aberdeen fans frequently taunt Celtic supporters with "You're in the wrong country" (January 28, 2006). Motherwell supporters chanted this towards Celtic's Aiden McGeady in February 2009 and to Hamilton's James McCarthy at a Scottish Premier League match the previous week. McCarthy is also Scottish born, third generation Irish who plays for Ireland in international soccer. In Glasgow (December 17, 2006), Rangers fans held a banner up to Celtic supporters with the slogan, "This is our city, where in Ireland is Glasgow?"

Rangers' fans drew some media attention during 2008 and 2009 when sections of their fans sang to Celtic supporters: "The Famine is over, why don't you go home?" When a discussion was aired on BBC Radio 4 on "Boxing Day" in December 2008, a Rangers fan interviewed on the show stated that in relation to "The Famine Song":

> The song is about people who are British but who wish to be Irish and would prefer to be Irish and we're saying "Ok, go to Ireland and be Irish or be British".

Another said:

> There's almost this plastic Paddyism that happens over here … but at every opportunity they keep telling us they're Irish … if you don't like it here then leave, it's the old when in Rome scenario, they're in our country now.

A different interviewee stated:

> They're clinging to this link to Ireland. This is a small country that can't incorporate a lot of ethnic minorities … this is about people purporting to be Irish when in fact they're not, they're Scottish.

These types of arguments are dominant throughout Scottish football fandom at club and international level, are replicated in the Scottish media, and unite opposition towards Irishness in Scotland. One popular TV, radio, and newspaper pundit discounted the possibility of any racist connotations or intentions in the singing of "The Famine Song" on BBC Radio Scotland's "Sportsound" (September 13, 2008) program. Further, when referring to Celtic supporters' Irishness, he derisively and mockingly added that having recently played Motherwell (the club he supports) he would congratulate them for "at last" having "sung a Scottish song at the match." This was because Celtic supporters had sung "Go home ya huns go home" to the tune of "Auld Lang Syne," a well known Scottish song. In 2001 a Scottish tabloid newspaper columnist and radio commentator aligned himself with the sentiments of the Famine song chorus when he stated to those of Irish descent in Scotland who are Celtic supporters (News of the World, May 6, 2001 & October 7, 2001):

> Plastic Irishmen and women who drink in plastic Irish pubs and don't know their Athenry from their Antrim ... perhaps they could do us all a favor and relocate to Dublin.

Celtic's third generation Irish player Aiden McGeady has been a recipient of many similar sentiments in the Scottish media. A typical comment towards McGeady was offered by one newspaper's columnist (The Daily Star, Scottish Edition, December 31, 2004, p.27):

> That wee traitor Aiden McGeady, who turned his back on the land of his birth to play international football for a foreign country ... McGeady got shirracked by Hearts fans at the weekend and will get booed wherever he goes because of his decision and I don't really see how he can expect anything else.

In wider Scottish society there exist similar discourses beyond Scottish football showing how the sport can reflect and inform broader cultural and national narratives regarding Scottish identity and otherness. This includes debates about the appropriateness and acceptability of Irish St Patrick's Day celebrations in Scotland. There have also been arguments in Scotland about memorials and monuments to Irish immigrants, some feeling that this detracts from the core meta-narrative of Scottish history and identity. Such examples show that anti-Irishness in Scotland and notions of Scottish authenticity are not limited to football.

CONCLUSION

Football is one of "the most representative aspects of mass and popular culture at the beginning of the twenty-first century" (Castro-Ramos, 2008, p.696). Mirroring this assertion, football is the most popular team sport in Scotland as is reflected in its high profile and prominence in the media as well as by the many thousands that attend as spectators on a regular basis. In terms of culture and identity, football takes a varying but significant meaning for many people.

Football does not exist in a social and cultural vacuum and can be seen as varyingly connected to, and as an extension of, everyday living (Stone, 2007, pp.169-184). John Sugden and Alan Tomlinson (1998, p.171) regard the world's most popular team sport as a critical site and source "for the expression of forms of collective belonging, affiliation, and identity." Through the use of interviews and by focusing on sports media narratives, this study has reflected an intertwining of ethnicity, religion, and national identity in Scotland and indicates that football has a significant role and meaning in wider Scottish society. The Scottish international football environment is a location and space for claims about shared social, cultural, national, religious, and sometimes political ideas, emotions, allegiances and identities. As a place for concomitant collective antagonisms, hostilities, resentments, rivalries, and prejudices, the Scottish football environment is also an arena for the contestation of numerous identities that help form modern Scottish society.

Although club teams create, nourish, and reflect distinctive community passions, on the international football stage support for Scotland is widespread and is shared by many fans throughout these clubs and, of course, in the sports media and in other parts of society. This support is a dominant feature of sporting life in Scotland, so much so that Giulianotti and Gerrard (2001, p.34) refer to the Scottish national team as "the sporting symbol of Scotland." Analysis of the Scottish international football environment shows nonetheless that, like all imagined communities, and as with the wider society, there are dominant narratives involving personal, community, ideological, and symbolic identities. As popular mass institutions, the Scottish sports media and international football followers significantly "participate in the idea of the [Scottish] nation ... and symbolic community" (Hall, 1196, p. 612).

This work reveals a grand narrative of Scottishness and supporting Scotland as a process, distinctive from or in opposition to other identities manifest in Scotland. These identities are not Mexican, Chinese, Ukrainian or any similar other, but essentially ethnic, religious, and national identities that have historical significance as to how Scotland and Scottishness have evolved, developed, and functioned in recent centuries. This is particularly so in terms of the British conquest of Ireland, including Scotland's key involvement in the plantation of the northern Irish province of Ulster, the subsequent evolution of the British Empire, Protestantism as Scotland's national faith, including a prevailing anti-Catholicism, and negative Scottish reactions against Catholic immigrants and their descendents from Ireland. These discursive constructions of dominant Scottishness and subjugated Irishness in turn both "shape and reflect their socio-historical contexts" (Hall, 1996, p.612).

The discourses that dominate within the Tartan Army and Scottish sports media function not only to reflect, but also to formulate and reproduce content, symbolic boundaries and markers of Scottishness, as well as aspirations about what Scottishness and Scotland "should" mean. These boundaries have evolved in the context of complex historical events and developments.

For the Tartan Army, other football fans and the Scottish sports media, the construction of Scottishness also invokes questions regarding the presence or otherwise of social and cultural spaces in Scotland that accepts and/or allows for the acknowledgement, representation, and expression of social and cultural distinctiveness not based on popular or dominant notions of Scottishness. For example, Britishness, Englishness, and religious identities form significant aspects of the direct or indirect discourses of identity that arise from the Tartan Army and the sports media, and it is evident that there are various levels of resentment and opposition, as well as affinity, towards these. This is particularly the case with regards to the ethnic Irishness of the offspring of Irish immigrants in Scotland, something that brings many people from within and beyond football together in mutual hostility and antagonism.

For many who are passionate about their Scottishness through football, "other" ethnic, national, and religious distinctions in Scotland can be dismissed as not conforming to the principal and prevailing narratives of cultural and national acceptance. In this instance, Scottishness can also be viewed as a symbolic boundary, a mark of acceptance assembled on the part of those that see themselves as "authentic" Scots. This paper has focused on how this authenticity is partly constructed via a process of "othering" with regards to Irishness in Scotland. In terms of immigrant Irishness in Scotland, this shows that Irishness is constructed as not simply distinctive, and even "negatively" different, but more revealingly as "oppositional" to Scottishness. This demonstrates that in Scottish football (and often beyond) there is little room for the acceptance of such ethnic variation. For these Scots, Scottishness is not only dominant and primary, but such "authenticity" requires the marginalization of an Irishness that should be forgotten, concealed, repulsed, denied, or erased.

The Tartan Army is, as expected, self-consciously assembled and conceptualized specifically and emblematically as "authentically" Scottish. Reflecting how they construct and imagine themselves, the purpose of the Tartan Army is to "be" Scottish and to passionately support the Scottish international football team as an expression of that patriotism. As with all such identities, this entails processes of assimilation, inclusion and exclusion. Nonetheless, in terms of the sports media in Scotland, it is worth considering how it might be socially advantageous as well as culturally reasonable and equitable to hear voices, see images, and receive positive representations of "other" substantial cultural and national affinities within Scotland. This is particularly so with regards the multi-generational Irish community, the largest and longest established of Scotland's minority ethnic groups. This paper shows that Scottishness is a consciousness and identity that is shared by many of Scotland's inhabitants, particularly those who follow football. However, it also shows that this Scottishness is continually constructed partly in the context of, or in opposition to, other important ethnic, national, and cultural identities and communities in Scotland. In this way, the dominant notion of "authentic" Scottishness in the Scottish football environment, and beyond, is one that frequently both reveals and obscures "historical conflicts, social tensions, and unequal power relations" (Ricento, 2003, p.625).

ENDNOTE

[1] http://www.scotland.gov.uk/News/Releases/2004/02/5072

REFERENCES

Archer, I & Royle, T. (Eds.). (1976) *We'll Support You Evermore: The Impertinent Saga of Scottish 'Fitba'*, Souvenir Press, London.

Armstrong, G and Giulionotti, R. (Eds.). (1997) *Entering the Field: New Perspectives in World Football*, Berg, Oxford.

Armstrong, G and Giulionotti, R. (Eds.), (2001) *Fear and Loathing in World Football*, Berg, Oxford.

Bairner, A. (1994) Football and the idea of Scotland, in G Jarvie and G Walker (Eds), *Scottish Sport in the Making of the Nation*, Leicester: Leicester University Press, 9-26.

Billig, M. (1995) *Banal Nationalism*, London: Sage.

Black, I. (1997). *Tales of the Tartan Army*, Edinburgh: Mainstream Publishing, Edinburgh

Blain, N and Boyle, R. (1994) Battling along the boundaries: The marking of Scottish identity in sports journalism, in G Jarvie and G Walker. (Eds.) *Scottish Sport in the Making of the Nation*, Leicester University Press, Leicester, 125-141.

Boyle, R. and Haynes R. (1996) The Grand old game': football, media and identity in Scotland, *Media, Culture and Society* 18, 4, 549-564.

Boyle, R. and Haynes R. (2000) *Power Play: Sport, the Media and Popular Culture*, Longman, London.

Bradley, J M. (1995) *Ethnic and Religious Identity in Scotland: Politics, Culture and Football*, Avebury, Aldershot.

Bradley, J M. (1998) 'We Shall Not Be Moved'! Mere Sport, Mere Songs?: a tale of Scottish Football, in Brown, A. (Ed.) (1998) *Fanatics: Power, Identity and Fandom in Football*, Routledge, London. , 203-218.

Bradley, J M. (2002) The Patriot Game, *International Journal for the Sociology of Sport, 37*, 2, 177-197.

Bradley, J M (2004) Orangeism in Scotland: Unionism, Politics, Identity and Football, *Eire – Ireland: An Interdisciplinary Journal of Irish Studies*, Vol 39, 1 & 2, pp. 237-261

Bradley, J M. (Ed.) (2004) *Celtic Minded: essays on religion, politics, society, identity and football*, Argyll Publishing, Argyll Scotland.

Bradley, J M. (Ed.) (2006) *Celtic Minded 2: Essays on Celtic Football Culture and Identity*, Argyll Publishing, Argyll Scotland.

Bradley, J M. (Ed.) (2009) *Celtic Minded 3: Essays on Celtic Football Culture and Identity*, Argyll Publishing, Argyll Scotland.

Brah, A Hickman ,M J & Mac an Ghaill, M. (1999) *Thinking Identities: Ethnicity, Racism and Culture*, MacMillan Press, London.

Brown, A. (Ed) (1998) *Fanatics: Power, Identity and Fandom in Football*, Routledge, London.

Brown, S.J. (1991) Outside the Covenant: The Scottish Presbyterian Churches and Irish Immigration 1922-1938, *The Innes Review*, Vol.XLII, No.1, Spring 19-45.

Burdsey D. (2004) 'One of the Lads'? Dual Ethnicity and Assimilated Ethnicities in the Careers of British Asian Professional Footballers, *Ethnic and Racial Studies 27*, 5, 757-779.

Burdsey, D & Chappell R. (2003). Soldiers, sashes and shamrocks: Football and social identity in Scotland and Northern Ireland, *Sociology of Sport Online* (SOSOL), School of Physical Education, 6, 1.

Castro-Ramos, E. Loyalties (2008) Commodity and fandom: Real Madrid, Barca and Athletic fans versus 'La Furia Roja' during the World Cup, *Sport in Society, 11*, 6, 696-710.

Crabbe, T. (2004) England fans—A New Club for a New England? Social Inclusion, Authenticity and the Performance of Englishness at 'Home and 'Away', *Leisure Studies, 23*, 1, 63-78.

Curtice, J and Seawright, D. (1995) The Decline of the Scottish Conservatives and Unionist Party 1950-1992: Religion, Ideology or Economics? *Journal of Contemporary History, 2*, 2, 319-342.

Della Porta, D & Diani, M. (1999) *Social Movements: An Introduction*, Oxford, Blackwell.

Devine, T M. (2000) *Scotland's Shame: Bigotry and Sectarianism in Modern Scotland*, Mainstream, Edinburgh.

Esplin, R. (2000) *Down the Copland Road*, Argyll Publishing, Argyll, Scotland.

Finley, R.J. (1991) Nationalism, Race, Religion and The Irish Question in Inter-War Scotland, *The Innes Review*, Vol.XLII, 1, 46-67.

Finn, G,.P, T. (1991) Racism, Religion and Social Prejudice: Irish Catholic Clubs, Soccer and Scottish Society—I The Historical Roots of Prejudice, *The International Journal of the History of Sport, 8*, 1, 72-95.

Finn G,P, T. (1991) Racism, Religion and Social Prejudice: Irish Catholic Clubs, Soccer and Scottish Society - II Social Identities and Conspiracy Theories, *The International Journal of the History of Sport, 8*, 3, 370-397.

Finn, G, P, T. (1994) Faith, Hope and Bigotry: Case Studies of Anti-Catholic Prejudice in Scottish Soccer and Society, *Scottish Sport in the Making of the Nation: Ninety-Minute Patriots*, Leicester University Press, Leicester.

Finn, G. P, T.(1994) Sporting Symbols, Sporting Identities: Soccer and Intergroup Conflict in Scotland and Northern Ireland, 33-55, *Scotland and Ulster*, I.S. Wood (ed.), Mercat Press, Edinburgh.

Forsyth, R. in Linklater M & Denniston R (eds.). (1992) *Anatomy of Scotland: how Scotland works*, Chambers, Edinburgh, 334-353.

Gallagher, T. The Catholic Irish in Scotland: In search of identity, in T M Devine (Ed.). (1991) *Irish Immigrants and Scottish Society in the Nineteenth and Twentieth Centuries*, John Donald, Edinburgh, 19-43.

Giulianotti, R. (1994) Scoring away from Home: A Statistical Study of Scotland Football Fans at International Matches in Romania and Sweden, *International Review for Sociology of Sport, 29/2,* 172-200.

Giulianotti, R. (1994) *Game Without Frontiers: Football, Identity and Modernity,* Arena Ashgate, Aldershot.

Giulianotti, R. (1995) Football and the Politics of Carnival: An Ethnographic Study of Scottish Fans in Sweden, *International Review for Sociology of Sport, 30/2,* 191-223.

Giulianotti, R & Gerrard, M, (2001) Cruel Britannia? Glasgow Rangers, Scotland and 'Hot' Football Rivalries, in Armstrong, G and Giulionotti, R. (Eds.), *Fear and Loathing in World Football,* Berg, Oxford, 23-42.

Hall, S. (1996) The Question of Cultural Identity, in Hall S & Hubert D (Eds.), *Modernity: An Introduction to Modern Societies,* Blackwell, London, 595-634.

Henderson, A. (1999) Political Constructions of National Identity in Scotland and Quebec, *Scottish Affairs, 29,* 121-138.

Hobsbawm, E. (1990) *Nations and Nationalism Since 1780: Programme, Myth, Reality,* Cambridge University Press, Cambridge.

Horne, J. (1995) *Racism, Sectarianism and Football in Scotland, Scottish Affairs, 12,* 27-51.

Jarvie, G & Reid, I. (1999) Sport, Nationalism and Culture in Scotland, *The Sports Historian, 19,* 1, 97-124.

Law, S. (2001) Near and far: banal national identity and the press, *Scotland, Media, Culture & Society, 23,* 299-317.

Lugton, A. (1999) *The Making of Hibernian,* John Donald, Edinburgh.

Miles R. & Muirhead L. (1986) Racism in Scotland: a matter for further investigation? *Scottish Government Yearbook,* 108-136.

Moorhouse, B. (1984) Professional Football and working class culture: English Theories and Scottish evidenc, in *Sociological Review, 32,* 285-315.

Moorhouse, B. (1987) Scotland Against England: Football and Popular Culture, *International Journal of the History of Sport, 4,* 189-202.

Mosely, P A, Cashman R, O'Hara J & Weatherburn H. (1997) *Sporting Immigrants,* Walla Walla Press, Crows Nest, NSW, Australia.

Muirhead, Rev. I.A. (1973). Catholic Emancipation: Scottish Reactions in 1829, *The Innes Review, 24,* 1.

Muirhead, Rev. I.A. (1973) Catholic Emancipation in Scotland: the debate and the aftermath, *The Innes Review, 24,* 2.

McClancy, J. (1996) Nationalism at Play: The Basques of Vizcaya and Athletic Bilbao, *Sport, Identity and Ethnicity,* J McClancy (Ed.), Berg, Oxford, England, 181-199.

McCrone, D. (1998) *The Sociology of Nationalism,* Routledge, London.

McCrone, D. (2001) *Understanding Scotland: The sociology of a nation,* 2nd edition, Routledge, London.

McCrone, D. (2002) Who do you say you are? *Ethnicities, 2,* 3, 301-320.

McDevitt, R. (1999) *A Life in the Tartan Army,* Glasgow, Zipo Publishing, Glasgow.

MacDonald, C M M. (1998) *Unionist Scotland 1800-1997,* Edinburgh, John Donald.

McFarland, E.W. (1990) *Protestants First: Orangeism in nineteenth Century Scotland,* Edinburgh University Press, Edinburgh.

Ricento, T. (2003) 'The discursive construction of Americanism', *Discourse and Society,* vol 15 (5), 611-637.

Reid, I. (1997) Nationalism, Sport and Scotland's Culture, Scottish Centre Research Papers in *Sport, Leisure and Society, 2.*

Schlesinger, P. (1991) Media, the Political Order and National Identity, *Media, Culture and Society, 13,* 3, 297-308.

Stone, C. (2007) The Role of Football in Everyday Life, *Soccer & Society, 8,* 2/3, 169-184.

Sugden, J & Tomlinson, A. (eds.). (1994) *Hosts and Champions: Soccer Cultures, National Identities and the USA World Cup,* Arena, Ashgate, Aldershot.

Sugden, J & Tomlinson, A. (1998) Sport, politics and identities: Football cultures in comparative perspective, in M Roche (ed.), *Sport, popular culture and identity,* CSRC Edition 5, Aachen, Meyer & Meyer, Germany, 169-192.

Walker, G. (1990) 'There's not a team like the Glasgow Rangers': football and religious identity in Scotland in G Walker & T Gallagher (Eds.) *Sermons and Battle Hymns: Protestant Culture in Modern Scotland,* Edinburgh University Press, Edinburgh.

Walvin, J. (1994) *The People's Game: The History of Football Revisited,* Edinburgh, Mainstream.

Wilson, B. (1988) *Celtic: A Century with Honour,* London, Willow Books (Collins).

Invisible but Not Absent: Aboriginal Women, Knowledge Production, and the Restructuring of Canadian Sport

BY **VICTORIA PARASCHAK** AND **JANICE FORSYTH**

They're there because of the impact that they know they can have.
They know they're needed.
– Interview with Participant B

INTRODUCTION

In February 2008, the two authors organized and hosted the first-ever national roundtable on Aboriginal women in Canadian sport. The round-table brought together twelve Aboriginal female athletes, coaches, administrators, organizers and officials from the mainstream (i.e., wider Canadian) sport system, the Aboriginal (i.e., solely Aboriginal participants) sport system, and traditional (i.e., activities of Aboriginal heritage) sport settings to discuss the place and importance of sport in their lives, examine the conditions that have helped and hindered their involvement in sport, and identify various strategies to enhance their participation. All participants were invited to participate in follow up interviews. In the end,

Janice conducted individual semi-structured interviews with nine of the delegates who attended that meeting to further explore the role of sport in their lives. In this paper we make reference to four of those interviews, which were the first four completed. After completing the analysis on the nine interviews, we are pleased to report that these findings remain representative of the nine women interviewed.

The stories the women told us at the national roundtable and in the interviews reminded us of an article that the second author (Vicky) published in 1995 entitled "Invisible but not absent: Aboriginal women in sport and recreation." In that brief critique, Paraschak argued that Aboriginal female contributions in mainstream sport are often overlooked because they are framed within a gendered understanding that values, privileges and rewards the involvement of boys and men more strongly than the involvement of girls and women. This reinforces the belief that Aboriginal girls and women do not take part in sport, and that sport is the proper domain for Aboriginal boys and men. This paper thus builds on the assertion that Paraschak made more than ten years ago by bringing into focus the enormous contributions that Aboriginal women make to community-level sport. In all, our findings from the national roundtable and interviews highlight the complex ways in which Aboriginal women experience sport, as well as the challenges they face in trying to gain recognition and support for their work and volunteering at the community level.

BEING COUNTED

Since the early 1990s, there have been a growing number of opportunities to participate in sport for Aboriginal people in Canada. These opportunities have focused primarily on athlete and coaching development at the regional and national level, which have expanded for a number of reasons, including Aboriginal efforts to implement their desired goals for sport, as well as increasing government support for Aboriginal sport. The emergence of the North American Indigenous Games in 1990, a sport and cultural festival for Aboriginal people in Canada and the United States, as well as the establishment of the Aboriginal Sport Circle in 1995, a national body with regional affiliates dedicated to Aboriginal sport development in Canada, are two highly visible examples of the organizational gains that have been made in Aboriginal sport in recent years.

The growing number of opportunities in Aboriginal sport has emerged at the same time as a desire by government and the non-profit sector to evaluate the policies and programs that have been created and implemented throughout the country. This had the effect of positioning research as a small but significant part of the development of Aboriginal sport in Canada. National strategies and federal documents such as *Sport Canada's Policy on Aboriginal Peoples' Participation in Sport* (Canadian Heritage, 2005) and *Best Practices to Increase Sport Participation: A Report by Sport Canada's Work Group on Participation* (Sport Canada, 2005) incorporated statements about the need for more research in Aboriginal sport to guide institutional practices, while other publicly available documents outlined issues needing immediate scholarly attention (Forsyth & Paraschak, 2006).

Within government, the recent emphasis on evidence-based decision-making in sport has elevated the importance of quantitative information in the construction of policies and programs. Without quantitative data, decision makers face significant challenges in assessing the effectiveness of established initiatives or in determining which areas need more attention. Moreover, it is difficult for sport leaders to achieve their goals without reliable quantitative data to support their requests for funding of selected projects. For example, statistical information would help to confirm or refute the often repeated claim that hockey is the most widely played sport by Aboriginal people in Canada. This unfounded assumption has led some organizations, like the Aboriginal Sport Circle, to focus its limited human and financial resources on hockey programs—a sport with high participant costs (Coakley & Donnelly, 2004) that limits participant accessibility in the mainstream sport system. Significantly, the data might also render visible approximately how many Aboriginal girls and women, as compared to boys and men, play and compete in organized hockey, and at what levels. The information gained from these studies could help sport leaders to make more informed decisions about where best to invest a limited amount of human and financial resources.

However, quantitative information on Aboriginal female participation in sport is scarce. Little is known about their level of participation as athletes, coaches, administrators, organizers, or officials. Without such basic demographic information, sport leaders do not know how many girls and women are taking part in the programs, whether or not those numbers have changed over time, or if they have the necessary baseline data to investigate why changes in participation rates occurred in the first place. This situation is similar to that in women's sport development more generally, wherein there remains an ongoing need to collect and analyze quantitative data in order to monitor and address emerging trends among female participants. Referring to quantitative data collection as 'distributive' research, Ann Hall (1996) calls attention to the political dimensions of this approach because it "provides proof of unequal allocation of or unequal access to limited resources, and it can be used to plot progress, or the lack of it, over time" (p. 12). What is more, it "continues to produce useful knowledge about women's position in the sports world and is sometimes used as a starting point for further analysis and action" (p. 72).

Where quantitative information does exist, it focuses almost exclusively on two areas: participation rates at major games and the number of male and female recipients of regional and national awards for sport. Each focus area poses distinct methodological challenges. For example, McPherson (1998) compared and contrasted athlete performances at the 1997 North American Indigenous Games (NAIG) and the 1997 Canada Summer Games and found that athletes at the latter event did better overall in terms of performance outcomes. There was no comparison of male and female performances; that is, whether or not the male athletes at the NAIG performed better or worse than female athletes at the NAIG in relation to their counterparts at the Canada Summer Games. A key (and perhaps critical) weakness with this comparison is that, within the context of the NAIG, it is possible for athletes who have little or no experience in their chosen sport to qualify and compete at the Games, an event that has historically encouraged mass participation rather than performance excellence. In short, there are currently no qualifying standards for participation in the NAIG as there are for the Canada Games. As a result, the depth of any field at the NAIG can be enormously uneven—which is not necessarily a negative. In 2006, at a symposium on Aboriginal sport development in Canada, Tara Hedican, a member of the Pikangikum First Nation in Ontario, spoke fondly of her experience at the 2002 NAIG, describing how the emphasis on participation, not competitive outcomes, was what she liked most about the Games. Tara, a World Junior and Pan-American Champion, described how one woman in her weight class at the NAIG was competing in her first wrestling competition ever (Forsyth & Paraschak, 2006). While there might be several thousand competitors at the NAIG, there may also be a significant portion of the population that does not engage in organized sport on a regular basis. Here we argue that this is most likely to be girls and women, in particular those who come from economically marginalized backgrounds, who have family responsibilities, or who are raised in an environment where males are more supported in their athletic endeavors, who do not regularly have access to organized sport, or the supports needed to succeed within that system (e.g., qualified coaching, competitive opportunities, etc.).

Compounding the problematic link between the lack of demographic information and participation rates is the image of gender equity that is implicitly promoted through such vehicles as the Tom Longboat Awards and the National Aboriginal Coaching Awards. Only in recent years have Aboriginal female sporting accomplishments been promoted as equal alongside Aboriginal male accomplishments. A case in point is the Tom Longboat Awards. Established in 1951, the Awards are given annually to Aboriginal athletes who have succeeded within the mainstream competitive sport system, a structure in which women generally have had (and continue) to struggle for recognition and support. It was not until 1999 that the Awards were split into two categories, male and female, thus allowing for equal recognition. Now, every year, one male and one female Award winner is identified and their accomplishments recognized primarily by Aboriginal newspapers and electronic media. Arguably, rewarding and elevating the profile of Aboriginal female athletes helps to provide role models for younger generations of athletes, female and male. Nevertheless, the lack of opportunity for both female and male Award winners to discuss and analyze their full experiences in sport is one way in which the silence around issues of gender is reinforced in Aboriginal sport (Forsyth, 2005). One way to help address this issue might be to provide Award winners with opportunities to offer their insights on sport through public speaking engagements, thus providing them with opportunities to be "heard." This could, for example, be one expectation attached to winning the Tom Longboat Award— that Award winners spend the next year sharing stories about their accomplishments (the challenges and the benefits) to Aboriginal and non-Aboriginal audiences across Canada.

The under representation of Aboriginal girls and women in sport was acknowledged in *The Report on Consultations with Provincial/Territorial Aboriginal Sport Bodies on the Draft Policy Framework* (Sport Canada, 2003). In the Report, respondents from British Columbia, Ontario, and the Northwest Territories stated explicitly the need for a gender equity policy to ensure that Aboriginal girls and women get equitable support and adequate funding for their chosen activities. As a result, and no doubt aided by efforts to encourage gender equity within the broader Canadian sport system, a brief statement about Aboriginal girls and women having "unique" needs were inserted into *Sport Canada's Policy on Aboriginal People's Participation in Sport* (Canadian Heritage, 2005). This was an important development for the practitioners in the field—the coaches, organizers, administrators, and other decision-makers—because there has not been a clear understanding of what these 'unique' needs are. We appreciate the benefits of leaving this "uniqueness" undefined (so that we do not inadvertently create dichotomies where none exist). However, we contend that the dearth of information reflects the low priority that has generally been accorded to addressing the needs and interests of Aboriginal girls and women. This absence of vital information remains an obstacle to the advancement of Aboriginal sport in Canada.

BEING HEARD

Arguments about the need for quantitative data can likewise be made for qualitative data. These are the stories that help us to make sense of the demographics and clarify the direction from which action can be taken. Although qualitative information about Aboriginal participation in sport continues to expand, there remains little information specific to women's experiences. For instance, in the *Annotated Bibliography of Aboriginal Women's Health and Healing Research* (Bennett, 2005), the most comprehensive resource to date on Aboriginal women's health in Canada, not one of the 900+ articles surveyed pertain to sport, recreation or physical activity. Similarly, the *Report of the Royal Commission on Aboriginal Peoples* (Government of Canada, 1996), which dedicates over 100 pages to describing issues pertinent to Aboriginal women, does not once refer to sport, recreation, or physical activity as meaningful parts of Aboriginal women's lives. The silence on this topic is particularly problematic considering the already invisible presence of Aboriginal women within the Canadian sport system.

This pattern of invisibility fits with earlier developments in mainstream sport, wherein research on women was largely absent from sport studies until the initiation of research specifically on women and sport in the 1970s. While the literature on mainstream women's sport has grown greatly since that time, there has been little analysis within that body of knowledge about the particular experiences of Aboriginal women. Furthermore, there is a limited exchange of ideas or concepts in the scholarly literature on Aboriginal women's experiences, resulting in disparate threads of knowledge production concerning their lives in sport: the field has barely moved at all since "Invisible but not absent" was made available in 1995. Of the existing information, the picture that emerges when we look at some of the key writings suggests that Aboriginal women are making significant contributions to sport and succeeding within that system in spite of the barriers that lie before them (c.f., Forsyth, 2007; Giles 2002, 2004, 2005; Hall, 2002; Hargreaves, 2000; O'Bonsawin, 2002, 2003; Paraschak, 1990, 1995, 1996, 2007).

REASSESSING THE INVISIBLE PRESENCE OF ABORIGINAL WOMEN IN SPORT

Returning to the discussion introduced at the start of the paper, one of the principle reasons for organizing the national roundtable and carrying out the follow-up interviews was to counter the ongoing invisibility of Aboriginal women as athletes, coaches, administrators, organizers, and officials. In each case we paid particular attention to the unequal gendered power relations in sport, the invisibility of Aboriginal women within that field, and the complexities that Aboriginal women contend with to gain access to, and maintain their positions in sport. Specifically, we examined how their invisibility is tied to gendered notions about caregiving, community development, work and volunteering, and the paradox of their invisibility in sport when the women identify their contributions as being absolutely meaningful to, and some of the most valued work from their perspective, in sport.

We introduce our first point of analysis, focusing on the intersection of caregiving, community, and work, with a brief quote taken from an interview with one of the Northern women (B): "They're there because of the impact that they know they can have. They know they're needed." She is speaking about her understanding as to why the majority of Aboriginal women in sport in her region remain solely as volunteers at the community level. These women rarely take on professional or volunteer positions tied to the structure of sport development *beyond* the community level, such as coaching, officiating, mission staff, program leaders, or board of directors positions. As she and the other women we interviewed each suggested, volunteering at the community level is one of the few spaces where Aboriginal women can meaningfully and consistently exert their agency in sport while concomitantly maintaining valued caretaker role(s) with their family. Jennifer Hargreaves (2000) likewise noted the preferred, extensive involvement of Aboriginal women in community volunteer positions in her study of Aboriginal sportswomen in Canada and Australia. However, she left unexamined *how* Aboriginal women came to occupy this role of the community volunteer, the meanings women attached to that time and space, the ways that the structure of sport intersected with discourses about community and volunteerism, and how these discourses influenced women's perspectives about their involvement in sport. These lines of enquiry can help to illuminate the different ways that Aboriginal women are challenging and reproducing the structure of community level sport in Canada.

For example, we found that the positive value Aboriginal women attribute to their support role is connected to their declared belief that women are best suited for community level positions because of their innate nurturing abilities. As one woman from Ontario (C) explained:

> I think it's the caregiving part of women. Women are the caregivers. I don't have any children, but my life has always been focused around children. Everyone else's children are a part of my life. As a young person growing up, right up to now, they come first.

This notion of women as 'natural' caregivers has been deconstructed in the literature on

gender and sport. For example, Boyle and McKay (1995) spoke about "'compulsory altruism' ... the belief that women are 'naturally' suited to performing expressive and compassionate duties in both the private and public spheres" (p. 557). We acknowledge this potential interpretation but also posit that the caregiver discourse can be further explored in relation to Western colonial beliefs that historically positioned Aboriginal women as unfit wives and mothers, and which are linked to various practices that attempted to correct such deficiencies through mechanisms including residential schooling and the child welfare system (Anderson, 2000). The interviewees' privileging of their position as caregiver actively challenges Western perceptions about their competency in this role. It is also a rebuttal to feminists who argue that women who willingly assume the place of caregiver are unwittingly consenting to their own subordination in a patriarchal society. These Aboriginal women, including those who have operated at some of the highest levels of the sport system, vigorously defended their status as *the* caregivers of their communities.

Our second point of analysis, focusing on the 'real' work of volunteering, begins with a quote from one of the interviewees (C): "Especially in the community, I'm always doing something for somebody's kids. And I'm not thinking, 'Well, how much can I get paid for this?'" Closely associated with the idea that Aboriginal women are 'natural' caregivers is the belief that women do not expect to be paid, and, perhaps more importantly, should not want to be paid for volunteering—as suggested in the above quote. This is because taking care of the children and youth, who constitute the foundation for coming together as a community, is presumed to be their 'proper' role in sport and society. This valorization of being a helpmate fits with Western knowledge about the unpaid work that caregivers—most of whom are women—do to support their families and communities. For example, a Canadian survey of 18,000 mothers noted that if women were paid for their unpaid contributions to the family, they would make $125,000 yearly for stay at home mothers and almost $75,000 for working mothers on top of their "real" salaries (*Windsor Star*, 2008).[1] This acknowledgement of the unpaid contribution of Aboriginal and non-Aboriginal women to family life helps to explain ongoing unequal gender relations in sport whereby women do the 'invisible' work while the men benefit from the women's work by gaining recognition (social, financial, material) for their visible contributions—what we have labeled the 'perk volunteer' roles. For example, in Chafetz and Kotarba's (1999) study of mothers involved in little league baseball in Texas, the authors documented how middle and upper class women reproduced gender by servicing the needs of the boys and men in their families, thus upholding community values including how to act as a 'competent' mother. They clearly document that women were working to be sure everything got done behind the scenes, while the men and boys just had to coach, spectate, or play—and receive the benefits tied to those positions.

Over time, men gravitate to these visible positions and dominate and control access to them. Women who recognize the invisible work needed to keep the system going (as they do in the home) develop a perspective that supports and valorizes their continuation in those roles. This does not mean, however, that women are unclear on the unequal gender relations underlying the sport system. One of the interviewees (D) noted the following:

> I haven't had a lot of support from the men, which is surprising because this is something for their people. I mean, I've been on my email or telephone saying, "Okay, I've got this clinic, pass the good word on," and what not, yet no response. I really try to get responses back from the men. So that was a big shock—that I'm here for our people and I'm not getting a whole lot of response from all of the men.

Another interviewee (A) explained women's invisible labor in relation to unequal gender relations at the community level this way:

> I'll give you an example from minor hockey. The dads are the coaches, and the whole support system to that are the moms. There are only two dads on the ice generally, but there are probably twelve moms who run the bingo, organize the potluck, organize the tournament, get the kids back and forth … That's what I mean in terms of more women at the local level.

In this sense, sport at the Aboriginal community level is a time and space shaped by gendered notions about women's work, whereby the women are there to support the men in an unpaid and unrecognized capacity, aligning with patterns identified by scholars such as Shona Thompson in her book, *Mother's Taxi* (1999). The women we interviewed thus actively facilitated the privileging of male involvement and recognition in sport as a byproduct of facilitating children's opportunities *for* sport. Male coaches were facilitated by female volunteer labor, thereby allowing them to focus on coaching. However, when a woman coached she also had to do everything else to provide for the team, such as fundraising, arranging travel, managing, etc.

Here again, the women shaped their own understanding of which roles in sport are the most valued at the community level. They made a distinction between unpaid volunteer roles and those that offer money and perks (e.g., status and travel), labeling the former as "real" volunteer work; that is, unpaid work that makes a concrete contribution to the community, versus paid and perk volunteer work, usually done by men. These women, while recognizing unequal gender relations in sport, framed women's work as being the "real volunteer"—a uniquely female and, for the moment, empowering space.

CONCLUSIONS

The need for research holds special relevance for Aboriginal girls and women in sport because the present dearth of information is an obstacle to planning (Paraschak, 1995). Through this chapter we hope that people who are not familiar with the subject of Aboriginal women in sport will walk away with a better understanding of the issues that influence their involvement, and that people who have some knowledge and experience working in this area will commit themselves to further action. While it is true that opportunities for Aboriginal people in sport are constantly expanding, there are still many Aboriginal people, but particularly girls and women, for whom these opportunities are still out of reach. If Aboriginal females experience sport and recreation differently than Aboriginal boys and men and other Canadian females, then these realities must be acknowledged, documented, and addressed through policies and programming.

To that end, we are paying attention to Ann Hall's argument that there are two hurdles to overcome in academic scholarship:

> One is that incorporating even some of the differences in women's sporting experiences is difficult because so much remains to be researched and written, but as more scholarship accumulates, it will become even more difficult unless we confront the problems of integration now. Second, merely adding minority women's experience is not good enough; we must pay attention to relations among women and retheorize at the same time (Hall, p. 44).

The Aboriginal women we interviewed, who all have professional training in sport and have worked extensively in both paid and volunteer capacities in the sport system, voiced their deep commitment to family and community while also being challenged by gendered ideas about work and volunteering. Their belief that women are "natural" caregivers not only facilitates the involvement of their own and other children in sports, but also facilitates the participation and advancement of men within the system by enabling them to concentrate on defined and visible roles in sport, like coaching, and using their networks to take advantage of perk volunteer opportunities that are not equally available to the women. It also appears that the growing number of perk volunteer opportunities that are available due to the growth in Aboriginal sport since the 1990s has further shifted men's attention (and one might argue their physical presence) away from the community, thereby leaving a void for the women to fill, which they do, thus reproducing the unequal gender relations found in sport.

What we are able to discern thus far, from our preliminary analysis, is that the women we interviewed are contributing to the development of a sport system that does not profile nor privilege them, but they find strength in what they do in keeping with their assumptions about the importance of community, along with women as the "natural" caregivers who serve as the "real" volunteers in the sport system. These Aboriginal women have claimed the community as their space in sport; they valorize the contributions that females make in that space by defining unpaid volunteer work at the community level as the most valued type of contribution possible. Their reinforcement of this perspective facilitates Aboriginal men, who can then focus on perk volunteer roles, which provide more limited but valued and rewarded roles within and beyond the community level. The women's perspective does not stem from a belief that men are more naturally suited to sport, but rather from recognition of the importance of sporting opportunities for the youth and the community, and the centrality of women's labor in providing for these opportunities. Family demands for their caretaker contributions then combine with community-based volunteer work demands to legitimize their decision to stay home while men take the trips and get the training and experience that will provide them with overt rewards within the sport system. Researchers are complicit as well in this process: each time we explore the sport system in terms of professional and perk volunteer elements, but ignore the real, invisible, and unpaid caregiving roles that women provide to the sport system, especially at the community level, which is a cornerstone of Aboriginal sport.

Part of the process for helping to ensure that programs and policies are appropriate for women includes engaging in meaningful conversation with them. While that statement might seem cliché, as government and other institutionalized agencies routinely call for grassroots participation in decision-making, it is striking how little information exists about how this form of engagement actually works in practice. People who are actively involved in this form of decision-making, wherein they attempt to relinquish some of their power to service users, know it is not a straightforward process and, sometimes, it does not result in anticipated outcomes. The reality for many Aboriginal women in sport is that they have few opportunities to publicly engage in discussions about gender and how it shapes their lives as women in sport. Aboriginal women lag behind men and well behind Canadian women as a whole on many social and economic indicators, but statistics do not reveal why. Women themselves provide a deeper understanding of the realities they face—realities that must be acknowledged and addressed for progress to be made. Statistics could provide us with a glimpse into the realities of women's lives; however, it is their stories that make those barriers real and tangible, and, ultimately, surmountable. What can researchers and practitioners do? The examples cited above demonstrate insights into how researchers and practitioners can understand and support Aboriginal girls and women as they work towards their vision for sport development in Canada. Furthermore, talking to, and researching with, Aboriginal girls and women is a good place to start understanding issues from their point of view.

ENDNOTE

[1] Salary calculations were based on the top ten jobs mothers said they did at home and the hours spent doing them each day. These numbers were compared to the market value each job was worth. Average base pay was about $41,600 Canadian; the high salaries were due to overtime—90 hours for stay at home mothers and 56.4 hrs for working women in addition to their jobs.

REFERENCES

Anderson, K. (2000). *A Recognition of Being: Reconstructing Native Womanhood*. Toronto, ON: Second Story Press.

Boyle, M., & McKay, J. (1995). 'You leave your troubles at the gate': A case study of the exploitation of older women's labor and leisure. *Sport, Gender & Society, 9*(5), 556-575.

Canadian Heritage. (2005). *Sport Canada's Policy on Aboriginal Peoples' Participation in Sport*. Ottawa, ON: Minister of Public Works and Government Services Canada.

Chafetz, J.S., & Kotarba, J. (1999). Little league mothers and the reproduction of gender. In J. Coakley, & P. Donnelly (Eds.), *Inside Sports* (pp. 46-54). New York, NY: Routledge.

Coakely, J., & Donnelly, P. (2004). *Sports in Society: Issues and Controversies: First Canadian Edition*. Toronto, ON: McGraw-Hill Ryerson.

Forsyth, J. (2007). To my sisters in the field. *Pimatisiwin: A Journal of Aboriginal and Indigenous Community Health, 5*(1), 155-168.

Forsyth, J., & Paraschak, V. (2006). *Aboriginal Sport Forum, Proceedings and Final Report. Report from the Aboriginal Sport Forum*. Report prepared for Sport Canada.

Forsyth, J. (2005). *The Power to Define: A History of the Tom Longboat Awards*. Unpublished PhD thesis. London, ON: University of Western Ontario.

Giles, A.R. (2002). Sport Nunavut's gender equity policy: Reality, rhetoric, and relevance. *Canadian Woman Studies Journal: Women and Sport, 21*(3), 95-99.

Giles, A.R. (2004). Kevlar, Crisco©, and menstruation: "Tradition" and Dene Games. *Sociology of Sport Journal, 21*(1), 18-35.

Giles, A.R. (2005). A Foucaultian approach to menstrual practices in the Dehcho, Northwest Territories, Canada. *Arctic Anthropology, 42*(2), 9-21.

Government of Canada. (1996). *Royal Commission on Aboriginal Peoples. Volume 1: Looking Forward, Looking Back.* Ottawa, ON: Royal Commission on Aboriginal Peoples.

Hall, A. (1996). *Feminism and Sporting Bodies: Essays on Theory and Practice.* Champaign, IL: Human Kinetics.

Hall, A. (2002). *The Girl and the Game: A History of Women's Sport in Canada.* Peterborough, ON: Broadview Press.

Hargreaves, J. (2000). *Heroines of Sport: The Politics of Difference and Identity.* New York, NY: Routledge.

McPherson, T.L. (1998). A Comparative Analysis of Athlete Participation and Performance for the 1997 North American Indigenous Games and the 1997 Canada Summer Games. M.A. Thesis, University of Ottawa.

O'Bonsawin, C. (2002). The construction of the Olympian Firth sisters by the Canadian Press. In K. B. Wamsley, R. K. Barney, & S. G. Martyn, *The Global Nexus Engaged: Past, Present, Future in Interdisciplinary Olympic Studies, Sixth International Symposium for Olympic Research* (pp. 193-198). London, ON: University of Western Ontario.

O'Bonsawin, C. (2003). Time to take notice: A biographical analysis of the firth sisters. In V. Paraschak, & J. Forsyth (Eds.), *2002 North American Indigenous Games Research Symposium Proceedings* (pp. 13-22). Winnipeg, MB: University of Manitoba.

Paraschak, V. (1990). Organized sport for Native females on the Six Nations Reserve, Ontario from 1968-1980: A comparison of dominant and emergent sport systems. *Canadian Journal of History of Sport, 21*(2), 70-80.

Paraschak, V. (1995). Invisible but not absent: Aboriginal women in sport and recreation. *Canadian Woman Studies: Women and Girls in Sport and Physical Activity, 15*(4), 71-72.

Paraschak, V. (1996). An examination of sport for aboriginal females on the Six Nations Reserve, Ontario from 1968 to 1980. In C. Miller, & P. Chuchryk (Eds.), *Women of the First Nations: Power, Wisdom, and Strength* (pp. 83-96). Winnipeg, MB: University of Manitoba Press.

Paraschak, V. (2007). Doing race, doing gender: First Nations, 'sport', and gender relations. In K. Young, & P. White (Eds.), *Sport and Gender in Canada, Second Edition* (pp. 137-154). Don Mills, ON: Oxford University Press.

Sport Canada. (2005). *Best Practices to Increase Sport Participation: A Report by Sport Canada's Work Group on Participation.* Ottawa, ON: Sport Information Resource Centre.

Sport Canada. (2003). *Report on Consultations with Provincial/Territorial Aboriginal Sport Bodies on the Draft Policy Framework.* Report prepared by Sport Canada.

Windsor Star, 13 May 2008: B6.

INDEX

ABOUT THE EDITOR

Daryl Adair (PhD),
Associate Professor, School of
Leisure, Sport, and Tourism,
University of Technology, Sydney, Australia
Adair has research interests in sport his-
tory, sport management, and sport media.
His recent work deals with sport and physical activity among
Aboriginal Australians, with a particular focus on stereotypes
about Aboriginal people as "natural" athletes.

ABOUT THE AUTHORS

Dean Allen (PhD),
Research Associate, Centre for Human Performance Sciences, Stellenbosch University, South Africa
Allen has published widely about the history and politics of sport in South Africa, with particular interests in colonialism, imperialism, and inter-group relations.

Douglas Booth (PhD),
Professor and Dean, School of Physical Education,
University of Otago, New Zealand
Booth has research interests in the social and cultural history of sport, the politics of sport, and historiography. His recent work delves into theory and narrative in sport history.

Joseph M. Bradley (PhD),
Senior Lecturer in at the School of Sport at the
University of Stirling in Scotland
Bradley's research interests lie in sport's relationship with ethnicity, identity, racism, religion, and politics. Dr. Bradley has authored, joint authored, and edited numerous books, and is published in sociology, ethnic, history, and politics-based journals. In 2001-02, he was a member of a group financed by the Economic and Social Research Council to explore ethnicity and identity amongst those who comprise the 2nd and 3rd generation Irish in Britain.

Sean Brawley (PhD),
Associate Professor of History, and Associate Dean (Education),
University of New South Wales, Sydney, Australia
Brawley's research interests in sport range from surf lifesaving to rugby union, from cultural diplomacy to terrorism. He has recently edited a collection on Australia's Asian sporting context in the 1920s and 30s.

Janice Forsyth (PhD),
Director & Assistant Professor, International Centre
for Olympic Studies, The University of Western Ontario,
London, Ontario, Canada
Forsyth's research interests include Canadian sport and cultural history, and Olympic studies, with a particular emphasis on Aboriginal people and sport. Recent projects include representational issues and Olympic Games, examinations of Aboriginal experiences in Canadian sport, sports and games at Canadian residential schools, and women/work and community sport development.

John Hoberman (PhD),
Professor of Germanic Studies, University of Texas at Austin, USA
Hoberman's research interests include the racial dimension of sport, the history of doping in elite sports, the politics of the Olympic movement, and sportive nationalism around the world. His most recent work deals with the origins and consequences of medical racism.

Graham Knight (PhD),
*Professor, Chair, Department of Communication Studies
and Multimedia, McMaster University, Hamilton, Canada*
Knight has research interests in corporate communication,
promotional culture, and the mass media and social movements. His recent work deals with the role of public relations
in the debate over global warming.

Nicole Neverson (PhD)
*Assistant Professor, Department of Sociology,
Ryerson University, Toronto, Canada*
Neverson has research interests in sport media, sport and
gender, and issues related to sport, race, and identity. Her recent work deals with digital television and the advancement
of women's sport.

Victoria Paraschak (PhD),
*Associate Professor, Department of Kinesiology,
University of Windsor, Ontario, Canada*
Paraschak has research interests in Aboriginal Peoples and
their physical cultural practices, as well as government policy
for underserved groups in sport. Her recent work deals with
an analysis of Sport Canada's Policy on Aboriginal Peoples'
Participation in Sport, and Aboriginal women's experiences
participating in, and organizing, sport and recreation.

Andrew Ritchie (PhD)
Ritchie researches and writes about the history of cycling. He is on the advisory board of the International Cycling History Conference, and edits its annual *Proceedings*. He is currently preparing a major study of the origins and early history of European and American cycling for publication. His book on the African-American champion, *Major Taylor,* has just been reissued in a new and enlarged edition, and he is adviser to the producer of a feature film based on Major Taylor's life, which is in pre-production.

Randy Roberts (PhD),
Distinguished Professor of History at
Purdue University, Indiana, USA
Roberts has written, co-written, or edited more than twenty book on American popular culture and sport, including *Winning is the Only Thing: Sports in America Since 1945* and the biographies *Jack Dempsey, the Manassa Mauler, Papa Jack: Jack Johnson and the Era of White Hopes,* and *Joe Louis: Hard Times Man.*

Colin Tatz (PhD),
Emeritus Professor of Politics, is now Visiting Fellow, Politics and International Relations, College of Arts and Social Sciences, Australian National University, Canberra, Australia
His fields include comparative race politics, Holocaust and genocide studies, migration studies, suicidology, and sport history.